# SUPERNATURAL
## PSYCHOLOGY

## ROADS LESS TRAVELED

EDITED BY TRAVIS LANGLEY
AND LYNN ZUBERNIS

www.sterlingpublishing.com
#SPNpsych

STERLING
New York

STERLING
New York

An Imprint of Sterling Publishing Co., Inc.
1166 Avenue of the Americas
New York, NY 10036

ISBN 978-1-4549-2661-0

Distributed in Canada by Sterling Publishing
c/o Canadian Manda Group, 664 Annette Street
Toronto, Ontario, Canada M6S 2C8
Distributed in the United Kingdom by GMC Distribution Services
Castle Place, 166 High Street, Lewes, East Sussex, England BN7 1XU
Distributed in Australia by Capricorn Link (Australia) Pty. Ltd.
P.O. Box 704, Windsor, NSW 2756, Australia

For information about custom editions, special sales, and premium and corporate purchases,
please contact Sterling Special Sales at 800-805-5489 or specialsales@sterlingpublishing.com.

Manufactured in Canada

2 4 6 8 10 9 7 5 3 1

www.sterlingpublishing.com

IMAGE CREDITS

Lynda Ciaschini: 278

iStock: © Ellerslie77: throughout (trees); © fandijki: 41; © GeorgePeters: 175; © ilbusca:31;
© jhorrocks: throughout (lightning); © kycstudio: 243; © MattGrove: 307; © nicoolay:
67, 205; © nikolaj2: 6, 150, 202, 258; © ninjaMonkeyStudio: 84; © TonyBaggett: 219

© Dustin McGinnis: 19, 238

Shutterstock.com: DoubleBubble: 9; Christos Georghiou: 163; intueri: 55; MaKars: 231;
Aleks Melnik: 187; Milan M: 275; Pinchuk Oleksandra: 75, 145, 199, 255, 321; Vera
Petruk: 289; Frolova Polina: 117, 153; Eduard Radu: throughout (hand); RomanYa: 87,
105; Anna Timoshenko: 133; tsaplia: 261

*Dedication*

To family not by blood,
Katrina, Marko, and Renee
—TRAVIS

To family by blood,
my children Emily and Jeffrey
—LYNN

To the fans, creators, cast, and crew of
*Supernatural* who over the years have truly become
"SPN Family" whether blood relations or not
—FROM US ALL

# CONTENTS

# ACKNOWLEDGMENTS

# The Family That Hunts Together

– I –

## TRAVIS LANGLEY, PhD

*Editor*

We traveled a long road to get here and would be hard pressed to say where the road began or when we merged onto it. Where does any journey begin, and when? When you get into a vehicle or before that when you pack your bags, when you make the choice, when you develop a preference behind the choice, where your parents met? My life's journey took a detour when my son Nicholas and I discovered our love of fan conventions, and my decision that summer to write about a bat-themed superhero has kept me off the main highway ever since.[1] Through the books that have followed, figures along this road have included zombies, dragons, time travelers, more superheroes, and mortals who must deal with them all.[2] Other psychologists and accomplices have joined this excursion, crossing space and time in the topics we've covered[3] before coming back to the here and now. Here, we have landed on a version of our contemporary world, one where ghosts lurk in shadows, monsters inhabit the countryside, demons and angels clash while humanity gets caught in between, and two brothers ride ready to take them all on. However ironic it might seem, *Supernatural Psychology: Roads Less Traveled* may be the most down-to-earth book we've written yet.

*Supernatural* is about family. For all the horror and adventure that characterize the stories, you miss the essence of

*Supernatural* if you don't discuss that, and so we dedicate this book to family. My daughter-in-law Katrina Hill, my son-by-other-mortals Mark Head, and Marko's fiancée Renee Cooey prove family does not end with blood. They aren't the only ones. Through sons Alex and Nicholas, my wife and I have also welcomed Carly Cate, Michael Dorman, Sarah Fuller, Stephen Huckabee, Ryne Johnston, Cordell Moss, Jimmy and Nicole Smith, and Tim Yarbrough into the Langley fold. Sister-in-law Sharon Manning is a great help to us. Wife Rebecca gets the greatest credit as my sounding board, proofreader, colleague, best friend, oracle, and partner who keeps up with all kinds of things when I lose myself in the lore.

For quite a while, I've wanted to cover *Supernatural*. Sterling Publishing editor Kate Zimmermann, publicist Blanca Oliviery, and I agreed during lunch one day that the time had come. Many other Sterling folks helped us bring these books to life: Ardi Alspach, Toula Ballas, Betsy Beier, Michael Cea, Sari Lampert, Damien Martinez, Marilyn Spetzer, Lauren Tambini, Theresa Thompson. Even though my original editor, Connie Santisteban, has left Sterling on her greatest adventure, raising little J. J., she still looks out for me and remains forever part of the team. Kate and company make me feel truly fortunate. They are a Sterling family.

We're different around here. I know of no other anthology series with such a close-knit and supportive team of professionals analyzing popular culture both independently and together. Because I met many of our contributing writers along with relevant writers, artists, actors, filmmakers, propmakers, and more through fan conventions, I thank the organizers who work hard to put the cons together. Most relevant for this particular collection are San Diego Comic-Con International (Eddie Ibrahim, Gary Sassaman, Cathy Dalton, Sue Lord, Adam Neese, Amy Ramirez, Chris Sturham), and many

Wizard World conventions (Ryan Ball, Donna Chin, Danny Fingeroth, Kate Gloss, Christopher Jansen, Jerry Milani, Peter Katz, Brittany Walloch-Key). I studied media effects during graduate school, mentored by Ed O'Neal at Tulane University, but my immersion in studying popular culture on a wider scale began with the Comics Arts Conference (Peter Coogan, Randy Duncan, Kathleen McClancy).

Henderson State University provides great support for this work. Our administrators—President Glendell Jones, Provost Steve Adkison, Dean Angela Boswell—encourage creative ways of teaching. Library director Lea Ann Alexander looks forward to my next strange request so she and her staff can keep the shelves full of unusual resources. David Bateman, Lecia Franklin, Carolyn Hatley, Ermatine Johnston, and Salina Smith help me and my students go all the places we need to go. My fellow department members offer endless encouragement and put up with my crazy schedule. Our faculty writers group (Jennifer Dawes, Angela Boswell, Matthew Bowman, Suzanne Tartamella, Michael Taylor) reviewed portions of this manuscript. Through groups such as our Comic Arts Club and the Legion of Nerds, our students prove that geeky passions belong in higher education, and they seem to enjoy the fact that some of their professors are also professional nerds.

For serving as muses, hunting partners, devil's advocates, keepers of arcana, and guardians at the gate, our writers thank Amy Blunt, Aaron Dickson, Jeffrey Henderson, Patty Hlava, Nina Taylor Kester, Barbara and James Kus, Eli Mastin, Dustin McGinnis, K. T. Rex, Bethany Souza, Brian Edward Therens, Jacqueline Traversa, and Sarah West. Family of many kinds encourage or at least tolerate us in these endeavors. FirstGlance Photography's Bill Ostroff and others shot our author photos. My literary agent, Evan Gregory of the Ethan Ellenberg Literary Agency, handles all kinds of details. Christine Boylan,

Joyce and Tim Cogburn, Jane Espenson, Maurice Lamarche, Chase Masterson, Ali Mattu, Jose Molina, Marc Nadel, Kaja Perina, Travis Richey, Matt Smith (not the one with fez and bowtie, though we love him, too), and Michael Uslan deserve mention for joining us at different stops along the way.

We owe series creator Eric Kripke for once upon a time envisioning his "*Star Wars* meets Truck Stop America" epic: "Who wouldn't want to watch Han Solo and Luke Skywalker with chain saws in the trunk?"[4] This book would not exist without him and the many others who put the show together: writers, directors, producers, hundreds upon hundreds of crew members doing everything from running spooky lights to designing yet another hotel room, and actors who bring the characters to life. For speaking with us and sharing their thoughts at different times, we heap thanks upon Jensen Ackles, Jared Padalecki, Misha Collins, Felicia Day, Adam Glass, Jay Gruska, Mark Sheppard, and Amanda Tapping. We especially thank best-selling author Jonathan Maberry for this book's foreword and actor Mark R. Pellegrino for the introduction.

There is no *Supernatural* family without the fans who transform it all into a wild and crazy phenomenon. Through conventions, message boards, social media, and more, fans share this common interest and make it something more. Conscientious volunteers who build resources such as supernaturalwiki.com and supernatural.wikia.com help us in many ways. While we always check the original sources, a wiki can point us to the right episode when we're double-checking details such as when viewers found out about Sam's fear of clowns or Dean's passion for pie.[5] It is a privilege to have superfan Lynn S. Zubernis ride shotgun as my co-editor this time. Lynn has already authored, co-authored, edited, and co-edited five books on *Supernatural* and the fandom, and this one would have been incomplete without her. Believe me, it's not hard to keep thinking of things to say about *Supernatural* characters and stories.

And thank *you* for riding with us. Hunt well and stay safe!

– II –
# LYNN S. ZUBERNIS, PHD
*Co-Editor*

Sometimes serendipity takes us in a direction we weren't anticipating, and it turns out to be a road that affords a view we never would have been able to appreciate otherwise. After falling hard for the television show *Supernatural* over a decade ago, I began researching its appeal to fans, eventually writing five books about the show and its passionate fandom.[6] So it wasn't surprising that *Supernatural* fans started excitedly tweeting me about a new book from someone whose name and reputation I'd encountered before at Comic Con panels: @Superherologist, a.k.a. Travis Langley. He was already working on this volume and invited me to jump on board as co-editor. It was a no-brainer, so on I jumped. The next few months were a whirlwind of playing catchup on the way this series works, getting to know the other contributors, and doing some more of what I love: writing about *Supernatural*. I'm grateful for the invitation, Travis, and have enjoyed every minute of the process!

Thanks to my family and friends for not shaking their heads in dismay when they heard the news that I was taking on yet another *Supernatural* book when the previous one wasn't even released yet, and to my university colleagues for never dismissing my research as anything but valid (even if they do roll their eyes at the Impala poster in my office). I'm also grateful

XIIACKNOWLEDGMENTS

to Kelsey Davis for her tireless technical assistance and to the Superwiki for being the invaluable resource that it is for all things Supernatural.

As always, thank you to the *Supernatural* fandom for welcoming me in with open arms twelve years ago and for teaching me that it was okay to be myself. The encouragement to express my creativity, in fan fiction and meta and art, was the catalyst to all my other writing. Equally important, that encouragement and the openness of the fan community brought me some of my closest friends—with whom I've traveled the world, waited in endless convention lines, and posed for some truly ridiculous photo ops. And finally, thanks to the *Supernatural* cast, who also welcomed me with open arms into their side of the *Supernatural* world and have given me countless hours of their time for interviews. I appreciate their willingness to step outside their comfort zones and write chapters, and their unflagging professionalism and sense of humor as we worked through the process together. Special thanks to Mark Pellegrino and composer Jay Gruska for their thoughtful contributions to this book.

1. *Batman and Psychology: A Dark and Stormy Knight* (2012).
2. *The Walking Dead Psychology: Psych of the Living Dead* (2015); *Game of Thrones Psychology: The Mind is Dark and Full of Terrors* (2016); *Doctor Who Psychology: A Madman with a Box* (2016); *Captain America vs. Iron Man: Freedom, Security, Psychology* (2016); *Wonder Woman Psychology: Lassoing the Truth* (2017).
3. Distant past—*Star Wars Psychology: Dark Side of the Mind* (2015); future—*Star Trek Psychology: The Mental Frontier* (2017).
4. Knight, N. (2014). *The Essential Supernatural: On the Road with Sam and Dean Winchester* (revised, updated ed.). San Rafael, CA: Insight. Quoted on p. 14.
5. Clowns—episode 2–2, "Everybody Loves a Clown" (October 5, 2006); pie—1–11, "Scarecrow" (January 10, 2006).
6. *Fan Culture: Theory/Practice* (2012); *Fandom at the Crossroads: Celebration, Shame, and Fan/Producer Relationships* (2012); *Fangasm: Supernatural Fangirls* (2013); *Fan Phenomena: Supernatural* (2014); *Family Don't End with Blood: Cast and Fans on How Supernatural Has Changed Lives* (2017).

# FOREWORD

# Born to Fire

JONATHAN MABERRY
*New York Times* best-selling author

People often ask me why I write about monsters.

The question still surprises me, and I think my answer surprises them. I tell them that I don't write about monsters. I write about people who *fight* monsters. And that, my friend, is a very big difference.

The difference is rooted in who I am. And it's the reason I've always gravitated to a certain kind of storytelling, both as a writer and as a lifelong fan. You see, I was raised by monsters. Real ones. My father was one. He was an intensely violent man. A criminal and an abuser who turned his own home into one of the outer rings of hell. He abused his children and assaulted friends and relatives. Mostly female, but not always. And he was a big, powerful man who knew how to hit and how to hurt. I had four sisters, but I was the youngest in the family. A little kid.

When I was young, on those quiet nights when nothing bad was happening at home or when it was happening to someone else behind a locked door, I tried to close it all out by escaping into a book or by crawling inside the worlds that unfolded on TV. This was the early sixties in Philadelphia and we had the reruns of *The Twilight Zone* and new episodes of *The Outer Limits* and *Dark Shadows*. We had late-night movies of the old Universal Pictures monster flicks and the newer Hammer horror films. I had a secret stash of Marvel comics and some of the old EC magazines like *Vault of Horror* and *Tales from the*

*Crypt*. That's where I learned about monsters. About the people they preyed on and the people who fought back.

I watched films like *The Thing from Another World, Invaders from Mars, The Haunting, The Last Man on Earth, Horror of Dracula, Invasion of the Body Snatchers, The Blob,* and so many others. In 1968, when I was ten, my buddy and I snuck into the cavernous old Midway Theater to see the world premiere of *Night of the Living Dead*.

The films I liked most, the ones I was determined to watch again as soon as they reran them, were the ones where someone, no matter how weak or ordinary, stood up against monsters of incredible power. If I had a cinematic hero, it was probably the smart, athletic, energetic version of Abraham Van Helsing, as portrayed by Peter Cushing. Okay, sure, he also played the evil Dr. Frankenstein in a series of flicks, but it was his Van Helsing who spoke to me. He was the one who, despite being dreadfully afraid, would nevertheless summon the courage, information, and resources necessary to force a showdown with Dracula. What mattered more was that he did not have to. He could have slipped away back to Vienna and not put himself at risk to protect people he didn't even know all that well. However, fighting monsters had become his calling, and he girded his loins, grabbed his hammer and stake, and went to war.

I wanted to be Van Helsing. That version of Van Helsing.

I took some steps toward that goal, too. I began studying martial arts on the sly. My best friend's dad enrolled me in a dojo and, I later found out, paid for my lessons. He knew who and what my father was, and though he was too afraid to openly confront the neighborhood monster, he resisted in his own quietly subversive way.

I was a very good student. Diligent, hungry to build my knowledge and my abilities. And . . . well, okay, since I was also reading comics I wanted to be able to fight like Daredevil.

I wanted to be as smart and capable as T'Challa, the Black Panther. I wanted to be as steadfast as Captain America.

Now, at the same time, I was learning about other kinds of monsters. My grandmother, who lived near us, was a wonderfully spooky old lady. Imagine Luna Lovegood from the Harry Potter series as an old woman. That's her. Nanny, as we called her, believed in everything. She had been 40 when she gave birth to my mother, and my mother was 41 when she had me. So, when I was born in 1958, Nanny was 81, which means she was born in 1877. She'd been raised in Alsace-Lorraine and was of Scottish descent. She grew up in a place and at a time where most people still believed in the supernatural. Over the course of her life, Nanny delved deep into what she called the "larger world," and she shared that knowledge with me. She told me about vampires, ghosts, werewolves, demons, fairies, imps, trolls, and more; and she gave me the folkloric versions of these monsters, not the version so often presented in fiction and film.

For example, in folklore, there are hundreds of different kinds of vampires, thousands of different kinds of shapeshifting monsters, countless demons—each with its own unique qualities, dozens of different kinds of ghosts, and so on. In her world, there were so many different kinds of monsters and they were also there, lurking just beyond the reach of a campfire or flashlight beam. Nanny told me about the powers and abilities of these monsters, but she also told me about their weaknesses. And about the people who hunted them: exorcists, vampire hunters, ghost breakers, warrior monks, wise women, and more.

She even talked about cases where good monsters hunted bad ones. Those fascinated me. Among my favorites were the *stregoni benefici*, vampires who had been captured by medieval priests and who, under torture (because, let's face it, some old-time church leaders really dug their version of enhanced interrogation), were brought back to faith. After which they would be like vampire assassins for the church. Wild. My other favorite was the race of heroic warrior werewolves called the *beñandanti*, who descended into hell via their dreams to fight evil monsters.

As the child of a monster, I was always afraid that I would grow up to be like my father. So reading about monsters who fought evil really, really mattered to me.

Nanny also collected what she called "dark tales" or, as they are more popularly known these days, "urban legends." Those were even scarier to me because they were not set in distant lands and they didn't involve people who had died long ago. Her dark tales were about people living in cities or small towns. People like me. Scary stuff.

These worlds all collided for me when I was 14. By then I was getting some adult mass and muscle, I'd had years of jujutsu, and I simply could not abide a monster in my house. I threw down against my father—who was six inches taller and had 80 more pounds of solid muscle as well as a lifetime of experience in back-alley fighting. When it was over, the entire downstairs of my home was wrecked and my father was being rushed to the hospital.

He survived, though it was touch and go for a while there, and thereafter he was a different man. No longer an abuser, no longer violent. He never touched my sisters again. Or me. He didn't dare hurt anyone after that.

I'd survived my own hell, had defeated my monster, and was—in a way—the hero of my own coming-of-age story.

I remember a day when I was sitting on the mats at the jujutsu dojo with my instructor. We were talking, drinking bottles of water, sweating, aching from a hard class, and we were the last ones in the place. It was one of the rare times when I opened up about my childhood, including what had just happened. My sensei told me his story, and I learned that he grew up in a similar hell.

He said, "Some people get lucky and they're born into TV-sitcom families. Happy parents and all their problems are minor and can be solved by the end of a 30-minute episode. Maybe once in a blue moon they'll get a whack across the fanny, but that's it. Those people are lucky, but they're also a long way from anyone I know. They're not like us."

"So," I said, "what does that make us? Freaks? Victims? Damaged goods?"

He looked at me for a long time and there were odd lights in his eyes. "No. We're different is all. Not worse, not better. Different."

"Different how?" I persisted.

And he said, "We weren't born wrong or bad or anything like that, but we aren't like the people who were born into happiness and light. It's more like we were born to fire."

Born to fire.

I truly understood what he meant. And it spoke to one of those great unanswerable questions we humans sometimes pause to consider: What if? What if my father had been a different person? What if I'd run away instead of staying in that hell? What if I hadn't finally stood up to my old man and used my martial arts skills to stop the cycle of abuse in our house? What if I hadn't watched all those movies and read all those books about people standing up to a seemingly unbeatable negative force?

What if, what if . . . ?

It can be a real killer of a mental exercise, too, because we can't ever really know if life would have been better had that one kind of threat or that one transformative cause not been there. In moments of self-deception and rationalization, we try to blame the circumstances of our lives on fate or destiny. In worse moments, we believe ourselves to be hounded by bad luck. It works out the same, though. We can never know what our lives would have been like had things played out a little differently.

But here's the thing . . .

Having the trajectory of one's life forever changed by a tragic incident isn't necessarily a bad thing. Sure, the event is bad—that's a given. But the *effect* doesn't necessarily have to be equally bad. Sometimes good things come out of bad.

Over the years that concept grew in meaning for me because it seemed to define a very specific part of our culture. Just as it defines a certain type of character in the stories I read and, later, wrote.

Being born to fire isn't a flaw. It's not a condition or a scar.

A lot of the most successful novels, comics, and short stories I've written are part of my desire to explore this phenomenon. In *Ghost Road Blues* and its sequels, a bunch of very ordinary people are pitted against an army of vampires. They prevail because they, like most people, are stronger and more resourceful than they think. My Joe Ledger thriller series pits the hero and his special ops team against massive international conspiracies and terrorist organizations. My Sam Hunter short stories feature a *benandanti* werewolf who has become a private investigator specializing in cases involving innocent women and children. I don't write about monsters, you see. I really do write about the people who fight them.

Which brings me to *Supernatural* and why I love that damn show so much. Sam and Dean Winchester were also born to fire. The tragic and horrific death of their mother left burn scars on their souls. As they peel back the layers of the complex history of their family, they see firsthand that there was always a darkness around them, and they feel the burn of that dreadful fire.

The Winchester brothers don't *have* to take up this fight, though. It is a calling that they answer, however reluctantly, because they can't stand the thought of the monsters winning. I get that. I get that.

Sometimes they go on a deliberate hunt and sometimes the hunt finds them. There is an argument to be made, at least from a "larger world" perspective, that once you peer into the darkness and see what's there then it also sees you. It knows you, and sometimes it goes hunting for you.

If you're ready, if you've trained and armed yourself with weapons and knowledge, then you are ready for that fight. Maybe even hungry for it, even though you know that winning can break your heart. Sam and Dean have had their hearts broken.[1] They've been brutalized, broken in places, robbed of peace, and lost in darkness, their optimism fractured.[2] But they keep coming back. They keep getting back to their feet. Each and every time.[3]

Why?

Because they were born to fire.

And man oh man do they love to make the monsters burn.

 **Jonathan Maberry** is a *New York Times* bestselling author, 5-time Bram Stoker Award-winner, and comic book writer. He writes in multiple genres including suspense, thriller, horror, science fiction, fantasy, and action, for adults, teens and middle grade. His works include the *Joe Ledger* thrillers, *Glimpse*, the *Rot & Ruin series*, the *Dead of Night* series, *The Wolfman*, *X-Files Origins: Devil's Advocate*, *Mars One*, and many others. Several of his works are in development for film and TV. He

is the editor of high-profile anthologies including *The X-Files,
V-Wars, Scary Out There, Out of Tune, Kingdoms Fall, Baker Street
Irregulars, Nights of the Living Dead,* and others. He lives in Del
Mar, California. Find him online at jonathanmaberry.com.

*Notes*

1. e.g., episodes 1–01, "Pilot" (September 13, 2005); 6–21, "Let It Bleed" (May 20,
   2011).
2. e.g., episodes 3–16, "No Rest for the Wicked" (May 15, 2005); 6–13, "Unforgiven" (February 11, 2011); 2–04, "Children Shouldn't Play with Dead Things"
   (October 19, 2006); 10–01, "Black" (October 7, 2014); 2–09, "Croatoan" (December 7, 2006).
3. Eventually, anyway. They both stay on the show, after all.—Editor.

# INTRODUCTION

# The Word and the Why

M A R K   R .   P E L L E G R I N O
"Lucifer" on *Supernatural*

When I came onto *Supernatural* (in what was to be the final season), I had no idea that the show would more than double its intended life span, and grow stronger and more potent with age. To me, it was just a job, like any other. Sure, I would be playing the iconic role of Lucifer, a being immortalized by brighter luminaries than I since Faust first crossed the boards to seal his deal with Mephistopheles. But Warner Bros. and the CW had very little in common with Marlow, Goethe, or Shakespeare, so I never anticipated having anything more than a minimal impact on the world at large.

Fast-forward and what was to be a four or five off in the final season turned into a few episodes here and a few episodes there in a never-ending saga. And as the character of Lucifer evolved through several iterations (and vessels)—from Apocalyptic Lucifer to Impish Lucifer; from Lucifer as potential savior to potential terminator—one thing remained constant and even grew: the love of the fandom.

After a time, not sure when exactly, an interesting phenomenon occurred. What was once show and audience, actors and fans, began a process of merging. It was a gradual but palpable evolution from many disparate individuals to a singular group identity. The metamorphosis first took the form of a tentative label, a verbal identifier that set the *Supernatural* fandom apart from other sci-fi/horror fandoms. It was a word, perhaps first tentatively thrown into the social mix by a passionate fan, or blurted out into the ether by an actor at his Q&A. The word probably got a couple of laughs at first but, for enough people, the word unlocked a deep truth and what started out as a half jest, became a serious reality. The word was *family*.

How did such an evolution happen? Was it the rebel spirit of the show? A mythology that irreverently turns classical religious images on their heads (angels not as guardians of men but arrogant pricks, and the Devil as the most honest guy in the room) can be very seductive, I imagine. Or was it the unique alchemy of the cast? (*Supernatural* is in the habit of hiring some pretty kind people who seem to have an aptitude for bonding with fans.) Well, not to pound the drum of "same old . . . ," but many shows with interesting mythologies and really nice people playing their roles still have mere fans, not families. So . . . what's the deal?

A family, if it is not by blood relation, implies a deeper connection than mere commonality of interests or attitudes. It implies a felt sense—an identification—of likeness, of similarity, of mutuality. In other words, you're family not so much because of shared interests, but because of shared souls. Family is that something in you that resonates with and recognizes that something in another. I have a theory as to what the "something" is that sits in the seat of the unconscious and is recognizable below words. I call it the "inner orphan."

An orphan is literally a child abandoned, usually by the death or absence of its parents. But the inner orphan is the displaced and disowned child in us all. Emptiness, displacement, and alienation have been feelings shared by many for generations. These feelings (and the attempts to grapple with them) have been the source of existentialist narratives and post-modernist novels for ages. Philosophers and social commentators have tried to find "alienation ground zero" for years and have entertained many possible loci: the complexities caused by civilization itself; the decline of religion and social tradition as our moral maps; the birth of technology. In short, everything beyond the "noble savage" has been blamed for dehumanizing us and forcing us further from our own authenticity. But, whatever the cause, whether by social construct or imperfect parenting, the inner orphan is in all of us and, like all sentient beings, seeks its own. Is it any wonder that the orphan in me seeks and finds comfort in camaraderie with the orphan in you? Is it any wonder that we gravitate to a show about . . . orphans?

Shakespeare rightly felt that art holds a mirror up to nature.[1] If that is so, and I believe it is, *Supernatural* (as art) cannot escape that noble human tradition. That mirror—the mirror of art— has a magical power of catharsis and transformation. By seeing, we are informed and healed. By knowing what's possible, we are transformed.

In the show, the mirror is held up to a family of literal orphans who face up to the whims of an indifferent and often hostile universe . . . and win. They win, not by the possession of some superhuman quality, but by the very human and attainable virtues of love, loyalty, certitude, courage, thought, and independence. I can think of nothing more cathartic and more empowering for the inner orphan to see and experience than the success of virtue in an indifferent (at best) or hostile world. But if that was all there was, we would still only be fans of a good, heroic narrative that used our common vulnerability as a story point. Right? As fans and actors we would still only interact on the imaginary level of the story. But what makes us a family is the exchange that takes place outside the show. If the show is the experience of orphans triumphant as a healing narrative, then the reality is the experience of orphans embracing one another in shameless acceptance. It's the virtues acted out in the show transferred to the community of "fandom," where life imitates art for the betterment of us all.

This show, like everything in our finite universe, will one

day end. But what can live on for many generations (besides the reruns) is the confidence that comes from recognizing our brokenness among our fellows; embracing it; and mending it with the virtues of love, courage, loyalty, certitude, and independence.

Embrace your inner orphan. He is the hero who will set you free.

 **Mark R. Pellegrino** is an actor and producer who has played Lucifer on *Supernatural* since 2009. He is well known for playing Jacob on *Lost*, along with many other television roles, and has appeared in films such as *The Big Lebowski* and *National Treasure*. Mark is also a martial arts practitioner and enthusiast.

*Note*

1. See William Shakespeare's *Hamlet*, Act III, Scene II (written sometime between 1599 and 1602).

The story begins at home.

# PART I

# FLESH AND BLOOD

## CHAPTER ONE

# The SPN Family:
# The Psychology of Fandom

## LYNN S. ZUBERNIS

*"Check it out, there's actually fans!*
*Not many of them, but still."*
—Dean Winchester[1]

> *"The source of basic anxiety is the feeling of being isolated*
> *and helpless in a potentially hostile world."*
> —psychoanalyst Karen Horney[2]

Fans experience the fictional characters and shows they love in powerful ways. We binge-watch for hours at a time, share experiences online, engage in spirited discussion with other fans about why Sam Winchester becomes addicted to demon blood or why Dean Winchester loves pie,[3] and travel to conventions. We collect memorabilia, write fan fiction or create fan art or fan videos, and restore classic 1967 Impalas.[4] Or maybe we just watch the show and love it. Psychological explanations for why people become fans have ranged from pathological—loneliness, attachment problems, even delusions—to an emphasis on normal developmental and social processes, such as identify formation, the importance of play, and the need to belong.[5]

*Supernatural* has been a cult fan favorite from the start, weathering near-cancellation season after season in its early years and surviving thanks to its passionate fan base.[6] *Supernatural* has won numerous People's Choice Awards, the cover of the very first *TV Guide* "Fan Favorite" magazine, and online polls about everything from "sexiest bad boy character" to "most tear jerker episode."[7] Why are some people so passionate about *Supernatural*—or any television show?

## Perspectives on Fan Passions
### Individual Psychology: Is This a Misery Thing?

Early research on individual psychological motivations for being a media fan leaned toward pathological explanations, emphasizing the most extreme kinds of fan behavior and largely ignoring the everyday fan.[8] One of the first researchers to conduct psychological studies of fans coined the frightening term *parasocial relationship* to describe the fan's one-way knowledge of a celebrity, which is not reciprocated, and even warned of the possibility of *erotomanic delusions* if a fan went too far down this slippery slope of fannish enthusiasm.[9] Fans were viewed as dysfunctional and obsessive, trying to shore up a missing sense of fulfillment and identity, and compensating for a lack of relationships, by becoming overly absorbed with a celebrity. Fans were hypothesized to be materialistic, insecurely attached, lonely, prone to fantasy and dissociation, and have lower cognitive functioning and a low level of well-being.[10] *Supernatural* has reflected this pathologizing view of fans, along with more positive models, in its tradition of incorporating its fans into multiple "meta" episodes (*meta* being a colloquialism for *metafiction*, fiction that somehow alludes to its own fictional nature). Series creator Eric Kripke wrote the first portrayal of fans into the show with fangirl/character Becky Rosen. Kripke's version of Becky can be seen as affectionately poking fun at his show's fans; the character in early seasons was portrayed as knowledgeable and even allowed to save the day.[11] Unfortunately, Becky returns later with a more pathologizing portrayal, as a lonely, insecure young woman whose unhealthy obsession with Sam Winchester reflects these absorption–addiction models.[12]

While some studies have found lower levels of psychological well-being, though, these were in small samples of self-categorized "celebrity worshippers"—those obsessed with individual celebrities—not television show "fans."[13] Eventually, the researchers concluded that celebrity worship was not problematic if carried out in moderation.[14] (Critics have noted that it would be conceptually flawed to treat *celebrity worshipper* as synonymous with *fan*.)[15]

A more positive view of fans emerges from psychologists studying sports fans, who took as a starting point a more neutral conceptualization of fans. This may be because sports fans continue to be less stigmatized than media fans, although the two types of fans have been found to be similar in motivation and behavior. Several studies found a positive, rather than a negative, relationship between identifying as a fan and overall well-being, with sports fans of local teams having higher self-esteem; more positive emotions; less neuroticism, loneliness, and feelings of alienation; and lower levels of depression.[16] Later portrayals of fans on *Supernatural* have been more positive as well, especially kick-ass tech whiz and self-professed geek Charlie Bradbury[17] and the playwright Marie, whose unique fan fiction interpretation of *Supernatural* is eventually explicitly embraced by the Winchesters themselves.[18]

*Supernatural* is also notable for the reciprocal relationship between fans and actors that has developed over the years, thanks to high levels of interaction on social media and an unprecedented number of conventions. The actors tend to have a more positive view of their fans thanks to this interaction.[19] Stereotypes and stigma tend to fall away when people interact face-to-face,[20] which is precisely what has happened with every-other-weekend conventions. In an early interview, series lead Jensen Ackles talked about how his view of *Supernatural* fans changed once he started meeting them:

> It was kind of surprising when the show really got its feet under it in the middle of the first season and we started getting feedback and recognition of the show. And it was from unlikely characters. The WB was a network focused on a demographic that was obviously much younger. The people coming up and talking to us or writing about the show online happened to be an older audience and a very intelligent audience. It wasn't "What side of the bed do you sleep on?" and "Do you wear boxers or briefs?" They wanted to know why this character said this and what did they mean by that, and could be there double meanings and how this character relates to that or not. It was kind of refreshing.[21]

Series lead Jared Padalecki also wanted to let fans know that he wasn't so different from them, identifying as a fan himself:

> One of the funnier things that happened at a con was when that sweet girl got up to ask a question

and started sobbing, and I wanted to say, "Oh my, it's okay—I'm a fan, too." If I saw Eddie Vedder, for example, I'd be like uhhhh, I—I—I don't even know what I'm going to say.[22]

In fact, it was series lead Jared Padalecki who first coined the term "SPN Family" to describe the reciprocal relationship that has developed between actors and fans.[23]

## Wanting to Be Just Like You: A Developmental View of Individual Identity

A similarly positive view of being a fan comes from a life-span development perspective. In contrast to the view of fans as dysfunctional and obsessive, this research emphasizes the healthy aspects of being a fan. *Psychosocial theory*[24] describes life as a series of stages, each driven by a crisis or challenge that needs to be negotiated. As we move through these stages, we develop our identity and self-concept. It is generally accepted that adolescents form attachments to celebrities and popular media characters as part of the process of identity development, and that this fosters the transition to adulthood in the same way that family and peers serve as models. The task of identity development, it is now understood, continues into adulthood, and adults also form attachments to popular media characters and celebrities, emulating the traits and characteristics they admire.[25] Having heroes and idols, such as the Winchesters or Castiel, is a normal part of identity development, allow-ing us to try on identities and forge our own in the process. Both fictional characters and the actors who portray them shape fans' identities by inspiring fans to take on similar atti-tudes, values and behaviors.[26] *Supernatural* fans have adopted

the Winchesters' mantra to "always keep fighting," wearing it
on T-shirts, inking it onto their bodies in tattoos, and making
it part of their value system. Individual cast members have also
inspired fans to support a wide range of charitable causes, from
animal rescue to juvenile diabetes, adopting these values as
their own.

Most fans fall into one of three developmental stages: adolescence, young adulthood, or middle adulthood.[27] Motivations
for being a fan differ, depending on a person's developmental stage. Adolescents, negotiating the challenge of establishing an identity, may become fans as a way of finding models
to emulate, particularly if there are no suitable models within
their family or community. Supernatural fans find plenty of
inspiration in Sam and Dean, especially in their loyalty to each
other and their determination to make the world a better place.
Fans also find the angel Castiel inspiring, as he struggles to fit
in, not entirely comfortable either in Heaven or on earth. In
addition, many of the actors who appear on the show serve as
role models for their fans. The show's female cast members—
including Kim Rhodes, Briana Buckmaster, Alaina Huff-
man, Kathryn Newton, and Ruth Connell—have modeled
the importance of being unapologetically genuine with their
"Wayward AF" message, which has been adopted by many
fans.[28] The actors explicitly encourage viewers to challenge
mainstream social norms. Most of the characters on the show
also repeatedly challenge societal norms, adding to the power
of this message.

The challenge for people in the young adult stage is learning
how to be comfortable with intimacy, instead of becoming
isolated. In a modern culture, which can necessitate frequent
moves and separations, this may be difficult. There are many
online Supernatural fan communities where fans congregate to
discuss the show and share opinions, news, photos, art, and

videos, and the feeling of belonging to such a group can reduce feelings of isolation.[29]

In the stage of middle adulthood, Erik Erikson described the crisis as *generativity*—finding meaning in life and focusing on leaving something behind—as opposed to *self-absorption*.[30] Fans in this developmental stage may focus on the charitable aspects of fandom as a way of giving back and as a means of generativity. The various charitable campaigns started by the *Supernatural* actors (including cast T-shirt campaigns and Misha Collins's international efforts through his nonprofit Random Acts) have been a huge success, allowing fans to make change in the world and to come together in doing so. Middle-aged fans may also find normative fan behaviors, which allow free expression of emotion, desire, and passion, to be a way of "staying young" with permission to bond with other fans and share that passion openly.[31]

People in all three stages may also be drawn to fandom during times of transition, especially when the developmental transition includes loss (death, divorce, etc.) or significant life changes. The relationships established within fan communities are particularly helpful at these times. In addition, the emotions that are generated by being a fan can be a way of reconnecting people to their feelings, making these transitions smoother.[32]

## Social Identity and the Experience of Belonging: We're All in the Same Boat

Early studies characterized fans as troubled individuals stalking a celebrity, perhaps with delusions about an imagined relationship (for example, an attempted assassin tried to kill President Ronald Reagan to attract a famous actress's attention).[33] So-called worshippers were viewed as isolated in their feelings about the celebrity, often lonely and disconnected.[34] Much fan behavior, by contrast, is highly social and community-based.

The academic field of fan studies pays particular attention to the role of community in fandom, emphasizing the creative and communal aspects. Instead of being an indication of pathology, being a fan is viewed as an expression of passion and enthusiasm that can enrich an individual's life,[35] based in part on the importance of "belongingness" for humans. We evolved to prioritize being part of a group and feeling included in that group; for the earliest humans, being excluded meant not surviving. Our emotional wiring evolved to meet these very needs.[36] This is an evolutionary lesson we have not forgotten, which means people will go to great lengths to belong. Fandom, it turns out, allows many people to do so.

In part, what fandom (and any community) offers is a group within which to develop one's identity. According to *social identity theory*,[37] our identities are created, developed, and strengthened through interaction with other people and tied to the groups to which we belong. Individuals figure out who they are by comparing themselves to others within the group (*in-group members*) and differentiating themselves from those outside the group (*out-group members*). We select these groups in order to maintain a positive identity: People want to feel good about themselves, so we want to belong to groups that can help us bolster that positive sense of self. Our connection to the group gives us a boost in self-esteem when whatever we are fans of is successful, whether that's a sports team winning a game, an individual actor winning an Emmy, or *Supernatural* winning a People's Choice Award or the show being renewed for yet another season. Many people want to belong to a group that is distinctive in some way, so becoming a fan of a genre television show like *Supernatural* fulfills that desire.[38]

The sense of belonging we feel when we affiliate with like-minded others is a benefit in itself. Social support networks can help us cope with anxiety, loneliness, and depression.[39] The benefits of social connection through fandom may be particularly important at a time in our culture when traditional modes of connection are not as readily available through nearby family, religious organizations, tight neighborhood bonds, or even the local pub. *Supernatural* fans and cast alike refer to themselves as the "SPN Family," making explicit reference to the function the community serves in their lives. In fact, fans view their fandom communities as more prominent in their lives than their face-to-face neighbors in terms of belongingness, emotional connection, shared values, and overall sense of community.[40] These perceptions translate to higher levels of collective happiness and a positive social identity. Importantly, fans perceive themselves to be part of the fandom group even when no face-to-face contact occurs; online fan communities serve the same role in establishing a sense of belongingness and acceptance.[41]

In online *Supernatural* fan communities, norms for interaction and for expressing passion for a favorite show are quite different than in the rest of the "real world." This opportunity to be genuine with others is another healthy benefit of fandom for many fans. Authenticity within relationships is associated with higher self-esteem and a stronger sense of well-being, whereas hiding who you really are to please others compromises identity development.[42] Fans often talk about finding like-minded others within fandom as feeling like "coming home," referring to a place where you can be yourself. The "disconfirmation of uniqueness" that we gain from being part of a group provides a relief, which results in greater self-esteem and a more positive sense of self.[43] When *Supernatural* fans share their real selves within the fandom community and find that other fans reach out and say, "OMG, me too!" that validation and reflection can be powerful.[44]

Of course, within any group there is contention and hierarchy, and that includes fandom. As we've seen, belonging to a group is extremely important; hence, there is a need to police the boundaries of that group and make sure other fans within it are "doing fandom right." Fans might look down on other fans who are lower in the social order, or perhaps more extreme in their fan behavior, which has the effect of raising self-esteem in the fan who can say, "Oh well, I wouldn't do *that*."[45] Within *Supernatural* fandom, some fans split into different camps, depending on which characters or which relationships are preferred (Sam Girls, Dean Girls, Cas Girls, Brothers Fans, or fans of certain romantic pairings between characters, known as "ships").[46] These intra-fandom arguments tend to be about interpretation of the show's canon. Because there is a strong affective attachment to these characters and their continued role in the show, adherents of each side can feel personally threatened when their interpretation is disputed.

Being a fan is connected to identity development through participation in the fandom community, but personal identity is also constructed through the fan's emotional connection to the show itself.[47] According to *social surrogacy theory*, a beloved television show can fulfill some of our human need to belong. Television shows are particularly powerful in creating feelings of belongingness because they allow viewers to regularly immerse themselves in an alternate universe that becomes familiar and comfortable.[48] The most powerful shows also have themes that activate social processing in viewers—*Supernatural*'s theme of family and its strong focus on relationships, for example. Although *Supernatural* viewers certainly are aware that Sam and Dean and Castiel are not real, when fans watch an episode, the brain is "tricked" into believing that some of the viewer's belonging needs have been met anyway.[49] When we identify strongly with a fictional character, we are able to be transported

# JARED PADALECKI ON "ALWAYS KEEP FIGHT-ING" AND THE SUPERNATURAL FAMILY

## Janina Scarlet

Jared Padalecki's "Always Keep Fighting" campaign ignited after he lost several friends to suicide and after his own experience with depression. Padalecki reports that he wanted to help reduce the shame and stigma associated with struggling with mental illness and wanted to send an encouraging message to his fans, reminding them to keep fighting.[50]

**Janina Scarlet:** "I'm a psychologist and I'm a big fan of your 'Always Keep Fighting' campaign. It's saving lives. I work with trauma survivors and, seriously, thank you so much for taking this initiative."

**Jared Padalecki:** "It's amazing to me. It's become much like *Supernatural*: It's greater than the sum of its parts. There's this kooky show about Hook Man, Bloody Mary, Wendigos,[51] and all of a sudden it's eleven years later. It's become this family, you know? We've all devoted so much time to each other, it's almost like being alumni of a college or something. When I meet somebody who's watched *Supernatural*, I'm like, 'Me, too! I've devoted way too much of my life to that as well!' So it's a fun camaraderie between the fandom and the writers and the actors, and I feel like truly we're all a part of this. The same with 'Always Keep Fighting.' It means something to me. That was something that I've always dealt with. Thank you."

Actor Jared Padalecki and Dr. Scarlet practice a mindfulness exercise.

into that world and enjoy the full experience of that character.[52] While these are still considered parasocial or one-way relationships, social surrogacy theory views the experience of belongingness delivered in this way to be an expression of a normal human need, instead of something pathological.[53]

In fact, when people are in the presence of a parasocial relationship partner (whether at a convention getting an autograph from Jensen Ackles or at home watching Dean Winchester on television), or even just thinking about the partner, fans react much as they would if they were with a real-life friend, with increases in empathy and greater openness to self-disclosure. There is even research to show that fans become closer to what they consider their ideal selves when in the presence of their favorite characters or actors, indicating the strength of the parasocial relationship.[54] Interestingly, the need to feel that one belongs is only met in this way by watching or thinking about one's *favorite* show or characters. Thus, this is not just escapism, which could be engaged in by watching whatever happened to be on TV. No one who has ever grieved over the cancellation of a favorite television show will be greatly surprised by the fact that the emotional connections that fans have to their favorite shows are quite powerful. When faced with feelings of rejection or loneliness, fears of being left out, or even having an argument with a loved one, watching a favorite television show can serve as a buffer for threats to belongingness and increase our sense of self-esteem and feelings of happiness.[55]

The question of why we have emotional responses to fictional characters we know are not real has been debated for decades. One explanation is that works of fiction are created out of real-life elements that we already recognize and react to emotionally, but are presented in a new configuration. The characters we relate to have psychological features and emotions that are meaningful to us; they are familiar to us from our own lives.

Thus, we react to them not only cognitively but emotionally. In fact, fictional stories invite an emotional reaction, and we may feel safer experiencing those emotions because of the lack of real-world ramifications.[56] A television show like *Supernatural* offers characters who grapple with strong emotions every week—universal emotions like love and loyalty and grief and loss. The story we're entering may give us a new perspective on our own emotional lives as well.

Certain personality traits impact the way people react to fictional characters and shows. One of the psychological characteristics that may predispose someone to being a fan is the ability to become highly involved with a media text, so that "transportation" into the fictional world can happen. Transportation is being absorbed into the story, so that the fictional narrative seems more real and has a more powerful impact.[57] Another trait that impacts becoming a fan is capacity for empathy, the ability to put ourselves in other people's shoes and thus understand how they're feeling. We become more emotionally involved with fictional characters when we experience empathy for them.[58]

Attachment theory can also help explain fans' emotional reaction to fictional characters and the actors who play them. Attachment is the emotional bond between humans, starting with the earliest bond between infant and caregiver and later shaping relationships in adulthood.[59] Attachment is spurred in part by our attraction to human faces,[60] which might explain the seemingly endless array of photos and gifs of Sam, Dean, and Castiel online. Centuries ago, we mostly saw the same faces day after day in our immediate neighborhood, so familiarity became a powerful determinant of what we valued. When fans say they fell into *Supernatural* fandom via social media without first seeing the show, this might be exactly what they mean. If you look long enough at a particular face, forming an attachment is likely. The brain doesn't necessarily make a distinction between the familiar neighbor across the way and the celebrity you see all day long on social media.[61] Once a fan feels an attachment to a show or an individual celebrity, the natural result is a desire for proximity—in other words, fans want to be close to whatever it is they're fans of. This can play out in repeated viewings of *Supernatural*, collecting character figures or miniature Impalas, getting photo ops and autographs at conventions, or pursuing closer connection with other fans.

## Fandom as Play Space: The *Supernatural* Sandbox

Fandom has also been conceptualized as a site of play, which is healthy for people of all ages. *Affective play* is all about the pleasure we feel when we engage in activities that allow us to challenge the boundaries between our internal reality and our external reality.[62] Play gives people outlets for experimenting, trying on other identities or perhaps expressing our own genuine identity more freely. Play space is therapeutic for the relaxation and freedom it offers. Online fan communities can be considered play space because of their different norms for self-expression. Fans who write fan fiction (stories about favorite fictional characters or the actors who portray them) often refer to the practice as "playing in the sandbox" of the show. The characters, in this sense, are toys for fandom to play with and then return. Creating fanworks can also serve this purpose.

Within the space of a fan convention, fans can engage with the world of their favorite show and with other fans in a playful way—the raucous karaoke party at Creation Entertainment's *Supernatural* conventions, or the costume contest, for example. Because play is carried out in a sphere that is not "ordinary life," people can immerse themselves temporarily in the fictional world of their favorite television show. Jenkins refers to these behaviors as "an escape from the mundane into the marvelous."[63] Play space—and fan space—can be seen as an example of the *magic circle*, a space dedicated exclusively to play and thus separated from everyday life, creating a safe space that is a temporary escape from everyday stressors and a place to explore identity.[64]

There is evidence that psychological well-being is connected to engaging in activities like these that are "happiness-relevant." Having a passion for something, whether it is football, coin collecting, or *Supernatural*, can improve well-being, especially when engaging in that activity results in repeatedly experiencing positive affect. When fans continually immerse themselves in something they love, they incorporate some of that passion into their own identity. As long as people retain the flexibility that prevents that passion from interfering with other life activities, this "harmonious passion" is beneficial to both well-being and personal growth.[65]

## Why *Supernatural? Supernatural* Has Everything!

Clearly there are many explanations for why people become fans and how the experience of being a fan impacts identity development and psychological health. But how do fans select the object of all that passion? There are hundreds of television shows, any of which could potentially attract the enthusiasm of fans. While genre shows are often the ones with passionate fan bases, few have attracted a fan community as loyal, vocal, and persistent as *Supernatural*. Why?

*Supernatural* began as a horror-themed show, focused on the Winchester brothers fighting monsters and demons while crisscrossing a quintessentially American landscape in their '67 Chevy Impala. The show incorporates the classic theme of the reluctant hero, and tosses in sibling rivalry and unresolved Oedipal drama. Creator Eric Kripke invested the show with an emphasis on family relationships from the beginning, allowing the show a surprising amount of flexibility within its genre.[66]

The Winchesters and Castiel are characters who don't fit in with the world around them, in keeping with *Supernatural's* tendency to focus on disaffected or odd-man-out characters; anyone who has experienced the sense of not belonging or not fitting in may find those characters and their experience compelling.[67] Fans tend to find themselves in certain stories and characters, and those are the ones who draw people in to become fans.

While characters in *Supernatural* are compelling, so are themes the show tackles. The Winchesters endure repeated losses and traumatic experiences, but ultimately their resilience allows them to keep going. This theme has been adopted by the actors and fans in a series of charity campaigns. The first was started by Jared Padalecki, echoing the show's message to "Always Keep Fighting." Themes of redemption also occur throughout the show's run, with all the main characters sometimes going off the path that's paved with good intentions, occasionally going to Hell quite literally as a result. Nevertheless, they are all redeemed eventually, which is a reassuring message for fans. Fans often rely on their favorite show for solace, comfort, and reassurance: *Supernatural's* message of redemption ultimately provides that solace.

*References*

Adorno, T., & Horkheimer, M. (2002). *Dialectic of enlightenment*. Stanford, CA: Stanford University Press.

Baumeister, R. F., & Leary, M. R. (1995). The need to belong: Desire for interpersonal attachments as a fundamental human motivation. *Psychological Bulletin, 117*(3), 497–529.

Boon, S. D., & Lomore, C. D. (2001). Admirer-celebrity relationships among young adults: Explaining perceptions of celebrity influence on identity. *Human Communication Research, 27*(3), 432–465.

# ROAD MUSIC

### "A Single Man Tear" from *Supernatural: The Musical*[68]

People crave belonging and acceptance.[69] Written for *Supernatural*'s 200th episode, the song refers to the fandom's love of Dean Winchester's complex negotiation of repressed masculinity and overt emotionality, as evidenced by scenes in which one tear escapes and rolls down his cheek during an emotionally powerful moment. Within the fan community, that is referred to as the OPT, or One Perfect Tear.[70] Such in-group references are markers of acceptance within the group.

Booth, P. (2016). *Crossing fandoms: SuperWhoLock and the contemporary fan audience.* London, UK: Macmillan.

Bowlby, J. (1969). *Attachment and loss* (vol. 1, *Attachment*). London, UK: Hogarth.

Branscombe, N. R., & Wann, D. L. (1991). The positive social and self-concept consequences of sport team identification. *Journal of Sport & Social Issues, 15*(2), 115–127.

Buckmaster, B. (2017). I am you. In L. S. Zubernis (Ed.), *Family don't end with blood: Cast and fans on how Supernatural has changed lives* (pp. 68–72). Dallas, TX: BenBella.

Caughey, J. (1984). *Imaginary social worlds: A cultural approach.* Lincoln, NE: University of Nebraska Press.

Clarke, J. W. (1990). *On being mad or merely angry: John W. Hinckley, Jr., and other dangerous people.* Princeton, NJ: Princeton University Press.

Cohen, J. (2006). Audience identification with media characters: In. J. Bryant & P. Vorderer (Eds.), *Psychology of entertainment* (pp. 183–197). Mahwah, NJ: Erlbaum.

Crisp, R. J., & Abrams, D. (2008). Improving intergroup attitudes and reducing stereotype threat: An integrated model. *European Review of Social Psychology, 19*, 242–284.

Derrick, J. L., Gabriel, S., & Hugenberg, K. (2009). Social surrogacy: How favored television programs provide the experience of belonging. *Journal of Experimental Social Psychology, 45*(2), 352–362.

Dino, A., Reysen, S., & Branscombe, N. R. (2009). Online interactions between group members who differ in status. *Journal of Language & Social Psychology, 28*(1), 85–93.

Erikson, E. H. (1959). *Identity and the life cycle.* New York, NY: Norton.

Erikson, E. H. (1968). *Youth and crisis.* New York, NY: Norton.

Fiske, J. (1989). *Understanding popular culture.* New York, NY: Routledge.

Gardner, W. L., & Knowles, M. L. (2008). Love makes you real: Favorite television characters are perceived as "real" in a social facilitation paradigm. *Social Cognition, 26*(2), 156–168.

Gaunt, R. (2011). Effects of intergroup conflict and social contact on prejudice: The mediating role of stereotypes and evaluations. *Journal of Applied Social Psychology, 41*(6), 1340–1355.

Gilligan, C. (1982). *In a different voice: Psychological theory and women's development.* Cambridge, MA: Harvard University Press.

Greenwood, D. (2008). Television as escape from self: Psychological predictors of media involvement. *Personality & Individual Differences, 44*(2), 414–424.

Gwinner, K., & Swanson, S. R. (2003). A model of fan identification: Antecedents and sponsorship outcomes. *Journal of Services Marketing, 17*(3), 275–294.

Hills, M. (2002). *Fan cultures.* London, UK: Routledge.

Horney, K. (1945). *Our inner conflicts: A constructive theory of neurosis.* New York, NY: Norton.

Horton, D., & Wohl, R. (1956). Mass communication and para-social interaction: Observations on intimacy at a distance. *Psychiatry, 19*(3), 215–230.

Impett, E. A., Sorsoli, L., Schooler, D., Henson, J. M., & Tolman, D. L. (2008). Girls' relationship authenticity and self-esteem across adolescence. *Developmental Psychology, 44*(3), 722–733.

Jenkins, H. (1992). *Textual poachers: Television fans and participatory culture.* New York, NY: Routledge.

Jenkins, H. (2006). *Fans, bloggers and gamers.* New York, NY: New York University Press.

Jenks1983 (2011, April 11). *Jensen Ackles panel Jibcon 2 Pt 3.* https://www.youtube.com/watch?v=GA3womj1zKA.

Jenson, J. (1992). Fandom as pathology: The consequences of characterization. In L. Lewis (Ed.) *The adoring audience: Fan culture and popular media* (pp. 9–29). London, UK: Routledge.

Karkanias, A. (2014). The intra- and inter-sub-community dynamics of fandom. *Summer Research,* paper 230. http://soundideas.pugetsound.edu/summer_research/230.

Kreitman, N. (2006). Fantasy, fiction and feelings. *Metaphilosophy, 37*(5), 605–622.

Larsen, K., & Zubernis, L. (2013). *Fangasm: Supernatural fangirls.* Iowa City, IA: University of Iowa Press.

Mackenzie, C. (2011, March 14). *'Supernatural': Jared Padalecki talks horseback riding and his charitable causes.* Screener TV: http://screenertv.com/news-features/supernatural-jared-padalecki-talks-horseback-riding-and-his-charitable-causes/.

Major, B., & Eccleston, C. P. (2005). Stigma and social exclusion. In D. Abrams, M. A. Hogg, & J. M. Marques (Eds.), *Social psychology of inclusion and exclusion* (pp. 63–88). New York, NY: Psychology Press.

Maltby, J., Day, L., McCutcheon, L. E., Gillett, R., Houran, J., & Ashe, D. D. (2004). Personality and coping: A context for examining celebrity worship and mental health. *British Journal of Psychology, 95*(4), 411–428.

Maltby, J., Day, L., McCutcheon, L. E., Houran, J., & Ashe, D. D. (2006). Extreme celebrity worship, fantasy proneness and dissociation: Developing the measurement and understanding of celebrity worship within a clinical personality context. *Personality & Individual Differences, 40*(2), 273–283.

Maltby, J., McCutcheon, L. E., Ashe, D. D., & Houran, J. (2001). The self-reported psychological well-being of celebrity worshippers. *North American Journal of Psychology, 3*(3), 441–452.

Martin, M. M., Cayanus, J., McCutcheon, L. E., & Maltby, J. (2003). Celebrity worship and cognitive flexibility. *North American Journal of Psychology, 5*(1), 75–80.

McCarley, N. G., & Escoto, C. A. (2003). Celebrity worship and psychological type. *North American Journal of Psychology, 5*(1), 117–120.

McCutcheon, L. E., Aruguete, M., Scott, V. B., & VonWaldner, K. L. (2004). Preference for solitude and attitude toward one's favorite celebrity. *North American Journal of Psychology, 6*(3), 499–506.

McCutcheon, L. E., Ashe, D. D., Houran, J., & Maltby, J. (2003). A cognitive profile of individuals who tend to worship celebrities. *Journal of Psychology, 137*(4), 309–322.

McCutcheon, L. E., Scott, V. B., Aruguete, M. S., & Parker, J. (2006). Exploring the link between attachment and the inclination to obsess about or stalk celebrities. *North American Journal of Psychology, 8*(2), 289–300.

Obst, P., Zinkiewicz, L., & Smith, S. G. (2002). Sense of community in science fiction fandom: Comparing neighborhood and interest group sense of community. *Journal of Community Psychology, 30(1)*, 105–117.

Padalecki, J. (2017). What does the fandom mean to me? In L. S. Zubernis (Ed.), *Family don't end with blood: Cast and fans on how Supernatural has changed lives* (pp. 217–246). Dallas, TX: BenBella.

Pinker, S. (1997). *How the mind works.* New York, NY: Norton.

Prudom, L. (2015, March 12). *"Supernatural" star Jared Padalecki talks depression and why you should "always keep fighting."* Variety: http://variety.com/2015/tv/people-news/jared-padalecki-always-keep-fighting-depression-suicide-twloha-1201451708/.

Reysen, S., & Branscombe, N. R. (2009). Fanship and fandom: Comparisons between sport and non-sport fans. *Journal of Sport Behavior, 33*(2), 176–193.

Rhodes, K. (2017). Wayward AF. In L. S. Zubernis (Ed.), *Family don't end with blood: Cast and fans on how Supernatural has changed lives* (pp. 60–67). Dallas, TX: BenBella.

Rubin, A. M., Perse, E., & Powell, M. P. (1987). Development of parasocial interaction relationships. *Journal of Broadcasting & Electronic Media, 31*(3), 279–292.

Ryan, M. (2009, August 26). *"It's the fun Apocalypse": Creator Eric Kripke talks "Supernatural."* Chicago Tribune: http://featuresblogs.chicagotribune.com/entertainment_tv/2009/08/supernatural-season-5-eric-kripke-cw.html.

Schaefer, M. (2014, July 31). *Supernatural series finale was supposed to happen in season 5? Cast reveals new spoilers of original ending.* International Business Times: http://www.ibtimes.com/supernatural-series-finale-was-supposed-happen-season-5-cast-reveals-new-spoilers-original-1645008.

Schorr, A. N. (2000). Attachment and the regulation of the right brain. *Attachment & Human Development, 2*(1), 23–47.

Stanfill, M. (2013). "They're losers, but I know better": Intra-fandom stereotyping and the normalization of the fan subject. *Critical Studies in Media Communication, 30*(2), 117–134.

Stever, G. (2008). The celebrity appeal questionnaire: Sex, entertainment or leadership. *Psychological Reports, 103*(1), 113–120.

Stever, G. (2010). Fan behavior and lifespan development theory: Explaining para-social and social attachment to celebrities. *Journal of Adult Development, 18*(1), 1–7.

Stever, G. S. (2011). Celebrity worship: Critiquing a construct. *Journal of Applied Social Psychology, 41*(6), 1356–1370.

Tajfel, H., & Turner, J. C. (1986). The social identity theory of intergroup behavior. In S. Worchel & W. Austin (Eds.), *Psychology of intergroup relations* (2nd ed., pp. 7–24). Chicago, IL: Nelson-Hall.

Taylor, L. D. (2014). Investigating fans of fictional texts: Fan identity salience, empathy and transportation. *Psychology of Popular Media Culture, 4*(2), 172–187.

Vallerand, R. J. (2012). The role of passion in sustainable psychological well-being. *Psychology of Well-Being: Theory, Research & Practice, 2*(1), 1–21.

Wakefield, K. L., & Wann, D. L. (2006). An examination of dysfunctional sports fans: Method of classification and relationships with problem behaviors. *Journal of Leisure Research, 38*(2), 168–186.

Wann, D. L. (2006). Examining the potential causal relationship between sport team identification and psychological well-being. *Journal of Sport Behavior, 29*(1), 79–95.

Wann, D. L., Dunham, M. D., Byrd, M. L., & Keenan, B. L. (2004). The five-factor model of personality and the psychological health of highly identified sport fans. *International Sports Journal, 8*(2), 28–36.

Wann, D. L., Melnick, M. J., Russell, G. W., & Pease, D. G. (2001). *Sport fans: The psychology and social impact of spectators.* New York, NY: Routledge.

Wertham, F. (1954). *Seduction of the innocent.* New York, NY: Rinehart.

Yalom, I. (1998). *The Yalom reader: Selections from the work of a master therapist and story-teller.* New York, NY: Basic.

Zubernis, L., & Larsen, K. (2014). *Fan phenomena: Supernatural.* Bristol, UK: Intellect.

## Notes

1. Episode 4–18, "The Monster at the End of This Book" (April 2, 2009).
2. Horney (1945), p. 41.
3. Sam's addiction, prominent throughout season 4; Dean's love of pie, first mentioned in episode 1–11, "Scarecrow" (January 10, 2006).
4. Larsen & Zubernis (2013), Zubernis & Larsen (2014).
5. Boon & Lomore (2001), Hills (2002), Jenkins (1992, 2006), Maltby et al. (2001, 2006), McCutcheon et al. (2003, 2004, 2006), Stever (2010).
6. Schaefer (2014).
7. Zubernis & Larsen (2014).
8. Adorno & Horkheimer (2002), Fiske (1989), Jensen (1992), Major & Eccleston (2005), Wertham (1954).
9. Horton & Wohl (1956);
10. Maltby et al. (2001, 2006), Martin et al. (2003), McCutcheon et al. (2004, 2006).
11. Episodes 5–1, "Sympathy for the Devil" (September 10, 2009); 5–9, "The Real Ghostbusters" (November 12, 2009).
12. Episode 7–8, "Season Seven, Time for a Wedding!" (November 11, 2011).
13. Maltby et al. (2001, 2006), Martin et al. (2003), McCarley & Escoto (2003), McCutcheon et al. (2004, 2006).
14. Maltby et al. (2004).
15. e.g., Stever (2011).
16. Branscombe & Wann (1991), Wakefield & Wann (2006), Wann et al. (2001), Wann et al. (2004).
17. Episode 7–20, "The Girl with the Dungeons and Dragons Tattoo" (April 27, 2012).
18. Episode 10–5, "Fan Fiction" (November 11, 2014).
19. Padalecki (2017).
20. Crisp & Abrams (2008), Gaunt (2011).
21. Larsen & Zubernis (2013), p. 221.
22. Larsen & Zubernis (2013), p. 217.
23. Mackenzie (2011).
24. Erikson (1959, 1968).
25. Caughey (1984).
26. Boon & Lomore (2001).
27. Stever (2008).
28. Buckmaster (2017), Rhodes (2017).
29. Stever (2010).

30. Erikson (1959).
31. Stever (2010).
32. Stever (2010).
33. Clarke (1990).
34. Jenson (1992), Rubin et al. (1987).
35. Jenkins (1992).
36. Baumeister & Leary (1995).
37. Tajfel & Turner (1986).
38. Gwinner & Swanson (2003), Reysen & Branscombe (2009).
39. Baumeister & Leary (1995).
40. Obst et al. (2002).
41. Branscombe & Wann (1991), Dino et al. (2009), Reysen & Branscombe (2009), Wann (2006).
42. Gilligan (1982), Impett et al. (2008).
43. Yalom (1998).
44. Larsen & Zubernis (2013).
45. Stanfill (2013).
46. Karkanias (2014).
47. Jenkins (1992).
48. Cohen (2006).
49. Pinker (1997).
50. Prudom (2015).
51. Respectively, episodes 1–7, "Hook Man" (October 25, 2005); 1–5, "Bloody Mary" (October 11, 2005); 1–2, "Wendigo" (September 20, 2005).
52. Cohen (2006).
53. Derrick et al. (2009).
54. Gardner & Knowles (2008).
55. Derrick et al. (2009).
56. Kreitman (2006)
57. Greenwood (2008).
58. Taylor (2014).
59. Bowlby (1969).
60. Schorr (2000).
61. Schorr (2000).
62. Hills (2002).
63. Jenkins (2006), p. 42.
64. Hills (2002).
65. Vallerand (2012).
66. Ryan (2009).
67. Booth (2016).
68. Written by R. Thomson & C. Lennertz (2014); performed in episode 10–5, "Fan Fiction" (November 11, 2014).
69. Baumeister & Leary (1995).
70. Jenks1983 (2011).

## CHAPTER TWO

# Family by Choice or by Blood

ELIZABETH KUS, CHRISTINE
DICKSON, AND JANINA SCARLET

*"Once a wise man told me, 'Family don't end in blood,'
but it doesn't start there either. Family cares about you.
Not what you can do for them. Family is there—for
the good, bad, all of it. They got your back. Even
when it hurts. That's family."*
—Dean Winchester[1]

> *"Life doesn't make any sense without
> interdependence. We need each other, and
> the sooner we learn that, the better for us all."*
—Joan Erikson, psychologist Erik Erikson's wife and collaborator[2]

Regardless of supposedly traditional views, a large percentage of families are single-parent and a growing number include same-gender parents, stepparents, adoptive parents, and chosen families.[3] When the Winchester family is first introduced, they are the seemingly average nuclear (two-parent) family. After Azazel the yellow-eyed demon kills the boys' mother Mary, their father John Winchester becomes a single parent to Sam and Dean, often being absent while hunting monsters and searching for Azazel.[4] While trauma can be hard enough on anyone, long-term consequences for children become complicated when such experiences result in the absence of their primary support system, their parents. For some, family not by blood—chosen family, such as Bobby Singer—may make all the difference in how deeply the repercussions impact such children.

## Family Systems

*Family systems theory* suggests that because an individual is part of an emotional family unit, he or she cannot be understood without considering the interactions with other family members.[5] Family interactions can affect a family member's thoughts, feelings, and actions, with some of these elements being passed down across multiple generations.[6] The Winchesters come from a long line of hunters, most of whom believe in killing all monsters indiscriminately without second chances. Sam breaks this rule by sparing his childhood friend, Amy, a *kitsune* (a human-like creature that feeds on human brains' pituitary glands), but Dean, influenced by generations of hunter training, finds the kitsune and kills her.[7]

In addition to multigenerational influences, family members might be affected by *triangulation* (or simply *triangle*, a three-person system). According to family systems theory, two people in a relationship are more likely to have a tension between them because small conflicts can destabilize the relationship. Adding a third person to the group boosts stability in the group because tension can shift between the three members. After his wife is killed and once he learns that Sam might become

# ROAD MUSIC

## "Thunderstruck" by AC/DC[8]

Healthy relationships—including friendships, romantic couples, and families—need trust and commitment. If trust is broken, individuals may become less satisfied with a relationship, feel less committed to it, or consider severing it altogether.[9] When Dean returns from Purgatory, he learns that Sam did not try to find him. Dean is angry with his brother, feeling betrayed that Sam did not try to help him.[10]

a demon, John Winchester and his older son, Dean, both watch over Sam.[11] In this case, the mission of protecting Sam eases some of the tension and strengthens commitment in the Winchester triangle. After John dies, his sons are able to form separate triangles with family friend Bobby Singer, surrogate sister Charlie Bradbury, angel Castiel, and demon Crowley.[12]

When enough tension builds in any relationship, conflict becomes likely. If a conflict grows severe enough, the individuals might emotionally cut off their family members. *Emotional cutoff* might include avoiding sensitive topics around other family members, moving away, or reducing or completely severing contacts with other members.[13] Sam and Dean spend enough time on the road together to have experienced a number of conflicts, prompting them to temporarily part or keep secrets from each other.[14]

Another way that families and other close-knit social groups might influence the thoughts, feelings, and actions of their members is through the degree of *member differentiation*. When people are able to establish differentiated (that is, independent and distinct) views from the group, they might be more likely to remain calm and are better able to regulate their emotions during a conflict, as compared to people who have a poor sense

# THE FAMILY BUSINESS

Any family business, including hunting, relies on adequately managing the needs of the individuals involved in the business. A number of factors might affect the way in which family members manage a family business.[15]

- *Tradition* encompasses family roles, customs, and history. Sam and Dean come from a long line of hunters. Their heritage and the desire to honor their family's traditions sometimes create conflicts between the brothers.[16]

- *Stability* is a way for family members to maintain a sense of balance. If a family member falls outside the rules or expectations set by the family (for example, by descending into heavy substance abuse), thereby creating instability, the family might take action to help the individual "return to normal" and regain balance. When Sam becomes addicted to demon blood, Dean and Bobby lock him up in Bobby's panic room in order to help him detox.[17]

- *Loyalty* is the sense of commitment to the family. After Sam leaves the family business and moves to college, Dean becomes visibly hurt and angry by Sam's apparent lack of loyalty.[18]

- *Trust* in the family business is the ability and willingness of members to be honest with one another. Upon discovering that Dean has been lying to him about allowing an angel, Ezekiel/Gadreel, to use his body as a vessel, Sam is furious, as Dean has broken his trust.[19]

- *Interdependency* is the extent to which family members support and rely on each other. Bobby Singer becomes a father-like figure to Sam and Dean. They rely on him for his expertise, as well as support,[20] so much so that his death initially leaves them unable to act.[21]

of self-differentiation.[22] Sam exemplifies someone with a good level of *self-differentiation* at the start of the series: He is working toward his law degree and a life he had chosen for himself. Dean, on the other hand, often acts in ways that closely resemble his father by blindly following John's instructions and demonstrating poorer ability to regulate his emotions than his younger brother shows.[23]

## Attachment Theory

*Attachment theory* looks at how the emotional connection within a family or between individuals positively and negatively affects their lives.[24] The theory holds that adult success, positive relationships, feelings of security, and even confidence can be traced back to strong, positive relationships between the infant and his or her primary caregiver. Alternatively, children whose parents are absent, abusive, dismissive of their emotional needs, or inconsistent in supporting them are more likely to struggle with commitment and emotion regulation.[25] John Winchester is frequently gone on a hunt, leaving Dean to watch over his brother and hardly ever conferring on him praise or affection. When Dean grows up, he struggles with regulating his emotions and opening up to others.[26]

## Winchesters Build a Family

Single-parent homes have become more prevalent in the contemporary United States than in previous generations.[27] Some children who lose a parent at a young age, as Sam and Dean do,[28] and are then raised in a single-parent home might be more likely to experience physical and psychological difficulties, compared to children from two-parent homes.[29] Though

research on children of historically normative two-parent families suggests that these tend to fare better compared to those
raised in single-parent families, other findings also suggest
that the well-being of children depends more on whether they
receive positive support and stability.[30]

Family structure appears to be less important than the degree
of family connection and support. Regardless of whether an
individual is raised in a single- or a two-parent home, and
regardless of whether the individual's parents are biological,
stepparents, or adoptive parents, parental support seems to be
most important influence on the child's well-being.[31] Chosen
(that is, non-blood-related) family members, such as Bobby
Singer, Castiel, or Ellen and Joe Harvelle, can help individuals
overcome adversity.[32]

Family, whether biological or chosen, can also help improve
the individual's resilience to psychological and physical
distress.[33] Specifically, connections with loved ones are related
to improved physical health, including strengthening immune
responses, and may positively impact length of life.[34] Sam and
Dean frequently rely on Bobby for support and mentorship.
In turn, he also experiences a sense of connection with them,
which helps him better cope with the loss of his wife, Karen.[35]

One of the ways people can benefit through their family
connections is by working together in a collaborative way.
Collaborating with loved ones can enhance a sense of balance
and cohesion and can help improve the individual's level of
commitment and satisfaction.[36] After Dean receives the Mark
of Cain and finds the First Blade, he turns into a bloodthirsty
killer and eventually becomes a demon. After Sam is able to
help him return to being a human, Dean immediately wishes
to return to hunting. He points out that hunting is "the only
normal thing" he knows and therefore believes that it is the
best way for him to recover.[37]

## Family Matters

People who experience adverse childhood events, including illness, personal threats, or deaths of loved ones, as Sam and Dean do,[38] might be more likely to struggle with physical or psychological problems, compared to people who do not experience such events.[39] The degree to which an individual can receive support from biological, adoptive, or chosen family can positively impact that person's well-being.[40] Family members who work together need to be cognizant of the effects of family traditions, the need for stability, loyalty, trust, and interdependence on their relationships.[41] Even though Sam and Dean often disagree about the best practices of working together and they sometimes keep secrets from each other, they also support and rely on each other.[42] Arguably, it is their commitment to each other and to their chosen families that gives them the resilience they need to cope with the great amount of adversity they face.

> *"On one level each family member is an individual.*
> *But on a deeper level the central family group is as one."*
> —psychiatrist Murray Bowen[43]

> *"Next time you hear me say that our family is messed up,*
> *remind me that we could be psycho goat people."*
> —Dean Winchester[44]

### References

Bowen, M. (2013). *The origins of family psychotherapy: The NIMH family study project.* New York, NY: Jason Aronson.

Collins, P. H. (1998). It's all in the family: Intersections of gender, race, and nation. *Hypatia, 13*(3), 62–82.

Couch, L. L., Jones, W. H., & Moore, D. S. (1999). Buffering the effects of betrayal. In J. M. Adams & W. H. Jones (Eds.), *Handbook of interpersonal commitment and relationship stability* (pp. 451–469). New York, NY: Kluwer Academic/Plenum.

Croghan, C. F., Moone, R. P., & Olson, A. M. (2014). Friends, family, and caregiving among midlife and older lesbian, gay, bisexual, and transgender adults. *Journal of Homosexuality, 61*(1), 79–102.

Erich, S., Leung, P., & Kindle, P. (2005). A comparative analysis of adoptive family functioning with gay, lesbian, and heterosexual parents and their children. *Journal of GLBT Family Studies, 1*(4), 43–60.

Felitti, V. J., Anda, R. F., Nordenberg, D., Williamson, D. F., Spitz, A. M., Edwards, V., Koss, M. P., & Marks, J. S. (1998). Relationship of childhood abuse and household dysfunction to many of the leading causes of death in adults: The Adverse Childhood Experiences (ACE) Study. *American Journal of Preventive Medicine, 14*(4), 245–258.

Goldberg, J. (2015, October 27). *Why family matters, and why traditional families are still the best.* Los Angeles Times: http://www.latimes.com/opinion/op-ed/la-oe-1027-goldberg-family-structure-20151027-column.html.

Goleman, D. (1988, June 14). Erikson, in his own old age, expands his view of life. *New York Times*, pp. C1, C14.

Grzywacz, J. G., Almeida, D. M., & McDonald, D. A. (2002). Work-family spillover and daily reports of work and family stress in the adult labor force. *Family Relations, 51*(1), 28–36.

Hooper, L. M. (2007). The application of attachment theory and family systems theory to the phenomena of parentification. *Family Journal, 15*(3), 217–223.

John, O. P., & Gross, J. J. (2004). Healthy and unhealthy emotion regulation: Personality processes, individual differences, and life span development. *Journal of Personality, 72*(6), 1301–1334.

Kerr, M. E. (2000). *One family's story: A primer on Bowen theory.* Washington, DC: Bowen Center for the Study of the Family.

Lansford, J. E., Ceballo, R., Abbey, A., & Stewart, A. J. (2001). Does family structure matter? A comparison of adoptive, two-parent biological, single-mother, stepfather, and stepmother households. *Journal of Marriage & Family, 63*(3), 840–851.

Lumpkin, G. T., Martin, W., & Vaughn, M. (2008). Family orientation: individual-level influences on family firm outcomes. *Family Business Review, 21*(2), 127–138.

Parke, M. (2003). *Are married parents really better for children? What research says about the effects of family structure on child well-being.* Washington, DC: Center for Law and Social Policy.

Raza, S., Adil, A., & Ghayas, S. (2008). Impact of parental death on adolescents' psychosocial functioning. *Journal of Psychosocial Research, 3*(1), 1–11.

Rutter, M. (1999). Resilience concepts and findings: Implications for family therapy. *Journal of Family Therapy, 21*(2), 119–144.

Seppälä, E. M. (2012, August 26). *Connect to thrive: Social connection improves health, well-being & longevity.* Psychology Today: https://www.psychologytoday.com/blog/feeling-it/201208/connect-thrive.

Traies, J. (2015). Old lesbians in the UK: Community and friendship. *Journal of Lesbian Studies, 19*(1), 35–49.

## Notes

1. Episode 10–17, "Inside Man" (April 1, 2015).
2. Goleman (1988).
3. Goldberg (2015), Collins (1998), Erich et al. (2005), Lansford et al. (2001).
4. Episode 1–1, "Pilot" (September 13, 2005).

5. Bowen (2013).
6. Kerr (2000).
7. Episode 7–3, "The Girl Next Door" (October 7, 2011).
8. Written by A. Young & M. Young (1990); played in episode 5–1, "Sympathy for the Devil" (September 10, 2009).
9. Couch et al. (1999).
10. Episode 8–1, "We Need to Talk about Kevin" (October 3, 2012).
11. Episode 1–18, "Something Wicked" (April 6, 2006).
12. Episodes 7–10, "Death's Door," (December 2, 2011); 8–10, "Torn and Frayed" (January 16, 2013); 8–20, "Pac-Man Fever" (April 24, 2013); 10–1, "Black" (October 7, 2014).
13. Kerr (2000).
14. e.g., episode 4–21, "When the Levee Breaks" (May 7, 2009).
15. Lumpkin et al. (2008).
16. e.g., episodes 1–1, "Pilot" (September 13, 2005); 6–7, "Family Matters" (November 5, 2010).
17. Episode 5–14, "My Bloody Valentine" (February 11, 2010).
18. Episode 1–1, "Pilot" (September 13, 2005).
19. Episode 9–9, "Holy Terror" (December 3, 2013).
20. Episode 7–10, "Death's Door" (December 2, 2011).
21. Episode 7–11, "Adventures in Babysitting" (January 6, 2012).
22. Kerr (2000).
23. Episode 1–1, "Pilot" (September 13, 2005).
24. Hooper (2007).
25. Hooper (2007), John & Gross (2004).
26. Episode 2–2, "Everybody Loves a Clown" (October 5, 2006).
27. Parke (2003).
28. Episode 1–1, "Pilot" (September 13, 2005).
29. Raza et al. (2008).
30. Goldberg (2015), Collins (1998).
31. Lansford et al. (2001).
32. Croghan et al. (2014), Traies (2015).
33. Rutter (1999), Seppälä (2012).
34. Seppälä (2012).
35. Episode 7–10, "Death's Door" (December 2, 2011).
36. Grzywacz et al. (2002).
37. Episode 10–5, "Fan Fiction" (November 11, 2014).
38. Episodes 1–1, "Pilot" (September 13, 2005); 7–10, "Death's Door" (December 2, 2011); 3–11, "Mystery Spot" (February 14, 2008); 4–20, "The Rapture" (April 30, 2009).
39. Felitti et al. (1998).
40. Croghan et al. (2014), Rutter (1999), Seppälä (2012), Traies (2015).
41. Lumpkin et al. (2008).
42. e.g., episodes 1–21, "Salvation" (April 27, 2006); 3–9, "Malleus Maleficarum" (January 31, 2008); 4–4, "Metamorphosis" (October 9, 2008); 7–3, "The Girl Next Door" (October 7, 2011).
43. Bowen (2013).
44. Episode 12–18, "The Memory Remains" (April 13, 2017).

## CHAPTER THREE

# Losing One Parent is Hard; Losing Them All is Hell

## LARA TAYLOR KESTER

*"Jess and Mom—they're both gone. Dad is God knows where. You and me, we're all that's left, so if we're gonna see this through, we're gonna do it together."*
—Sam Winchester[1]

*"All that I am, or hope to be, I owe to my angel mother."*
—US President Abraham Lincoln[2]

The death of a parent is an experience that is tough to manage at any age.[3] Parents are the people most children turn to when they need help, whether they are hungry infants crying for a bottle or 30-year-olds who can't navigate the current housing market. Parents guide their children, teach them, and shape them, sometimes until they have been molded into mini versions of themselves. They are the caregivers, the protectors, and the indestructible ones—until they aren't.

Sam and Dean Winchester lose their mother, Mary, at a very young age when they are still in the prime of building the attachment systems that will shape the way they form relationships throughout their lives. Their understandably broken father, John, tries his best to raise them to be good men, until the day he suddenly dies. Afterwards, the Winchester boys have several years to bond with their dad's friend Bobby, whom they come to view as a father, only to have him die in front of them as well. Hunters expect to lose loved ones all the time; that's part of the job. Losing everyone who has ever taken care of you before your midlife crisis? That probably wasn't in the job description.

## Hitting the Highway: Attachment

Our earliest attachments, typically formed in the first three to four years of life, build the foundation for how we look at others and form relationships throughout our entire lives.[4] *Attachment figures* are typically someone a child seeks proximity to, resists separation from, sees as a safe haven while under stress, and uses as a secure base for exploration, risk taking, and interacting with the world.[5] Some people in an adult's life are seen as attachment figures as well, although these are different from other close relationships. For Sam and Dean, only a handful of people fit this description.

*Attachment behavior* is different from attachment itself. It involves any type of behavior that gains proximity to an attachment figure, or resists separating from them.[6] Sam and Dean call each other, even when they're fighting, to check up on each other, and constantly call either John or Bobby for help, as a way of keeping proximity to them, even though they are miles apart.

Sam cannot cope with his brother's repeated deaths caused by the Trickster, at this location from a falling piano. Episode 3-11, "The Mystery Spot" (February 14, 2008).

## Types of Attachment

The goal of the attachment system is to find an emotionally responsive caregiver who provides a sense of security, facilitates exploration, and minimizes fear.[7] Growing up in a world full of extreme hazards—whether they are demons, werewolves, and vampires, or drug dealers, drive-by shooters, and sexual predators—may not be the easiest task, but it's still possible. The types of attachment Sam and Dean seem most aligned with are secure, anxious-avoidant, and anxious-resistant.

*Secure attachment* happens when everything goes the way people think it's supposed to: A baby has a parent or other caregiver who cares for him or her, answers cries, feeds the child, and mirrors emotions. Securely attached children generally feel

safe in their caregivers' absence and confident that their caregivers will protect them when they return.[8] Mary and John are
these types of parents before Mary is killed, and Dean becomes
somewhat of a secure attachment figure for Sam as they are
growing up.[9]

Children with *anxious-avoidant attachment* show their insecu-
rity by avoiding their caregivers. They do not show distress
when their caregivers leave, do not expect anything from them,
typically ignore them when they are present, and have learned
to care for their needs on their own. This is usually the result
of unavailable, rejecting, and unresponsive caregivers. While
Dean may have been able to form some secure attachment to
his father in the first four years of his life, he shows many signs
of being anxious-avoidant later on in life. Dean doesn't see the
need for attachments outside of family, and makes it clear to
everyone around him that he can take care of himself.[10]

*Anxious-resistant* children will cling to their caregivers and
then resist that attachment by fighting against the closeness.
Sam does this with his father John, even as an adult.[11] Anxious-
resistant children try to stay close to their caregivers and do not
explore their surroundings. As an example, Sam doesn't even
try to leave the hotel room when John is off hunting.[12] When
the caregiver leaves an anxious-resistant toddler, the child cries
and yet also pushes away when the caregiver returns. This is the
result of caregivers who are inconsistently responsive to their
children's needs, leading the children not to know whether to
count on their caregiver's care, and to become worried about
whether or not someone will care for them. Until young Sam
is able to attach to Dean, this is his experience of the world.

The experiences up to age four create a *generalized attachment
model*, to influence how we interact with people we come in
contact with. *Specific attachment models* are developed for each
of our individual attachment figures, based on the patterns of

their interactions with us.[13] This is how Dean, who has a more anxious-avoidant attachment pattern, is able to establish some more secure attachments later on in life to Bobby and Lisa, and Sam is able to attach securely to Dean after starting out anxious-resistant.

## Loss as a Child

What happens if a child's main attachment figure dies before the attachment has finished forming? Grief is a physical, emotional, behavioral, and cognitive response to loss.[14] Children haven't fully developed in any of these areas, and may have more difficulty understanding what is happening when a caregiver dies. Infants are capable of grief once they have developed object permanence—the ability to recognize that people and objects still exist when they're out of sight—at around six to eight months of age. Sam is six months old when Mary is killed, so he may be at this stage.

Toddlers do not understand death, but they know when a significant figure in their life is missing.[15] Because they can remember what happened, but haven't fully developed their emotional repertoire, toddlers often relive the loss through each stage of development throughout their lives, with grief reemerging in different forms. Dean is four when Mary dies, meaning he may have had a harder time coping with her death as he relives it several times throughout his life. No wonder he flips out on Sam every time he brings her up.[16]

Children under the age of five who lose a parent are prone to poor adjustment, especially if the surviving caregiver is unable to cope with his or her own grief or if communication about the parent's death is avoided.[17] Sam and Dean aren't allowed to talk about their mom, and their dad doesn't exactly guide them into a normal routine of school, sleepovers, and family dinners.[18] Maternal death in infancy and parental death in childhood have been linked to an increased risk of early death, persisting into adulthood.[19] Hereditary health issues could be to blame, but there is also an increased risk of unnatural death in individuals whose parents have suffered an unnatural death, such as in a car accident, while choking on food, or in a demon attack. More high-risk behaviors and lifestyle changes, including becoming a hunter, can lead to unnatural death. Sam and Dean definitely follow suit, having died over and over and over again.[20]

### Personality

Traumatic loss in childhood can have an effect on how person- ality develops in a person as he or she grows up.[21] The personal- ity subtypes that are most common in adults who have suffered a traumatic loss as a child are *psychopathic, hostile/paranoid, inter- nalizing/avoidant*, and *resilient*. People can have more than one of these subtypes interacting with the other, as we see in Dean and Sam.

People with a *psychopathic* personality subtype is just about as friendly as they sound. They are manipulative and impulsive, lack empathy, and have a tendency to engage in criminal acts. At a quick glance, this sounds a lot like Dean, especially when people first meet him.[22] Dean also seems to fit into the *hostile/ paranoid* subtype, usually associated with a history of sporadic parental care. People in this subtype are often rigid, critical, and angry. They lack close relationships and are suspicious of others. Sometimes they have a negative self-view beneath a façade of superiority.[23] Dean is hard on everyone around him who isn't in his circle of trust, and it takes a lot for him to let others in. Dean can also be hard on himself, and blame himself for everything that goes wrong, even when he claims to be the toughest hunter around.[24]

While Sam can sometimes fit into the *internalizing/avoidant* subtype, which is characterized by a depressed mood, low self-esteem, and feeling like an outsider, more often he exemplifies the *resilient* subtype.[25] Resilient individuals are likable, energetic, and articulate. They also pursue goals and create meaningful relationships, much like Sam's goals of going to Stanford, attending law school, and forging a relationship with Jess.[26]

## Finding a New Attachment

In the aftermath of Mary's death, John becomes obsessed with revenge and spends the next 22 years of his life diving into the hunter way of life, researching the yellow-eyed demon, and leaving his boys to care for themselves. Dean has lost the life where he was able to have the crust cut off his PB&J sandwiches and hug his mom every day.[27] Instead, he finds himself taking care of his little brother, hiding a gun under his pillow, and being reprimanded for finding time to be a kid.[28] While John may not have done a very good job of making the boys feel safe, Dean is still able to attach to him and looks up to him, to the point that he believes that being a good son means doing whatever his father says.[29]

Sam has a very different experience. He has no memories of what John was like before the demon killed their mother, so he grows up not being able to form attachments as easily. Dean becomes Sam's primary caregiver while John is on the road, meaning that Dean becomes Sam's model of attachment. Even though Dean is still just a kid himself, he is able to soothe Sam's fears, set up a Christmas celebration overnight, and give up the last bowl of Lucky Charms,™ even if he wants it for himself.[30] Dean is the one who explains to Sam what monsters really lurk in the world. When John doesn't show up for Christmas, Sam gives Dean the special present meant for John, symbolizing that Sam sees Dean in a parental role. Sam also shows preference for Dean over John time and time again, when (a possessed) John and Dean argue about whether or not John is possessed, and when Dean and John are hurt in a car accident.[31] The attachments the Winchester boys form in the wake of their mother's death will guide how they cope with all the other major losses in their lives.

### Loss as an Adult

Typically, when a loved one dies, those left behind feel sorrow over the death, have an intense yearning for the person they lost, and may lose some interest in daily activities, but these symptoms fade over time.[32] For Dean, this isn't the case. Dean's need to dismiss emotional displays and push his emotions down causes his grief to come out in other ways. After John dies, Dean shuts down and refuses to talk to Sam about his feelings. He insists he's fine. He also takes it out on an already-beat-up Impala with a crowbar[33]—the same Impala that John has given him and that has been Dean's reminder of John when they are separated.

Sam's reaction to John's death is (relatively) healthier. While he knows his sudden interest in continuing to be a hunter is only because he feels guilty about arguing with John right before he died, he is open about talking about not being okay. Sam also wants to keep to his current routine and working jobs as a hunter, and he tries to connect with those who knew his father (Bobby, Dean, and Ellen).[34]

Dean's stronger reaction to John's death may be due to the feelings it brings up about the loss of his mother. They could also be due to his attachment style and the fact that he has now lost two attachment figures in a row. Or it could be the fact

# AMBIGUOUS LOSS

With John constantly on the road, hunting for weeks on end, Sam and Dean have to take care of themselves. The boys sit in a hotel room, left to wonder how long it will take John to come back for them or if he is even alive.[35] This could be comparable to what happens to children of those in the military who are deployed in war zones. Both the Winchester boys and many children of deployed soldiers have periods of limited (or no) contact with their parents or knowledge of where they are or what they are going through. Their imaginations about what is happening can run wild.

Uncertain situations like these can lead to ambiguous loss. *Ambiguous loss* is the type of loss people feel when they are unsure of whether if there a loss to mourn.[36] Even as adults, Sam and Dean wonder if their father is still alive, except when he is actively giving them clues or jobs.[37] This uncertainty can be processed in different ways, which can be seen in Sam's distancing himself from John and Dean's repeated insistence that John is okay.[38] Attachment to any other caregiver who is left behind increases, which could be the reason Sam seems to be so attached to Dean.

that John traded his life for Dean's and Dean blames himself for that. Any of those things alone might make someone grumpy and give up hitting on women for a while, but all of them together become a large burden to bear.

### Loss of a Surrogate

> **Samuel Campbell (grandfather):** "You must be the guy pretending to be their father."
> **Bobby Singer:** "Somebody ought to."[39]

Not all attachment figures are family members, and not all attachments are formed in childhood.[40] After losing both their

# ROAD MUSIC

parents, Sam and Dean build a strong bond with Bobby, even looking up to him as a father figure. Both of them have a stronger emotional reaction to Bobby's death than they did even to their own father's. Dean's anger is particularly intense, with him punching a glass display case when asked about donating Bobby's organs. Dean starts off with a vulnerability due to his difficulties adapting after Mary and John's deaths, leaving him unable to manage his feelings, and even says that they've been through enough.[43]

In the aftermath of Bobby's death, Sam and Dean disagree on how to best honor Bobby's memory.[44] Sam is almost ready to move on and get back into a routine after two weeks, proposing the idea of calling Bobby's friends to notify them that Bobby has died. Meanwhile, Dean is too focused on getting revenge to hear Sam, and becomes angry at the thought of taking the step of letting others know. Dean's difficulties stem from losing all the only attachment figures he has ever known.[45] Sam, on the other hand, seems to be able to test the waters of moving on because his main attachment figure, Dean, is still there for him.

## Getting Back on the Road

From the very beginning, Sam and Dean Winchester have a difficult life. Their mother dies when they are young, they manage on their own while their father hunts monsters, they lose their father just as they have begun to become a family again, and they lose their father figure as they are settling into life without their father. Through all of it, they develop very different types of attachments, at times healthy and at others not so healthy. Sam and Dean are an example of how no two children, even in the same family, attach or grieve in the same way. They grow up together, raised to be warriors, but learn to interact with the world in different ways.[46] In the end, Mary, John, and Bobby manage to teach their boys to take care of each other and to get back up and hit the road together no matter what evil gets in the way.

*References*

Bowlby, J. (1982). Attachment and loss: Retrospect and prospect. *American Journal of Orthopsychiatry, 52*(4), 664–678.

Bretherton, I. (1992). The origins of attachment theory: John Bowlby and Mary Ainsworth. *Developmental Psychology, 28*(5), 759–775.

D'Antonio, J. (2011). Grief and loss of a caregiver in children: A developmental perspective. *Journal of Psychosocial Nursing & Mental Health Services, 49*(10), 17–20.

Ellis, J., & Lloyd-Williams, M. (2008). Perspectives on the impact of early parent loss in adulthood in the UK: Narratives provide the way forward. *European Journal of Cancer Care, 17*(4), 317–318.

Holland, J. G. (1866). *Life of Abraham Lincoln.* Springfield, MA: G. Bill.

Huebner, A. J., Mancini, J. A., Wilcox, R. M., Grass, S. R., & Grass, G. A. (2007). Parental deployment and youth in military families: Exploring uncertainty and ambiguous loss. *Family Relations, 56*(2), 112–122.

Letzter-Pouw, S., & Werner, P. (2012). The relationship between loss of parents in the Holocaust, intrusive memories, and distress among child survivors. *American Journal of Orthopsychiatry, 82*(2).

Li, J., Vestergaard, M., Cnattingius, S., Gissler, M., Bech, B. H., Obel, C., & Olsen, J. (2014). Mortality after parental death in childhood: A nationwide cohort study from three Nordic countries. *PLoS Medicine, 11*(7).

Malone, J. C., Westen, D., & Levendosky, A. A. (2011). Personalities of adults with traumatic childhood separations. *Journal of Clinical Psychology, 67*(12), 1259–1282.

Raveis, V. H., Siegel, K., & Karus, D. (1999). Children's psychological distress following the death of a parent. *Journal of Youth & Adolescence, 28*(2), 165–180.

Shear, K., & Shair, H. (2005). Attachment, loss, and complicated grief. *Developmental Psychobiology, 47*(3), 253–267.

## Notes

1. Episode 1–11, "Scarecrow" (January 10, 2006).
2. Holland (1866), p. 23.
3. Bowlby (1982).
4. Bowlby (1982); Letzter-Pouw & Werner (2012).
5. Shear & Shair (2005).
6. Bowlby (1982).
7. Shear & Shair (2005).
8. Bretherton (1992).
9. Episodes 1–1, "Pilot" (September 13, 2005); 3–8, "A Very Supernatural Christmas" (December 13, 2007).
10. Episodes 1–1, "Pilot" (September 13, 2005); 1–16, "Shadow" (February 28, 2006); 2–2, "Everybody Loves a Clown" (October 5, 2006).
11. Episodes 1–11, "Scarecrow" (January 10, 2006); 1–20 "Dead Man's Blood" (April 20, 2006); 2–1, "In My Time of Dying" (September 28, 2006).
12. Episodes 1–18, "Something Wicked This Way Comes" (April 6, 2006); 3–8, "A Very Supernatural Christmas" (December 13, 2007).
13. Shear & Shair (2005).
14. D'Antonio (2011).
15. D'Antonio (2011).
16. Episodes 1–1, "Pilot" (September 13, 2005); 3–8, "A Very Supernatural Christmas" (December 13, 2007).
17. Ellis & Lloyd-Williams (2008), Raveis et al. (1999).
18. Episode 3–8, "A Very Supernatural Christmas" (December 13, 2007).
19. Li et al. (2014).
20. Episodes 1–22, "Devil's Trap" (May 4, 2006); 2–22, "All Hell Breaks Loose, Part 2" (May 15, 2007); 3–11, "Mystery Spot" (February 14, 2008); 3–22, "No Rest for the Wicked" (May 15, 2008); 4–8, "Wishful Thinking" (November 6, 2008); 5–4, "The End" (October 1, 2009); 5–13, "The Song Remains the Same" (February 4, 2010); 5–16, "Dark Side of the Moon" (April 1, 2010); 5–22, "Swan Song" (May 13, 2010); 6–11, "Appointment in Samarra" (December 10, 2010); 7–23, "Survival of the Fittest" (May 18, 2012); 9–23, "Do You Believe in Miracles?" (May 20, 2014).
21. Malone et al. (2011).
22. Episode 1–1, "Pilot" (September 13, 2005).
23. Malone et al (2011).
24. Episodes 1–18, "Something Wicked This Way Comes" (April 6, 2006); 4–3, "In the Beginning" (October 2, 2008); 4–13, "After School Special" (January 9, 2008).
25. Depressed mood: episodes 4–13, "After School Special" (January 9, 2008); 4–21, "When the Levee Breaks" (May 7, 2009).
26. Episode 1–1, "Pilot" (September 13, 2005).
27. Episode 5–16, "Dark Side of the Moon" (April 1, 2010).
28. Episodes 1–18, "Something Wicked This Way Comes" (April 6, 2006); 3–8, "A Very Supernatural Christmas" (December 13, 2007).
29. Episode 1–11, "Scarecrow" (January 10, 2006).

30. Episodes 1–18, "Something Wicked This Way Comes" (April 6, 2006); 3–8, "A Very Supernatural Christmas" (December 13, 2007).
31. Episodes 1–22, "Devil's Trap" (May 4, 2006); 2–1, "In My Time of Dying" (September 28, 2006).
32. Shear & Shair (2005).
33. Episode 2–2, "Everybody Loves a Clown" (October 5, 2006).
34. Episode 2–2, "Everybody Loves a Clown" (October 5, 2006).
35. Episodes 1–18, "Something Wicked This Way Comes" (April 6, 2006); 1–22, "Devil's Trap" (May 4, 2006); 3–8, "A Very Supernatural Christmas" (December 13, 2007).
36. Huebner et al. (2007).
37. Episode 1–11, "Scarecrow" (January 10, 2006).
38. Episodes 1–11, "Scarecrow" (January 10, 2006); 3–8, "A Very Supernatural Christmas" (December 13, 2007).
39. Episode 6–16, ". . . And Then There Were None" (March 4, 2011).
40. Shear & Shair (2005).
41. Written by J. Fogerty (1969); played in episode 2–1, "In My Time of Dying" (September 28, 2006).
42. Malone et al. (2011).
43. Episode 7–10, "Death's Door" (December 2, 2011).
44. Episode 7–11, "Adventures in Babysitting" (January 6, 2012).
45. Shear & Shair (2005).
46. Episode 1–1, "Pilot" (September 13, 2005).

## CHAPTER FOUR

# Carrying on After Parental Loss

## DENISSE MORALES

*"I had to be more than just a brother. I had to be a
father and I had to be a mother to keep him safe,
and that wasn't fair. And I couldn't do it."*
—Dean Winchester[1]

*"Young children, who for any reason are deprived
of the continuous care and attention of a mother
or substitute-mother, are not only temporarily
disturbed by such deprivation, but may in some
cases suffer long-term effects which persist."*
—psychoanalyst John Bowlby[2]

The death of a parent shakes the entire family system. It is a type of injury that never quite heals completely. Such a loss can propel a change in the family structure, as family members struggle to fill the sudden void, switching up responsibilities and taking on new roles.[3] For young children, this affects their overall development, including personality, how they feel about themselves and others, and how they navigate their world. For the Winchester boys, their mother's death marks the beginning of the family business and the end of a normal childhood.[4]

## The Parentification of Dean Winchester

When Mary dies, John is left a widower, determined to avenge her death. Hunting becomes his life purpose, which means he is often gone for days at a time, leaving Dean to take care of Sam. When a parent dies, taking on extra responsibilities is not uncommon for a child.[5] However, the responsibilities placed on Dean are much greater than what is appropriate for his age. As the older son, Dean is placed in the role of a parent while still a child himself. This process, called *parentification*, can create positive or negative consequences later in life. Children who are parentified often learn not to trust others. However, they may also develop positive qualities, such as responsibility and resourcefulness. In families where a child is parentified, boundaries in terms of who has parental authority are usually unclear.[6] Even though John is absent, he still creates a clear hierarchy: Dean and Sam are to follow his orders. John's clear position of authority may have been a protective factor allowing his sons to develop resiliency and eventually find meaning in what they do. Despite this protective factor, though, early parental loss is a trauma that had consequences in terms of the Winchesters' behavior.

## Impact of Trauma on Brain Development

*"The number it must've done on your head . . ."*
—John Winchester[7]

*". . . when a child grows up in an environment permeated*
*with chaos or violence, that child perceives this state of*
*hypervigilance and distractibility as the norm . . .*
*to him this is normal. This is his baseline."*

—neuroscientist Bruce Perry[8]

Sam is a six-month-old infant when Mary dies, and Dean is four years old. In terms of brain development, both Winchesters are in the most crucial years of life. Trauma, especially that of a parent's death, can have a severe impact when it occurs in childhood. The boys not only lose their mother, but at the same time they lose the stability of a home life and the stability of a consistent father. The loss of a caregiver at an early age places a child at greater risk of experiencing mental health problems later in life—such as depression.[9] There are moments when the Winchester brothers exhibit significant distress. For example, when Sam and Dean admit themselves into a psychiatric hospital while hunting a wraith, it becomes evident that Sam is coping with severe anger issues that may at times make him prone to aggressive impulses. In this same episode, the wraith makes a mockery of how the patients' brains are soaked in "all sorts of chemicals that make them more delicious."[10] As unsavory as the comment is, there is some truth to it.

The system governing stress and how the body reacts to it is the *hypothalamic-pituitary-adrenocortical* (HPA) system, which controls the stress hormone *cortisol*. When cortisol levels are consistently high for prolonged periods, that can be detrimental to the developing brain, as cortisol keeps it in a constant state of increased stress, which is associated with depression, anxiety, and a number of physical problems.[11] During his time with the Mark of Cain, Dean shows multiple behaviors usually associated with depression, including isolation, apathy, avoidance of his family, lack of interest in the things he usually enjoys, and, ultimately, thoughts of dying.

Studies have suggested a link between parental loss and function of the HPA system.[12] One study found adult men who experienced the death of a parent at a young age and who were otherwise healthy to have higher levels of cortisol.[13] Dean and Sam are both in peak physical condition, and at least Sam is very mindful of what he eats. However, they both experience emotional distress often, which makes it likely that they have both learned to function with consistently high levels of stress.

## Impact on Personality Development

Experiencing a trauma in early life can lead to the development of unhealthy personality characteristics.[14] One particularly unhealthy aspect of Dean's personality is guilt. Growing up in the role of a parentified child, Dean develops a sense of *omnipotent responsibility guilt* regarding his little brother. Omnipotent responsibility guilt refers to the idea that a person feels an "exaggerated sense of responsibility and concern for the happiness and well-being of others."[15] On one occasion while hunting a Shtriga, Dean reveals that this is a monster that attacked Sam at one point in their childhood while Dean was supposed to be watching him. Dean, a child himself at the time, was unable to kill the Shtriga. He therefore feels guilty not only for the attack on Sam, but for all attacks the monster has perpetrated since.[16] Omnipotent responsibility guilt usually co-occurs with other types of guilt, like *survivor guilt* and *separation guilt*. Survivor guilt is often seen among veterans who have lost peers during combat.[17] It refers to a sense of guilt related to being alive while others died, and is something that Dean seems to exhibit multiple times throughout the series, for

# ROAD MUSIC

### "Knockin' on Heaven's Door" by Bob Dylan[18]

*Parentification* is the act of placing a child in the role of a parent. That child is burdened with responsibilities that should be that of a parent, such as caring for younger children.[19] As he has always taken care of his younger brother, it is no wonder that Dean's version of heaven is being able to watch Sam enjoy his childhood, evidently by blowing up a field with Fourth of July fireworks.

example, after Sam falls in Lucifer's Cage. Dean also appears to have a strong sense of separation guilt, which is guilt related to leaving the family to become independent.[20] He is so loyal to his family and so against leaving his brother and father that when Sam decides to go to college, he sees it as a betrayal, and describes the night Sam leaves as "one of the worst nights of my life."[21] Men whose fathers are less emotionally available to them while they are growing up tend to show lower self-esteem.[22] Upon telling Dean why he has pulled him out of Hell, Castiel reflects, "You don't think you deserve to be saved."[23]

Parental loss, be it by death or by absence, affects Sam's personality in different ways. As a result of Mary's death, Sam is very protected throughout his childhood. He is kept from the reality of Mary's death, finally discovering the truth by reading his father's journal on his own.[24] Overprotection in childhood may be associated with anxiety and internalizing feelings of low self-worth,[25] the latter of which Sam exhibits on multiple occasions. Sam also seems to have negative interactions with his father, which tend to lead a child to form negative views of himself or herself.[26] From young Sam's perspective, it is unfair that his brother has participated in hunting activities from a very young age but Sam isn't allowed to do so. Feeling left out or abandoned by loved ones, despite being perhaps the safest option in Sam's case, tends to make a child feel that he or she is not important enough.[27] Not only is Sam supposed to obey his father and remain indoors, but the family also moves around quite frequently, which can have an impact on emotional development. The instability that accompanies frequent moving can lead to feelings of anger, sadness, and loneliness,[28] all of which Sam expresses at various points throughout the series.

Being torn from a primary caregiver in early life, especially in infancy, means losing the first significant *object* in the child's life. The object, as described in *object-relations theory*, is the primary caregiver who provides safety, nurture, and meets all the infant's needs.[29] When an infant loses the object at an early age, it may make him or her more likely to develop a depressive personality and a pessimistic view of others.[30] To determine whether Sam has a depressive personality requires more information, but he was a very lonely child. He craves connection, as viewers can discern by the times he ran away[31] and the fact that a Zanna named Sully appears to him to be his "imaginary friend" when he needs guidance.[32] Perhaps Sully serves as an object that allows Sam to resolve his feelings of loneliness until he begins to feel included in family activities.

## Two Brothers against the World

Throughout the series, viewers see many flashbacks of a young Dean navigating adolescence, getting into legal trouble, and giving little importance to school. Children who lose a parent to unnatural causes and who face other adversity are more likely to get lower grades and fail in school when compared to children who lose a parent to a natural causes such as cancer.[33] Boys who suffer maternal loss may also engage in more delinquent behaviors.[34] However, an appropriately nurturing environment can be a protective factor. As a teen, Dean is once caught stealing peanut butter and bread, and spends two months in a home for troubled teenage boys. He has a stable environment and his performance in school improves. He makes friends, makes the wrestling team, and makes plans to attend his first school dance.[35] In just two months, he adjusts into a typical adolescent's life. This teaches us the importance of the environment and shows that a person can thrive after trauma when given the right opportunities.

Our relationship with our primary caregivers throughout childhood affects how we approach relationships in adulthood.[36] The lack of a secure attachment to their parents, whether due to early death or absence, may place the Winchesters in a position of being less likely to have romantic relationships of better quality.[37] For example, Dean has many one-night stands and occasionally goes on dates, but almost never forges long-term relationships. For Sam, the only truly significant romantic relationship he experiences after his fiancé Jess dies is with Amelia, a woman who truly connects with him and whom he eventually decides to leave.[38]

## A Father's Sacrifice

Shortly before sacrificing himself for his sons, John realizes how his choices have affected Sam and Dean's lives in a negative way, and he has the opportunity to achieve a sort of redemption.[39] In their eyes, John's sacrifice, though tragic, allows the Winchester brothers to experience and express authentic feelings toward their father, which ultimately lead to an empathetic understanding of him. Research suggests that children who lose a parent in adulthood tend to experience a decrease

# A LEGACY OF GRIEF

*"You gotta understand something. After your mother passed, all I saw was evil, everywhere. And all I cared about was— was keepin' you boys alive. I wanted you prepared, ready. So somewhere along the line, I, uh, I stopped being your father. And I, I became your—your drill sergeant."*
—John Winchester[40]

*"A man who becomes conscious of the responsibility he bears toward another human being who affectionately waits for him, or to an unfinished work, will never be able to throw away his life. He knows the 'why' to his existence, and will be able to bear almost any 'how.'"*
—psychiatrist Viktor Frankl[41]

The Winchester brothers lose their father long before John's death. After Mary dies, John focuses on training his boys to hunt monsters. Research suggests that finding and engaging in new activities can help widowers cope with their grief, and that making decisions about what happens in the lives of their children is especially important.[42] Perhaps throwing himself and his children into hunting is the best way that John can process his own grief and find meaning in their tragedy.

in psychological well-being.[43] It is not until after his father dies that Sam begins to express some of the aggression he has been holding on to. Perhaps their father's death is the catalyst for Sam to express some of that anger.

The act of forgiving and letting go of resentments may potentially lead to better health.[44] During a visit to the past to save their parents from the angel Anna, Sam finds himself explaining his father's choices and expresses his understanding that John was doing his best to "keep it together."[45] This teaches us the concept that even though the effects of parental loss are not erased, forgiving one's parents for their mistakes after they are gone can be an important step toward beginning to heal.[46]

*References*

Agid, O., Shapira, B., Zislin, J., Ritsner, M., Hanin, B., Murad, H., Troudart, T., Bloch, M., Heresco-Levy, U., & Lerer, B. (1999). Environment and vulnerability to major psychiatric illness: A case control study of early parental loss in major depression, bipolar disorder and schizophrenia. *Molecular Psychiatry, 4*(2), 163–172.

Ainsworth, M. D. S. (1969). Object relations, dependency, and attachment: A theoretical review of the infant-mother relationship. *Child Development, 40*(4), 969–1025.

Allen, D. M. (2012, March 26). *Does one need to forgive abusive parents to heal?* Psychology Today: https://www.psychologytoday.com/blog/matter-personality/201203/does-one-need-forgive-abusive-parents-heal.

Anderson, R. A., & Heydenburk, L. (1999). Relocation effects on American children. *TCA Journal, 27*(2), 78.

Berg, L., Rostila, M., Saarela, J., & Hjern, A. (2014). Parental death during childhood and subsequent school performance. *Pediatrics, 133*(4), 682–689.

Berg, L., Rostila, M., & Hjern, A. (2016). Parental death during childhood and depression in young adults: A national cohort study. *Journal of Child Psychology & Psychiatry, 57*(9), 1092–1098.

Boszormenyi-Nagy, L., & Spark, G. M. (1973). *Invisible loyalties: Reciprocity in intergenerational family therapy.* New York: Harper & Row.

Bowlby, J., Ainsworth, M., Boston, M., & Rosenbluth, D. (1956). The effects of mother-child separation: A follow-up study. *British Journal of Medical Psychology, 29*(3–4), 211–247.

Bowlby-West, L. (1983). The impact of death on the family system. *Journal of Family Therapy, 5*(3), 279–294.

Cas, A. G., Frankenberg, E., Wayan, S., & Thomas, D. (2014). The impact of parental death on child well-being: Evidence from the Indian Ocean tsunami. *Demography, 51*(2), 437–457.

Dick, G. L., & Bronson, D. (2005). Adult men's self-esteem: The relationship with the father. *Families in Society, 86*(4), 580–588.

Firestone, L. (2013, July 30). *How your attachment style impacts your relationship.* Psychology Today: https://www.psychologytoday.com/blog/compassion-matters/201307/how-your-attachment-style-impacts-your-relationship.

Frankl, V. (1959/2006). *Man's search for meaning.* Boston, MA: Beacon.

Hooper, L. M. (2007). Expanding the discussion regarding parentification and its varied outcomes: Implications for mental health research and practice. *Journal of Mental Health Counseling, 29*(4), 322–337.

Huprich, S.K. (2001). Object loss and object relations in depressive personality analogues. *Bulletin of the Menninger Clinic, 65*(4), 549–559.

Juby, H., & Farrington, D. P. (2001). Disentangling the link between disrupted families and delinquency. *British Journal of Criminology, 41*(1), 22–40.

Lachmann, S. (2013, December 24). *10 Sources of low self-esteem*. Psychology Today: https://www.psychologytoday.com/blog/me-we/201312/10-sources-low-self -esteem.

Laurin, J. C., Joussemet, M., Tremblay, R. E., & Boivin, M. (2015). Early forms of controlling parenting and the development of childhood anxiety. *Journal of Child and Family Studies, 24*(11), 3279–3292.

Marks, N. F., Jun, H., & Song, J. (2007). Death of parents and adult psychological and physical well-being: A prospective U.S. national study. *Journal of Family Issues, 28*(12), 1611–1638.

Mayo Clinic (2016, April 21). *Chronic stress puts your health at risk*. Mayo Clinic: http://www.mayoclinic.org/healthy-lifestyle/stress-management/in-depth/stress/art-20046037.

O'Connor, L. E., Berry, J. W., Weiss, J., Bush, M., & Sampson, H. (1997). Interpersonal guilt: The development of a new measure. *Journal of Clinical Psychology, 53*(1), 73–89.

Rademaker, A. R., Vermetten, E., Geuze, E., Muilwijk, A., & Kleber R. J. (2008). Self-reported early trauma as a predictor of adult personality: A study in a military sample. *Journal of Clinical Psychology, 64*(7), 863–875.

Ross, C. A. (2013). Self-blame and suicidal ideation among combat veterans. *American Journal of Psychotherapy, 67*(4), 309–322.

Rushton, P. N. (2007). Widower responses to the death of a wife: The impact on family members. *Topics in Advanced Practice Nursing eJournal, 7*(2). Medscape: http://www.medscape.com/viewarticle/560196_4.

Simpson, J. A. (1990). Influence on attachment styles on romantic relationships. *Journal of Personality & Social Psychology, 59*(5), 971–980.

Soffer-Dudek, N., & Shahar, G. (2008). The relationship of childhood emotional abuse and neglect to depressive vulnerability and low self-efficacy. *International Journal of Cognitive Therapy, 1*(2), 151–162.

Supin, J. (2016, November). The long shadow: Bruce Perry on the lingering effects of childhood trauma. *The Sun* (pp. 4–13).

Tyrka, A. R., Wier, L., Price, L. H., Ross, N. S., Anderson, G. M., Wilkinson, C. W., & Carpenter, L. L. P. (2008a). Childhood parental loss and adult hypothalamic-pituitary-adrenal function. *Biological Psychiatry, 63*(12), 1147–1154.

Tyrka, A. R., Wier, L., Price, L. H., Ross, N. S., & Carpenter, L. L. P. (2008b). Childhood parental loss and adult psychopathology: Effects of loss characteristics and contextual factors. *International Journal of Psychiatry in Medicine, 38*(3), 329–344.

Worthington, E. L., Witvliet, C. V. O., Pietrini, P., & Miller, A. J. (2007). Forgiveness, health, and well-being: A review of evidence for emotional versus dispositional forgiveness, dispositional forgiveness, and reduced unforgiveness. *Journal of Behavioral Medicine, 30*(4), 291–302.

*Notes*

1. Episode 12–22, "Who We Are" (May 18, 2017).
2. Bowlby et al. (1956), p. 211.
3. Bowlby-West (1983).
4. Episode 1–1, "Pilot" (September 13, 2005).
5. Cas et al. (2014).
6. Hooper (2007).
7. Episode 5–13, "The Song Remains the Same" (February 4, 2010).

8. Supin (2016).
9. Agid et al. (1999).
10. Episode 5–11, "Sam, Interrupted" (January 21, 2010).
11. Mayo Clinic (2016).
12. Tyrka et al. (2008a)
13. Tyrka et al. (2008b).
14. Rademaker et al. (2008).
15. O'Connor et al. (1997), p. 76.
16. Episode 1–18, "Something Wicked" (April 6, 2006).
17. Ross (2013).
18. Written by Bob Dylan (1973), featured in episode 5–16, "Dark Side of the Moon" (April 1, 2010).
19. Boszormenyi-Nagy & Spark (1973).
20. O'Connor et al. (1997).
21. Episode 5–16, "Dark Side of the Moon" (April 1, 2010).
22. Dick & Bronson (2005).
23. Episode 4–1, "Lazarus Rising" (September 18, 2008).
24. Episode 3–8, "A Very Supernatural Christmas" (December 13, 2007).
25. Laurin et al. (2015).
26. Soffer-Dudek & Shahar (2008).
27. Lachmann (2013).
28. Anderson & Heydenburk (1999).
29. Ainsworth (1969).
30. Huprich (2001).
31. Episode 7–3, "The Girl Next Door" (October 7, 2011).
32. Episode 11–8, "Just My Imagination" (December 2, 2015).
33. Berg et al. (2014, 2016).
34. Juby & Farrington (2001).
35. Episode 9–7, "Bad Boys" (November 19, 2013).
36. Firestone (2013).
37. Simpson (1990).
38. Episode 8–10, "Torn and Frayed" (January 16, 2013).
39. Episode 2–1, "In My Time of Dying" (September 28, 2006).
40. Episode 1–20, "Dead Man's Blood" (April 20, 2006).
41. Frankl (1959/2006), p. 80.
42. Rushton (2007).
43. Marks et al. (2007).
44. Worthington et al. (2007).
45. Episode 5–13, "The Song Remains the Same" (February 4, 2010).
46. Allen (2012).

## CHAPTER FIVE

# The Good, the Bad, and the Balanced: Q & A with Felicia Day and Amanda Tapping

## TRAVIS LANGLEY AND JENNA BUSCH

*"Good? Bad? I think I'll just settle for balanced."*
—Charlie Bradbury[1]

*"The road to hell is paved with good intentions."*
—proverb, possibly derived from Saint Bernard of Clairvaux[2]

What does it mean to be good? How can actions meant to accomplish good be perceived as evil? Is it ever good to hack into computer systems, to rob political organizations, to kill innocent bystanders? How does a person decide what number of civilian casualties is okay for a good cause?

Lawrence Kohlberg, one of the most prominent psychologists of the 20th century,[3] offered an explanation regarding how people wind up making their particular moral choices and what each choice says about each person's level of moral maturity. Based on his observations and extensive testing, he concluded that people go through a series of *stages of moral development*: two *pre-conventional stages* during preschool years before learning and utilizing moral conventions, two *conventional stages* in which the child or adolescent knows moral conventions and begins to apply them in simple ways, and possibly one or two *post-conventional stages* for mature individuals who move beyond conventional morality to develop ethical principles and priorities more advanced than conventional morality.[4]

Because neither Charlie nor Naomi tends to let personal consequences—good or bad—deter her from doing what she considers to be right (most obviously when each sacrifices herself for others[5]), each has progressed beyond the pre-conventional morality of early childhood, but how far? To evaluate an individual's morality, Kohlberg would have each one read a series of scenarios, such as one about a man with the opportunity to steal medicine to save a life. Kohlberg did not base his assessment of moral development on whether the respondent would indicate *yes* or *no* when asked if the man should steal the lifesaving medicine. At any stage, a person might give either answer. Moral development is instead indicated by the respondent's reasoning behind that answer.[6] Either might simply demonstrate a specific type of conventional morality—Charlie, if motivated to do things popularly considered to be good; Naomi, if driven by a law-and-order mentality that values rules for the sake of social order. Even if they might begin conventionally, though, each develops greater complexity in moral reasoning over time, showing post-conventional prioritization of human need over popular expectations or orderliness. In the end, each serves the greatest good for the most human beings.

For a better look at these complicated characters, we spoke with the actors who have played them: Felicia Day (Charlie) and Amanda Tapping (Naomi).

# ROAD MUSIC

## "Behind Blue Eyes" by The Who[7]

*Attribution theory* holds that we regularly try to make the world seem less chaotic and more predictable than it necessarily is by attributing people's observable behavior to internal thoughts and consistent dispositions, and yet none of us truly knows what goes on inside someone else's head. Written as the lament of a villain who considers himself to be a good guy,[8] "Behind Blue Eyes" addresses the fact that, despite suffering emotional turmoil and disdain, a person's intentions may be deeper and more morally based than they might outwardly appear to others. Charlie and Naomi commit wrongful acts for the sake of what each considers the greater good, regardless of how others might perceive their intent.

## Felicia Day Interview: Chatting About Charlie

Felicia Day, creator and star of *The Guild*, has portrayed characters in *Eureka*, *Buffy the Vampire Slayer*, *Dr. Horrible's Sing-Along Blog*, *Mystery Science Theater*, and many other programs and films. On *Supernatural*, she appears as the hacker-turned-hunter Celeste Middleton, best known by the alias Charlie Bradbury,[9] whom the Winchesters grow to accept as a surrogate sister.[10] The character's own feelings evolve from hoping she never sees them again to thinking of them as family: "Sam and Dean are like my brothers."[11] Despite her need for frequent interactions with others, those contacts tend not to be marked by *self-disclosure* (sharing private information). Basing relationships on fantasy and game as a form of *sublimation* (a healthier defense mechanism) or *social withdrawal* (often less healthy)[12] helps her avoid thinking of her own past. Sometimes detachment is necessary, though, and her disengagement never appears to take the form of *schizoid fantasy* in which fantasy replaces socializing.[13] (See chapter 6, "A Trunk Full of Defense Mechanisms.") Over time, she grows in her ability to experience *disclosure-based intimacy* (closeness through personal revelation) and develops connections with greater *tie strength* (fortitude of social connections).[14]

Felicia Day spoke with us about the character's coping behavior, dark side, and personal growth.

> **Q:** Before she becomes known as Charlie Bradbury, Celeste Middleton suffers a horrible family tragedy when a drunk driver kills her father and leaves her mother on life support.[15] How does she cope?
>
> **Day:** I think Celeste copes by becoming isolated and secretive about her past. By not telling anyone what happened to her, she's able to deny what happened herself. She chooses to live a life where she has nothing and no one to tie her down, so she, in a sense, can be whatever she wants to be—including, for brief periods of time, happy.
>
> **Q:** Charlie has trouble acknowledging the severity of her mother's condition. Did you see that as being delusional or as a normal human reaction?
>
> **Day:** I think it can be easy to reframe reality to suit ourselves, especially when it allows us to compartmentalize feelings of guilt or trauma. The ability to move on, to grow a scab over those most sensitive parts of our pasts, is healthy in some ways. As long as the remaining emotions don't unduly influence your actions in the present.
>
> **Q:** Trauma can affect people in many different ways, not just leading to PTSD. There is also a phenomenon called *posttraumatic growth*, in which reaction to trauma helps an individual find purpose and grow as a person.

Where does Charlie fall in this range, as you see it? Did trauma destroy her, eventually make her stronger, or something else?

**Day:** I think trauma motivates Charlie in a lot of ways, especially in her Robin Hood–esque actions against big corporations. I think she had to work through a lot of adversity as a teenager, but as an adult she's resilient and determined and relies on her own means to get her through life. I admire that about her.

**Q:** Charlie has spent much of her life on the run, and she loves games that might help her escape from reality.[16] Is Charlie afraid to face life, or does she just face it in a different way?

**Day:** I think there are aspects of her past that Charlie is afraid to face, and we saw a few of those moments in the show. But I think escapism isn't necessarily a bad thing, and Charlie likes to be more active in her hobbies than passive. Thus, video games versus TV. She's not one who necessarily avoids reality; she just uses it to relieve the pressure valve of everyday life.

**Q:** Why does Charlie have the same taste in women that Dean has? Why does she go for bad girls?

**Day:** Charlie is a very carefully controlled person and overall is a paladin type. She has a very strong sense of right and wrong and honor. I think she's drawn to her opposite side. Or perhaps just her dark side, as we saw personified in an episode in season 11.

**Q:** We know Charlie has a dark side that's ruthless and out for revenge.[17] Could Charlie's interest in bad girls have something to do with the part of her that wants to feel strong and be "bad" herself?

**Day:** Absolutely. Breaking rules is a rush, and she does that in her hacking, but not in person as much.[18] I think

# OFF TO SEE THE ID

Though Sigmund Freud's ideas remain controversial, rejected by many, his views on human nature nevertheless influence popular discussion to this day. He believed that personality at the beginning of life consists entirely of *id*: the inborn, amoral self that does not restrain its impulses. Freud said the id operates on the *pleasure principle*, seeking immediate gratification.[19] After magic splits Charlie into two separate beings (whom the Winchesters dub Good Charlie and Dark Charlie), Good Charlie meets Clive Dillon, a Man of Letters who was similarly split into two and whose darker self has become the Wizard of Oz. "A coven of witches grabbed me," Good Clive explains. "They used the Inner Key on me, unleashed my id."[20] More amoral than evil, the id represents impulsive animal nature. As each person learns some self-control, Freud said, each will develop the *ego* (the part we think of as ourselves, including the conscious mind), and then around kindergarten age each normally develops the *superego* (essentially the conscience). In a well-balanced individual with a healthy sense of self, the ego supposedly balances the demands of the id and the superego to meet the person's needs realistically (the *reality principle*).[21] When magic splits Charlie into id-dominated and superego-dominated selves, neither is a whole and healthy individual. Only after the two merge back together does Celeste become complete.

Charlie feels that walking the knife edge of danger is a turn-on and being with someone who pushes her into that territory is probably her weakness.

**Q:** Do you like Charlie?

**Day:** I love her! She's strong and vulnerable at the same time. She doesn't back down, even though she's afraid. She's a woman of dichotomies who is loyal to those she loves. She fights for the little guy. And over four seasons she inspired me to be a better, stronger person myself.

## Amanda Tapping Interview: But What About Naomi?

One person breaks rules for the sake of helping others, engaging in a bit of chaos for the sake of good, as Charlie does, while another person may hurt people for the sake of reinforcing rules, engaging in evil actions for the sake of order, as a number of *Supernatural*'s angels do. Both may believe they are doing what's just and right, that they serve the greater good. Executive angel Naomi reportedly oversees the biblical murder of firstborn children and later, simply to get Castiel's attention, orders the massacre of everybody in a restaurant.[22] She brainwashes Castiel, robbing him of his free will, out of her authoritarian belief that Heaven's security is more important than individual freedom.[23] In the basic human dilemma of freedom versus security, many people hoping to feel safe will more readily relinquish liberty than fight for it.[24] When the angels suddenly have free will, Naomi desperately strives to stamp it out.

Amanda Tapping, actress and director known for her work on the series *Stargate SG-1*, played the angel Naomi, who leads an angelic faction fighting for control of Heaven on *Supernatural*. Tapping has also gone ghost hunting with our own Jenna Busch, and she shared some thoughts with us about her angelic role.

> **Q:** Would you consider Naomi a villain?
>
> **Tapping:** No. No, I wouldn't. I think that she really felt like she had a clear purpose and her focus was always to protect Heaven. I mean, she may have meandered off her path a little bit, but ultimately her goal was to protect Heaven. And so, she would do it through whatever means necessary. Not in the most angelic way [laughs], but, I mean, ultimately, when she saw the

truth of everything, she just really wanted to protect
Heaven.[25] I don't think she wanted to be a bad guy. I
don't think she set out to be a bad guy. I think that she
got sidetracked. I think that, in essence, as hokey as it
sounds, her heart was pure. Pure-ish.

**Q:** What would you consider to be her human qualities?

**Tapping:** You know, it's funny, because even though I
played her, I never thought of her as *not* human. Do
you know what I mean? In the sense that I think she
feels a lot of the negative human emotions—like jeal-
ousy, rage, manipulation. She enjoyed manipulation.[26]
I say this after saying that I think she wasn't a villain.
*[laughs]* So it may sound a bit weird. She did so much
live on the side of the bad guy, not the nicest of human
elements, but I think, especially at the end, she felt
remorse. And I don't think that is something, necessarily, that supernatural beings normally feel. She definitely felt remorse, and I think that's very human. And
I don't know why—because she didn't really spend that
much time on Earth—why she was able to feel those
kinds of things, but she did. I think she most definitely, in the end, was more human than she was in
the beginning. I think in the beginning she was very
mission-driven: "I'm going to do this. I'm going to get
the information I need by whatever means necessary,
even if it hurts." And at the end, she was like, "Maybe
this is not the right way to do it." *[laughs]* And then she
dies, which sucks![27]

**Q:** What do *Supernatural*'s angels, as much as you can
generalize about angels, think of humanity?

**Tapping:** If you're talking about the good angels, I think
they feel sorry for them. I think they feel like they're
all ants in this raging war and they're just trapped on

this little planet. Even though they're created by God, I think the angels feel sorry for them overall. I think that the nastier angels are kind of disgusted by them. It's like they're just in the way. You just want to brush them off.

**Q:** Do you think that Naomi redeemed herself at the end?

**Tapping:** I do. I know that there are mixed reviews on that one out there. But I do feel like she did. I think that when she came to them and said, "Here's what I can offer, and I'm sorry," essentially, that she did. She became very honest, the most honest that we've ever seen her. I do feel she did redeem herself. I feel that the only way to redeem herself was to come clean.[28]

**Q:** Why are *Supernatural*'s angels such jerks?

**Tapping:** *[laughs]* I don't know! They are, though, aren't they? You know what it is? They're jerks to us. We have a different way of thinking as human beings: We believe in justice and in fair play and in being honest with each other. Not all the time, obviously, but at the core of the human element is that we believe in the good of people. And angels don't necessarily follow those same rules. Like they'll do what they have to do, to do what they need to get done. Damn the consequences. And it's not that they're being nasty, necessarily, but that's just who they are. That's what they do. Whereas humans are like, "That's really shitty! We don't act like that! Decent human beings don't do that;" and the angels are like, "Yeah, but we've got to get our stuff done." It's like they're operating on a different set of moral standards. Ironic, considering that we, as humans, throughout history, have been taught that the angels are the higher power and better than us. And yet, the cool thing about *Supernatural* is it kind of twists that paradigm and says, well, maybe the angels have gotten a bit too full of themselves! *[laughs]* Or maybe the humans are not so bad. It plays up all the qualities we think humans are; that's what the angels appear to be. So, yeah, they are kind of jerks by our set of standards, but not by theirs. *[laughs]*

## A Hacker and a Halo

In evaluating people's moral maturity, Lawrence Kohlberg looked less at their specific moral choices and more at the standards that guide their choices. He did not judge them by their own standards. Instead, he judged the standards themselves and looked at how those standards compared the kind of reasoning that people applied at different levels of maturity.[29] Standards change as we mature and as we encounter different circumstances. Charlie goes from trying to hide from the world and telling Sam and Dean to "never contact me again, like, ever" at the end of their first adventure together,[30] to becoming a hunter who eventually sacrifices herself in an effort to save Dean and protect the world.[31] Even though she becomes more selfless over time, Charlie always cares whether others get hurt, whereas Naomi's priorities shift. "That's my job—to protect Heaven," Naomi tells Dean at one point,[32] but later remembers the angels' true duty: "Our mission was to protect what God created. I don't know when we forgot that."[33] Morality can change greatly and in ways more complicated than Kohlberg ever knew.[34]

*References*

Ammer, C. (1997). *The American Heritage dictionary of idioms*. Boston, MA: Houghton Mifflin Harcourt.

Cortese, A. J. (1984). Standard issue scoring of moral reasoning: A critique. *Merrill-Palmer Quarterly, 30*(3), 227–246.

Freud, S. (1920). *Beyond the pleasure principle*. London, UK: Norton.

Freud, S. (1923/1927). *The ego and the id*. London, UK: Hogarth.

Freud, S. (1940). An outline of psychoanalysis. In *Standard edition of the complete works of Sigmund Freud* (vol. 23, pp. 141–207). London, UK: Hogarth.

Fromm, E. (1941). *Escape from freedom*. New York, NY: Rinehart.

Granovetter, M. S. (1973). The strength of weak ties. *American Journal of Sociology, 78*(6), 1360–1380.

Grantley, S., & Parker, A. G. (2010). *The Who by numbers: The story of The Who through their music*. Berkeley, CA: Helter Skelter.

Haggbloom, S. J., Warnick, R., Warnick, J. E., Jones, V. K., Yarbrough, G. L., Russell, T. M., Borecky, C. M., McGahhey, R., Powell, J. L., Beavers, J., & Monte, E. (2002). The 100 most eminent psychologists of the 20th century. *Review of General Psychology, 6*(2), 139–152.

Kohlberg, L. (1976). Moral stages and moralization: The cognitive-developmental approach. In T. Lickona (Ed.), *Moral development and behavior: Theory, research, and social issues* (pp. 31–53). New York, NY: Holt, Rinehart, & Winston.

Kohlberg, L. (1981). *Essays on moral development, vol. I: The philosophy of moral development*. San Francisco, CA: Harper & Row.

Krebs, D. L., & Denton, K. (2005). Toward a more pragmatic approach to morality: A critical evaluation of Kohlberg's model. *Psychological Review, 112*(3), 629–649.

Maschette, D. (1977). Moral reasoning in the real world. *Theory into Practice, 16*(2), 124–128.

Rubin, K. H., & Burgess, K. B. (2001). *Social withdrawal and anxiety*. New York, NY: Oxford University Press.

Tsujimoto, R. N., & Nardi, P. M. (1978). A comparison of Kohlberg's and Hogan's theories of moral development. *Social Psychology, 41*(3), 235–245.

Vaillant, G. E. (1977/1998). *Adaptation to life*. Cambridge, MA: Harvard University Press.

## Notes

1. Episode 10–11, "There's No Place Like Home" (January 27, 2014).
2. "*L'enfer est plein de bonnes volontés ou désirs*." ["Hell is full of good wishes."]—Bernard of Clairvaux (circa 1150; cited in Ammer, 1997).
3. Haggbloom et al. (2002).
4. Kohlberg (1976).
5. Charlie—episode 10–21, "Dark Dynasty" (May 6, 2015); Naomi—8–23, "Sacrifice" (May 15, 2013).
6. Kohlberg (1981).
7. Written by P. Townsend (1971); played in Charlie's last episode before dying, 10–18, "Book of the Damned" (April 15, 2015).
8. Grantley & Parker (2010).
9. Recurring from Charlie's debut in episode 7–20, "The Girl with the Dungeons and Dragons Tattoo" (April 27, 2012) until her death in 10–21, "Dark Dynasty" (May 6, 2015).
10. Growing from Dean's early assessment that Charlie is "kinda like the little sister I never wanted" soon after they meet her in episode 7–20, "The Girl with the Dungeons and Dragons Tattoo" (April 27, 2012).
11. Episode 10–21, "Dark Dynasty" (May 6, 2012).
12. Rubin & Burgess (2001).

13. Vaillant (1977/1998).
14. Granovetter (1973).
15. Episode 8–20, "Pac-Man Fever" (April 24, 2013).
16. Demonstrated most clearly in episodes 8–11, "LARP and the Real Girl" (January 23, 2013); 8–20, "Pac-Man Fever" (April 24, 2013).
17. Episode 10–11, "There's No Place Like Home" (January 27, 2014).
18. Demonstrated in Charlie's every appearance, beginning with episode 7–20, "The Girl with the Dungeons and Dragons Tattoo" (April 27, 2012).
19. Freud (1920, 1923/1927).
20. Episode 10–11, "There's No Place Like Home" (January 27, 2014).
21. Freud (1923/1927, 1940).
22. Episode 8–21, "The Great Escapist" (May 1, 2013).
23. Episode 8–17, "Goodbye Stranger" (March 20, 2013).
24. Fromm (1941).
25. As Naomi said in episode 8–19, "Taxi Driver" (April 3, 2013).
26. Demonstrated over the course of episodes 8–7, "A Little Slice of Kevin" (November 14, 2012); "Hunteri Heroici" (November 28, 2012); 8–10, "Torn and Frayed" (January 16, 2013); 8–17, "Goodbye Stranger" (March 20, 2013); 8–19, "Taxi Driver" (April 3, 2013); 8–21, "The Great Escapist" (May 1, 2013); 8–23, "Sacrifice" (May 15, 2013).
27. Episode 8–23, "Sacrifice" (May 15, 2013).
28. Episode 8–23, "Sacrifice" (May 15, 2013).
29. Kohlberg (1976, 1981).
30. Episode 7–20, "The Girl with the Dungeons and Dragons Tattoo" (April 27, 2012).
31. Episode 10–21, "Dark Dynasty" (May 6, 2015).
32. Episode 8–19, "Taxi Driver" (April 3, 2013).
33. Episode 8–23, "Sacrifice" (May 15, 2013).
34. Cortese (1984), Krebs & Denton (2005), Maschette (1977), Tsujimoto & Nardi (1978).

# Denial

### TRAVIS LANGLEY

*"You know you can't cheat Death."*
—Death[1]

*"I am so much more than five stages. And so are you."*
—psychiatrist Elisabeth Kübler-Ross[2]

One of the most misused and misunderstood concepts in psychology or psychiatry is Elisabeth Kübler-Ross's model of how people face death. Best known as the "stages of grief" once extended to include bereavement over the loss of others, the framework began with her observations on how people face their *own* deaths.[3] In fact, she had referred to them as *stages of dying*, having developed her ideas about this while working with terminally ill adults and children.[4] She and a colleague later wrote that the so-called stages "were never meant to tuck messy emotion into neat packages. They are responses to loss that many people have, but there is not a typical response to loss, as there is no typical loss. Our grief is as individual as our lives," and they stressed that "they are not stops on some linear timeline of grief. Not everyone goes through them or goes in a prescribed order."[5] Treating these five responses as stages might not be the best way to view them because empirical evidence has not demonstrated that people typically move through all five, going from one to the next.[6] When an electric shock injures Dean's heart so severely that a doctor says he'll have at most a month to live, Dean does not undergo a series of stages but instead promptly resigns himself to his fate[7] and this is one of the many ways different people react to terminal diagnoses.[8]

Of Kübler-Ross's five particular reactions to facing one's own impending death, *denial* may be the most common.[9] It is interesting that this was not Dean's reaction to his terminal diagnosis, given that denial is a default behavior he uses to plod his way through much of life. When asked how he deals with the mistakes that haunt him day and night, he says outright, "Whisky. Denial."

Kübler-Ross noted that denial about one's own upcoming death tends to take the form of disbelief and differs from denial about the loss of someone else, which consists more of difficulty feeling and staying conscious of the fact that the other person is gone.[10] Many a person will say, "I keep expecting him to walk in," and for others this involves trying not to think about it, as if thinking about it makes it real. When their father is absent and his fate unknown, Dean repeatedly rejects any suggestion that John Winchester is dead: "He's not dead! He can't be!"[11] So when his father's death is merely hypothetical, Dean shows disbelief, but once he knows that his father has truly died,[12] Dean won't talk about that, avoids thinking about it, mocks Sam for trying to bring it up, and distracts himself by working on the Impala.[13]

On *Supernatural*, the characters most often in denial about their own deaths are ghosts. Refusing to accept death may keep real people alive, whether by helping them find the strength to survive or simply not give up,[14] but could it also keep the spirit of someone who has died from passing over into the afterlife? Objective science has trouble answering such a question,[15] to say the least, but stories can explore it. Each year on the anniversary of her death in a car accident, a woman who does not know she's dead is hunted and tormented by another ghost, a farmer struck down in the same accident. Sam Winchester tells her that the reason she hasn't remembered much of this is "because you couldn't see the truth, Molly," and Dean says they didn't tell her that truth as soon as they met her "because you wouldn't have believed us."[16] The basic defense mechanism of denial has shielded her from guilt over accidentally killing the man, but it has also prevented her from escaping him. (For more on how we employ denial and other coping behaviors throughout life, see chapter 6, "A Trunk Full of Defense Mechanisms.")

This mainly applies to the nonviolent ghosts, though. The vengeful spirits Sam and Dean fight most tend to fume in anger over their deaths.

## References

Beilin, R. (1981–1982). Social functions of denial of death. *Omega: Journal of Death & Dying*, 12(1), 25–35.

Bonanno, G. A. (2004). Loss, trauma, and human resilience: Have we underestimated the human capacity to thrive after extremely aversive events? *American Psychology*, 59(1), 20–28.

Bonanno, G. A. (2010). The other side of sadness: What the new science of bereavement tells us about life after loss. New York, NY: Basic.

Corr, C. A., Doka, K. J., & Kastenbaum, R. (1999). Dying and its interpreters: A review of selected literature and some comments on the state of the field. Journal of Death & Dying, 39(4), 239–259.

Friedman, R., & James, J. W. (2012). The myth of the stages of dying, death, and grief. *Skeptic Magazine, 14*(2), 37–41.

Kastenbaum, R. (2000). The psychology of death (3rd ed.). New York NY: Springer.

Kübler-Ross, E. (1969). On death and dying: What the dying have to teach doctors, nurses, clergy, & their own families. London, UK: Routledge.

Kübler-Ross, E., & Kessler, D. (2005/2014). On grief and grieving: Finding the meaning of grief through the five stages of loss. New York, NY: Simon & Schuster.

Nickell, J. (2012). The science of ghosts: Searching for the spirits of the dead. Amherst, NY: Prometheus.

Tippett, K. (2010). Einstein's God: Conversations about science and the human spirit. London, UK: Penguin.

Varki, A., & Brower, D. (2013). Denial: Self-deception, false beliefs, and the origins of the human mind. Lebanon, IN: Twelve.

## Notes

1. Episode 5–21, "Two Minutes to Midnight" (May 6, 2010).
2. Kübler-Ross & Kessler (2005/2014), p. 216.
3. Kübler-Ross (1969).
4. e.g., Kübler-Ross (1969), Kübler-Ross & Kessler (2005/2014).
5. Kübler-Ross & Kessler (2005/2014), p. 7.
6. Bonanno (2004), Corr et al. (1999), Friedman & James (2012).
7. Episode 1–12, "Faith" (January 17, 2006).
8. Corr et al. (1999), Kastenbaum (2000).
9. Kübler-Ross (1969).
10. Kübler-Ross & Kessler (2005/2014).
11. Episode 1–22, "Devil's Trap" (May 4, 2006); see also 1–10, "Asylum" (November 22, 2005).
12. Episode 2–1, "In My Time of Dying" (September 28, 2006).
13. Episode 2–2, "Everybody Loves a Clown" (October 5, 2006).
14. Beilin (1981–1982), Varki & Brower (2013).
15. Nickell (2012), Tippett (2010).
16. Episode 2–16, "Roadkill" (March 15, 2007).

The first time he meets a Reaper, Dean does not accept his death. John Winchester also refuses to accept Dean's death, at great cost. Riverview Hospital, shooting location for episode 2–1, "In My Time of Dying" (September 28, 2006).

# PART II

# LOCK AND LOAD

# CHAPTER SIX

# A Trunk Full of Defense Mechanisms

## TRAVIS LANGLEY

*"Sometimes a cigar is just a cigar."*
—Bobby Singer[1]

*"Sometimes a cigar is just a cigar."*
—attributed to psychoanalyst Sigmund Freud, who probably never said it[2]

We lie to ourselves. We avoid problems, distract ourselves from sources of obsession or pain, and do one thing when we'd rather do something else, all in order to reduce stress in our lives. We have to. Just as we focus our attention on specific sights and sounds, instead of letting the stimuli that surround us bombard all at once, we select which stressors we will confront and which we will circumvent whether we realize that's what we're doing or not. For all the controversy and criticisms over Sigmund Freud's ideas about human nature, one area where many professionals view him more favorably is that of defense mechanisms. Even those who disagree with his beliefs about the unconscious motives behind these defenses tend to recognize that we often go to great lengths to protect ourselves from anxiety.[3]

Firefighters, police officers, soldiers, spies, and others in high-risk, high-stress occupations must stay alert for potential danger. If this readiness to spot danger becomes excessive or carries over into low-risk everyday activities, this may be referred to as *hypervigilance*, which can impede relationships, threaten health, and interfere with functioning in many areas of life.[4] *Supernatural*'s hunters, who fight fiends that frequently look like regular human beings, have reason to be vigilant, but heightened readiness to perceive threats can make it hard to open up, interact with others, and find enjoyment in life. Not all warriors find comfort in suburbia. The person who is ready to see danger anywhere and in anyone has trouble living a normal life. When the car's trunk is full of weapons, there's no room for luggage and a beach ball.

Sigmund Freud speculated on the mental weapons we carry for defense,[5] the *ego defense mechanisms*, but it was his daughter Anna Freud who named most of those safeguards against stress, catalogued them, and clarified their definitions.[6] Later investigators identified additional defense mechanisms. Psychiatrist George Vaillant classified them as *mature, neurotic, immature,* and *psychotic* according to how they correspond with healthy psychological development. How many of these coping mechanisms are there? According to Vaillant, "As many as the number of angels who can dance on the head of a pin."[7]

## The Good: Healthier Stress Management

Some of the ways we cope with stress are healthy and mature. They can potentially help us deal with our world, our relationships, and our private thoughts and feelings through rational, realistic means.[8] Unlike some of the unhealthy defenses, these provide real benefits, not imaginary ones, without simply trading one problem for another.

*Altruism* involves helping others without expectation of reward. The greater the risk or cost to the helper, the more altruistic the behavior is seen by others.[9] Long after the Winchesters brothers avenge their parents' deaths,[10] helping others despite repeated cost to themselves drives their continuing mission.

*Anticipation* can reduce stress by helping a person feel better prepared for the future. While obsessing about the future can cause worry, possibly to the point of suffering conditions such as *generalized anxiety disorder*,[11] feeling prepared can make future-oriented thinking less stressful and enhance performance when the time comes.[12] John Winchester raises his sons to be ready for whatever may come: "After your mother passed, all I saw was evil—everywhere—and all I cared about was, was keepin' you boys alive. I wanted you prepared."[13]

*Humor* in the face of hardship can help a person express ideas, feelings, and concerns and mentally process the situation without letting it bring them down.[14] Many people whose occupations put them in traumatic situations (*primary traumatic stress*) or make them feel vicariously traumatized through contact with trauma victims (*secondary traumatic stress*) try to cope by means of *gallows humor*, grim jokes about grave topics,[15] "whatever gets you through today."[16] When Sam says, "I miss conversations that didn't start with 'this killer truck,'"[17] he speaks lightheartedly about a deadly situation, but does so without belittling the ghost-driven truck's victims or making light of their deaths. Such dark humor can give individuals a sense of control in out-of-control circumstances, elicit social support from others, and help them distance themselves from feelings that might get in the way of doing their jobs.

*Sublimation* redirects someone from an impulse the person cannot or should not act on, so that he or she channels that energy into a more constructive or creative activity instead.[18] *Supernatural* includes many examples of such behavior. When Dean prefers to investigate spontaneous combustion instead of facing his personal problems, for example, Sam refers to this defense mechanism by name, "Dean, it's called sublimation"— which Dean acknowledges, "Yeah, it's kinda my thing."[19]

*Suppression*—a.k.a. *thought suppression*, deliberately trying not to think about a specific impulse or conflict—is often listed among the healthy defense mechanisms, even though the Freuds considered it too conscious a behavior to include among what they considered to be unconscious defenses (a distinction made more clearly by Anna Freud because her father Sigmund did not precisely clarify the terms).[20] It is a valuable coping behavior, though. By telling Dean, "Don't worry about the Mark. We'll figure out the Mark later," Sam is not suggesting that they ignore the issue, but is instead recommending that they temporarily suppress thought and associated worry about it while another life-threatening emergency is at hand.[21]

Even these healthier defenses can be used excessively or inappropriately,[22] as Sam points out when he chastises Dean that "I'm pretty sure six seconds is too soon" to joke about a man's death.[23] Humor that mocks victims is less common than humor at the expense of perpetrators, and it may indicate greater difficulty managing stress.[24] Joking excessively can also keep the person from facing feelings that sooner or later must be addressed. Dean exemplifies the risk of overusing this coping behavior. Sam admonishes him for overusing humor as a defense: "You know this whole 'I laugh in the face of death thing' thing? It's crap."[25]

## ROAD MUSIC

## The Bad: Trading One Problem for Others

Even though we develop defense mechanisms to protect us from stress, some of those mechanisms risk solving one problem simply by creating another. This could be represented by the Winchesters' long history of resolving one yearlong story arc by causing their next big problem or unleashing whatever evil they'll have to fight next.[30]

### "Neurotic" Defenses

The so-called *neurotic* defenses are the ones that psychoanalysts believe make individuals vulnerable to developing *neuroses*, Freud's term for nonpsychotic mental illnesses such as anxiety disorders. Regardless of whether these behaviors really fit Freudian notions about neurotic symptoms, most of them are not difficult to observe in people every day.[31]

*Displacement* relocates our feelings and impulses, transferring them from their real target and onto other targets. Instead of venting at the boss, a person might instead start snapping at co-workers, displacing those feelings away from the true object of frustration because standing up to the boss involves a threat to one's livelihood. An apt example of displacement might be when Cyrus Dorian turns his hatred of one African-American into a murderous vendetta against all black men.[32] Angry when a woman rejects him for another man, Dorian displaces his fury onto available men of that other man's race, becoming angry enough to kill each of them.

*Dissociation* (short for *dis-association*) occurs when different parts of the mind function at the same time without sharing information with each other. The simplest everyday example would be *highway hypnosis*, in which one part of the person daydreams while another part successfully drives the car until the part that was daydreaming realizes it "zoned out" and has no memory of the last few miles. Although *Supernatural* does not veer into extreme, psychologically induced dissociative conditions, such as *dissociative identity disorder* (DID, the modern term for *multiple personality disorder*), some of the characters who become werewolves or lose their souls have similar experiences in terms of memory gaps.[33] People vary in their ability to recall what has happened to them while dissociated. Some who receive the controversial diagnosis of DID describe knowing what someone else seemed to be doing while in control of their bodies—*co-consciousness*, being conscious at the same time as the personality that is in charge. Jimmy Novak reports having few memories from when the angel Castiel occupies his body, but the ghost of Meg Masters says she was brutally aware of the atrocities committed by the demon who possessed her.[34] Historically, some dissociative disorder cases may have been mistaken for demonic possession,[35] whereas in *Supernatural* demonic possession can duplicate dissociative symptoms.

*Intellectualization* uses thought to avoid feeling. In Vaillant's typology, this is an umbrella term that covers several different defense mechanisms, such as magical thinking, ritual, or rationalization. One of the most important defenses, as the Freuds saw it, *rationalization* involves coming up with a rational-seeming explanation for something in order to avoid feeling stressed by it—in other words, making excuses. When Castiel fumbles to explain how he lost track of a young woman who has been impregnated by Lucifer, Mary Winchester snaps, "Stop making excuses!"[36] She is, in effect, accusing him of rationalizing his actions instead of admitting he failed.

*Reaction formation* is a variant of sublimation, albeit a less helpful and possibly more destructive form: Rather than finding a useful alternative to acting on an unacceptable impulse, the person does the opposite—such as a pornography-obsessed individual who campaigns against the evils of porn or a person who vandalizes a car he or she adores but cannot afford. Hurt when his recently resurrected mother does not spend more time with her sons, Dean becomes resentful, pushes her away, and even ignores her text messages[37] not long after worrying why she wasn't answering his messages to her.[38]

Freud considered *repression*, locking disturbing thoughts or feelings away in the unconscious, to be the most important defense mechanism ("the cornerstone on which the whole structure of psychoanalysis rests"[39]), and yet modern empirical evidence suggests that it might occur rarely.[40] People more commonly engage in deliberate thought suppression without making information inaccessible by the conscious mind. In *Supernatural*, repression and other defense mechanisms can be the result of supernatural means. Sam's magically induced repression serves the purpose of protecting him from horrifying memories, but, as Freud described happening with real people, the memories also come out through dreams, flashes of memory, and other *slips* until they finally overwhelm Sam.[41]

### Immature Defenses

Some coping behaviors are common among children but not adults; therefore they seem not only neurotic but outright childish. While defenses in the "neurotic" category distress the person who performs them, immature defenses seem harmless to the performer but undesirable and juvenile to observers.[42] Immaturity is unappealing. *Supernatural* includes examples of such behavior, over which father figure Bobby Singer regularly chastises the boys for being "idjits." Wrapped up in their own needs, the Winchester brothers often take Bobby for granted, so much so that when he's the one who needs their help with something important for a change, he bellows: "You two are the whiniest, most self-absorbed sons of bitches I ever met!"[43]

Unlike many other defense mechanisms that keep the person from acting on an unhealthy impulse, *acting out* lets the individual take action in order to avoid acknowledging emotions. It includes delinquent misbehavior, impulsive actions, and chronic substance abuse.[44] These negative actions may result from circumstances ranging from mere annoyances to real tragedies. When Dean knocks a board game to the floor out of exasperation with Castiel[45] or beats his beloved Impala with a crowbar once he finally unleashes some rage over his father's death,[46] he is acting out in both instances. This behavior is not displacement because he does not convince himself that he is mad at the game or the car.

As opposed to *active aggression*, which is actively doing something to inflict hurt, *passive aggression* is about aggressively *not* doing something. Examples include procrastination, avoidance, stubbornness, sullenness, lateness, or neglecting to keep promises. Right after Kevin Tran gets Sam and Dean to promise to "get over" a rift they've been having, the brothers instead show annoyance by heading to their separate rooms and shutting their doors, rather than talking to each other.[47]

*Projection* downplays the importance of our worst qualities by projecting them onto other people, letting us perceive those unfavorable traits in others because they seem socially acceptable if they're commonplace. A gossipy individual may assume most people gossip, a cheater may assume most cheat, or a bigot may assume everybody harbors strong prejudices. A promiscuous individual, such as Dean Winchester,[48] may overestimate other people's promiscuity and will pay more attention to examples that support this expectation (*confirmation bias*).[49]

Fantasy can be useful, valuable, and productive. *Schizoid fantasy*, however, lets the person withdraw from engagement with other people by retreating into daydreams and other fantasies. Fantasizing replaces socializing. Fans who connect in real life,[50] like characters who gather for a *Supernatural* fan convention within a somewhat metafictional episode of *Supernatural*,[51] are *not* examples of people doing this because their shared love of the fantasy brings them together. While Lucifer is in control of Castiel's body, the angel occupies himself with schizoid fantasy by contentedly watching imaginary television deep within his own mind instead of worrying about what's going on out in the world.[52] Because he knows the fantasy isn't real, Castiel is not delusional. That would be psychotic.

## The Ugly: Losing Touch with Reality

An individual might experience a *psychotic episode*, briefly losing touch with reality perhaps in reaction to a traumatic experience, or suffer a long-lasting *psychotic disorder* such as schizophrenia or dementia.[53] The most obvious psychotic symptoms are *delusions* (beliefs severely out of touch with reality) and *hallucinations* (perceptions out of touch with reality). Clinicians who mistake clients' unusual circumstances or cultural differences for such symptoms can misdiagnose those clients and incorrectly label them psychotic.[54] Sam and Dean infiltrate a mental hospital simply by describing their life honestly, which sounds delusional,[55] and a psychologist diagnoses Anna with schizophrenia because she seems to be hallucinating but really is hearing angels' voices.[56] However bizarre a belief or perception might be, it is not psychotic if it accurately assesses bizarre reality. At a time when he is overwhelmed by hallucinations about Lucifer, Sam can no longer tell what is real and what is not, and he has therefore entered a psychotic state.[57]

Vaillant looked mainly at three "psychotic" *defense mechanisms*, those that alter reality beyond common misinterpretation or merely neurotic misrepresentation. A person in *denial*, the least pathological of the three, refuses to perceive a disturbing truth, more often about events ("That wasn't my fault" or "I am not an alcoholic") but sometimes about inner experience ("I am not angry").[58] In the show, characters are often in denial after being turned into a werewolf or other fantastical creature. Recently turned into a vampire, a young woman named Lucy refuses to believe that she has killed people for their blood, even though sunlight hurts her skin and she can hear blood pumping: "No! No, it wasn't real!"[59]

*Delusional projection* unrealistically casts blame on others for one's own problems and inner experience.[60] Those suffering this symptom tend to feel that others are out to get them (*persecutory delusions*). A clear-cut example would be Daniel M'Naghten, whose 1843 trial established our world's modern insanity defense. Convinced that the British prime minister, Sir Robert Peel, personally caused M'Naghten's hardships, the man attempted to shoot the prime minister but instead killed

# JENSEN ACKLES ON DEAN'S DEFENSE MECHANISMS

An audience member at JusInBelloCon asked actor Jensen Ackles what it would take for Dean to give up his defense mechanisms.[61]

**Ackles:** "It would take years of therapy, and Dean has broken down some of those walls but a lot of them are how he survives. They're defense mechanisms. Tearing them down might leave him so vulnerable he couldn't live the life that he lives. Obviously, I'm no psychologist, so I don't know how deep that goes. . . .

"He uses that not just to defend against emoting, but he uses it to give him strength and courage to do the things that he does. Some of them are good and some are not, but it's what makes Dean *Dean*. He's a complex character and that's part of his complexity, just like we are all complex. There are certain issues we all have emotionally, maybe physically, and that's all part of what makes us *us*. Sometimes you need to face those issues, deal with them head-on and ask for help, or sometimes you just have to learn to live with them and deal with them as best you can. I think Dean is trying to do the best he can but some of those walls he needs; he relies on them as crutches."

*[Ackles turned to this book's co-editor, Lynn Zubernis.]* "How'd you like that, Lynn?"

Peel's secretary.[62] A less clear-cut example is computer hacker Frank Devereaux—"a jackass and a lunatic," according to Bobby, and "bipolar with delusional ideation," according to Frank—who habitually perceives conspiracies and other threats in any situation. This seems to fit delusional projection but sometimes he's right in the supernatural world of the show.[63]

Hallucinations and other delusions are covered by the defense mechanism *distortion*, "grossly reshaping external reality to suit inner needs," including megalomaniacal beliefs.[64] This would include three patients studied by real-life psychologist Milton

Rokeach, each of whom believed himself to be Jesus Christ.[65] An example of delusional thinking is apparent in one of *Supernatural*'s vengeful spirits, the ghost of Father Thomas Gregory, who believes he is an angel and begins delivering "divine" messages, telling people to kill sinners, until Sam and another priest convince him of the truth.[66] Unlike Sam who succeeded with Father Gregory, Rokeach enjoyed no success with his delusional patients. His experiment did not cure them but it "did cure me of my godlike delusion that I could manipulate them out of their beliefs."[67]

## The Best Defense

The best defense mechanism is the one that best reduces stress to an optimal level in a given situation while enhancing the individual's grasp on reality and without creating new problems as a result. Originated by Sigmund Freud and fleshed out by Anna Freud,[68] the idea that we use psychological coping mechanisms to manage stress is supported by much evidence, even if we do not always agree with the Freuds as to how, when, or why we do these things. George Vaillant and others added to the list of defense mechanisms, and our understanding of them may grow and change.[69] If defense mechanisms are real, the ghost of Sigmund Freud does not own them,[70] even if he does haunt their literature.

> "Bobby, don't go all Sigmund Freud on me.
> I just got drugged by a sandwich."
> —Dean Winchester[71]

> "Resilience isn't a single skill. It's a variety of
> skills and coping mechanisms."
> —journalist Jean Chatzky[72]

## References

Alsentali, A. M., & Anshel, M. H. (2015). Relationship between internal and external acute stressors and coping style. *Journal of Sport Behavior, 38*(4), 357–375.

American Psychiatric Association (2013). *Diagnostic and statistical manual of mental disorders* (5th ed.) (DSM–5). Washington, DC: American Psychiatric Association.

Amjad, F., & Bokharey, I. Z. (2015). Comparison of spiritual well-being and coping strategies of patients with generalized anxiety disorder and with minor general medical conditions. Journal of Religion & Health, 54(2), 524–539.

Baruss, I. (2003). *Alterations of consciousness: An empirical analysis for social scientists.* Washington, DC: American Psychological Association.

Batson, C. (1991). The altruism question. Mahwah, NJ: Erlbaum.

Baumeister, R. F., Dale, K., & Sommer, K. L. (1998). Freudian defense mechanisms and empirical findings in modern social psychology: Reaction formation, projection, displacement, undoing, isolation, sublimation, and denial. *Journal of Personality, 66*(6), 1081–1124.

Berney, S., de Roten, Y., Beretta, V., Kramer, U., & Despland, J. (2014). Identifying psychotic defenses in a clinical interview. *Journal of Clinical Psychology, 70*(5), 428–439.

Boyd-Wilson, B. M., Walkey, F. H., & McClure, J. (2002). Present and correct: We kid ourselves unless we live in the moment. *Personality & Individual Differences, 33*(5), 691–702.

Carton, A. M., & Aiello, J. R. (2009). Control and anticipation of social interruptions: Reduced stress and improved task performance. *Journal of Applied Social Psychology, 39*(1), 169–185.

Casper, M. F. (2014). Family don't end with blood: Building the Supernatural family. In L. Zubernis & K. Larsen (Eds.) *Fan phenomena: Supernatural* (pp. 76–87). Fishponds, Bristol, UK: Intellect.

Chatzky, J. (2011, June 22). How to be an entrepreneur: Qualities you can learn to develop the next big thing. New York Daily News: http://www.nydailynews.com/news/money/entrepreneur-qualities-learn-develop-big-article-1.128118.

Collins, M. (2014). Life changing: Supernatural and the power of fandom. In L. Zubernis & K. Larsen (Eds.) *Fan phenomena: Supernatural* (pp. 100–105). Fishponds, Bristol, UK: Intellect.

Cramer, P. (2000). Defense mechanisms in psychology today: Further processes for adaptation. *American Psychologist, 55*(6), 637–646.

Cramer, P. (2015). Defense mechanisms: 40 years of empirical research. *Journal of Personality Assessment, 97*(2), 114–122.

Craun, S. W., & Bourke, M. L. (2014). The use of humor to cope with secondary traumatic stress. *Journal of Child Sexual Abuse, 23*(7), 840–852.

Craun, S. W., & Bourke, M. L. (2015). Is laughing at the expense of victims and offenders a red flag? Humor and secondary traumatic stress. *Journal of Child Sexual Abuse, 24*(5), 592–602.

Diamond, B. L. (1964/1977). On the spelling of Daniel M'Naghten's name. In D. J. West & A. Walk (Eds.), Daniel McNaughton: His trial and the aftermath. Ashford, Kent, UK: Gaskell.

Elms, A. C. (2001). Apocryphal Freud: Sigmund Freud's most famous "quotations" and their actual sources. In J. A. Winder & J. W. Anderson (Eds.), Sigmund Freud and his impact on the modern world: The annual of psychoanalysis (vol. 29, pp. 83–104). Hillsdale, NJ: Analytic.

Fata, C. (2009, May 1). PTSD: True battle scar? Psychology Today: https://www. psychologytoday.com/articles/200905/ptsd-true-battle-scar.

Finzi-Dottan, R., & Karu, T. (2006). From emotional abuse in childhood to psycho- pathology in adulthood: A path mediated by immature defense mechanisms and self-esteem. *Journal of Nervous & Mental Disease, 194*(8), 616–621.

Freud, A. (1936). *The ego and the mechanisms of defence.* London, UK: Imago.

Freud, S. (1905/1960). *Jokes and their relation to the unconscious.* London, UK: Routledge & Kegan Paul.

Freud, S. (1914/1957). On the history of the psychoanalytic movement. In J. Strachey (Ed., trans.), *The standard edition of the complete psychological works of Sigmund Freud* (vol. XIV, pp. 45–61). London, UK: Hogarth.

Gantt, E. E., & Burton, J. (2013). Egoism, altruism, and the ethical foundations of personhood. *Journal of Humanistic Psychology, 53*(4), 438–460.

Gilmartin, K. M. (1986). Hypervigilance: A learned perceptual set and its conse- quences in police stress. In J. T. Reese & H. A. Goldstein (Eds.), *Psychological services for law enforcement* (pp. 443–446). Washington, DC: US Government Printing Office.

Haugen, P. T., Evces, M., & Weiss, D. S. (2012). Treating posttraumatic stress disorder in first responders: A systematic review. *Clinical Psychology Review, 32*(5), 370–380.

Horesh, D., Solomon, Z., Zerach, G., & Ein-Dor, T. (2011). Delayed-onset PTSD among war veterans: The role of life events throughout the life cycle. *Social Psychia- try & Psychiatric Epidemiology, 46*(9), 863–870.

Inzana, C. M., Driskell, J. E., Salas, E., & Johnston, J. H. (1996). Effects of preparatory information on enhancing performance under stress. *Journal of Applied Psychology, 81*(4), 429–435.

Keber, K. W. (1984). The perception of nonemergency helping situations: Costs, rewards, and the altruistic personality. *Journal of Personality, 52*(2), 177–187.

Kihlstrom, J. F. (2006). Repression: A unified theory of a will-o'-the-wisp. *Behavioral & Brain Sciences, 29*(5), 523.

Kim, E., Zeppenfeld, V., & Cohen, D. (2013). Sublimation, culture, and creativity. *Journal of Clinical Psychology, 70*(5), 478–488.

Kleiger, J. H., & Khadivi, A. (2015). *Assessing psychosis: A clinician's guide.* Abingdon, UK: Routledge.

Langley, T. (2014, July 6). Haunted by Sigmund Freud: Adaptation or defense mecha- nisms? *Psychology Today:* https://www.psychologytoday.com/blog/beyond-heroes- and-villains/201407/haunted-sigmund-freud-adaptation-or-defense-mechanisms.

Larsen, K., & Zubernis, L. S. (2013). *Fangasm: Supernatural fangirls.* Iowa City, IA: University of Iowa Press.

Macatee, R. J., Albanese, B. J., Allan, N. P., Schmidt, N. B., & Cougle, J. R. (2016). Distress intolerance as a moderator of the relationship between daily stressors and affective symptoms: Tests of incremental and prospective relationships. *Journal of Affective Disorders, 206*, 125–132.

Manning-Jones, S., de Terte, I., & Stephens, C. (2016). Secondary traumatic stress, vicarious posttraumatic growth, and coping among health professionals: A compar- ison study. *New Zealand Journal of Psychology, 45*(1), 20–29.

Marks, M. J., & Fraley, R. C. (2006). Confirmation bias and the sexual double stan- dard. *Sex Roles, 54*(1–2), 19–26.

Metzger, J. A. (2014). Adaptive defense mechanisms: Function and transcendence. *Journal of Clinical Psychology, 70*(5), 478–488.

Moran, R. (1981). *Knowing right from wrong: The insanity defense of Daniel McNaughtan.* New York, NY: Free Press.

Nasar, S. (1998). *A beautiful mind*. New York, NY: Simon & Schuster.

Norem, J. K. (1998). Why should we lower our defenses about defense mechanisms? *Journal of Personality, 66*(6), 895–917.

NPR (2014, May 2). The three Christs of Ypsilanti. NPR: http://www.npr.org/2014/05/02/309004267/the-three-christs-of-ypsilanti.

Ojeda, A. E. (Ed.) (2008). The trauma of psychological torture. Westport, CT.

Paulhus, D. L., Fridhandler, B., & Hayes, S. (1997). Psychological defense: Contemporary theory and research. In S. Briggs, R. G. Hogan, & J. W. Johnson (Eds.), *Handbook of personality psychology* (pp. 543–579). Boston, MA: Academic Press.

Rassin, E. (2008). Individual differences in susceptibility to confirmation bias. *Netherlands Journal of Psychology, 64*(2), 87–93.

Rofé, Y. (2008). Does repression exist? Memory, pathogenic, unconscious, and clinical evidence. *Review of General Psychology, 12*(1), 63–85.

Rokeach, M. (1964). *The three Christs of Ypsilanti: A narrative study of three lost men*. New York, NY: Knopf.

Rowe, A., & Regehr, A. (2009). Whatever gets you through today: An examination of cynical humor among emergency service professionals. *Journal of Loss & Trauma, 15*(4), 448–464.

Sansom-Daly, U. M., Bryant, R. A., Cohn, R. J., & Wakefield, C. E. (2014). Imagining the future in health anxiety: The impact of rumination on the specificity of illness-related memory and future thinking. *Stress & Coping: An International Journal, 27*(5), 587–600.

Sappenfield, B. R. (1948). Review of The ego and mechanisms of defense. *Journal of Abnormal & Social Psychology, 43*(1), 122–123.

Sar, V., Alioglu, F., & Akyüz, G. (2014). Experiences of possession and paranormal phenomena among women in the general population: Are they related to traumatic stress and dissociation? *Journal of Trauma & Dissociation, 15*(3), 303–318.

Sliter, M., Kale, A., & Yuan, Z. (2014). Is humor the best medicine? The buffering effect of coping humor on traumatic stressors in firefighters. *Journal of Organizational Behavior, 35*(2), 257–272.

Suedfeld, P. (1990). *Psychology and torture*. Abingdon, UK: Taylor & Francis.

Tanielian, T., & Jaycox, L. (2008). *Invisible wounds of war*. Santa Monica, CA: RAND.

Thorson, J. A. (1985). A funny thing happened on the way to the morgue: Some thoughts on humor and death, and a taxonomy of the humor associated with death. *Death Studies, 9*(3–4), 201–216.

Tracy, S. J., Myers, K. K., & Scott, C. W. (2006). Cracking jokes and crafting selves: Sensemaking and identity management among human service workers. *Communication Monographs, 73*(3), 283–308.

Vaillant, G. E. (1977/1998). *Adaptation to life*. Cambridge, MA: Harvard University Press.

Varki, A., & Brower, D. (2013). *Denial: Self-deception, false beliefs, and the origins of the human mind*. Lebanon, IN: Twelve.

Violanti, J. M. (1997). *Traumatic stress in critical occupations: Recognitions, consequences, and treatment*. Springfield, IL: Thomas.

Wheelis, A. (1950). The place of action in personality change. *Psychiatry, 13*(2), 135–148.

Wilkinson, J. (2014). Post, reblog, follow, tweet: Supernatural fandom and social media. In L. Zubernis & K. Larsen (Eds.) *Fan phenomena: Supernatural* (pp. 46–55). Fishponds, Bristol, UK: Intellect.

Wu, J. Q., Szpunar, K. K., Godovich, S. A., Schacter, D. L., & Hofmann, S. G. (2015). Episodic future thinking in generalized anxiety disorder. *Journal of Anxiety Disorders, 36*(1), 1–8.

Zubernis, L. (2016, June 4). JiB Con 2016—Part 2! Fangasm: https://fangasmthebook. wordpress.com/2016/06/04/jibcon-2016-part-2/.

## Notes

1. Episode 5–15, "Dead Men Don't Wear Plaid" (March 25, 2010).
2. Despite claims by Wheelis (1950, p. 139—possibly the earliest such attribution in print) and others, extensive investigation by Elms (2001) found no source to confirm that Sigmund Freud ever said anything of the sort.
3. Norem (1998), Paulhus et al. (1997).
4. Fata (2009), Gilmartin (1986), Haugen et al. (2012), Horesh et al. (2011), Violanti (1997).
5. Freud, S. (1905/1960).
6. Freud, A. (1936), Sappenfield (1948).
7. Vaillant (1977/1998), p. 79.
8. Metzger (2014), Vaillant (1977/1998).
9. Batson (1991), Gantt & Burton (2013), Keber (1984).
10. Episode 2–22, "All Hell Breaks Loose," part 2 (May 17, 2007).
11. Boyd-Wilson et al. (2002), Sansom-Daly et al. (2014), Tanielian & Jaycox (2008), Wu et al. (2015).
12. Carton & Aiello (2009), Inzana et al. (1996).
13. Episode 1–20, "Dead Man's Blood" (April 20, 2006).
14. Freud, S. (1905/1960), Vaillant (1977/1998).
15. Craun & Bourke (2014, 2015), Manning-Jones et al. (2016), Sliter et al. (2014), Thorson (1985), Tracy et al. (2006).
16. Rowe & Regehr (2009).
17. Episode 1–13, "Route 666" (January 31, 2006).
18. Kim et al. (2013).
19. Episode 12–5, "The One You've Been Waiting For" (November 10, 2016).
20. Freud, A. (1936).
21. Episode 9–23, "Do You Believe in Miracles?" (May 20, 2014).
22. "Under increased stress, they may *change* to less mature mechanisms."—Vaillaint (1977/1998), p. 385.
23. Episode, 6–17, "My Heart Will Go On" (April 15, 2011).
24. Craun & Bourke (2015).
25. Episode 4–16, "On the Head of a Pin" (March 19, 2009).
26. Written by R. Johnson (1937); played in episode 2–08, "Crossroad Blues" (November 16, 2006).
27. Episode 6–22, "The Man Who Knew Too Much" (May 20, 2011).
28. Ojeda (2008), Suedfeld (1990).
29. Alsentali & Anshel (2015), Amjad & Bokharey (2015), Macatee et al. (2016).
30. e.g., episode 1–21, "Devil's Trap" (May 4, 2006), which leads to John Winchester's death in 2–1 "In My Time of Dying" (September 28, 2006); 2–22, "All Hell Breaks Loose," part 2 (May 17, 2007), which unleashes scores of demons into the world; and so on with every season finale.
31. Baumeister et al. (1998), Cramer (2000, 2015).
32. Episode 1–13, "Route 666" (January 31, 2006).
33. Werewolf—episode 2–17, "Heart" (March 22, 2007); Sam after recovering his soul—episode 6–13, "Unforgiven" (February 7, 2011).
34. Jimmy—episode 4–20, "The Rapture" (April 30, 2009); Meg—4–2, "Are You There, God? It's Me, Dean Winchester" (September 25, 2008).

35. Baruss (2003), Sar et al. (2014).
36. Episode 12–9, "First Blood" (January 26, 2017).
37. Episode 12–14, "The Raid" (March 2, 2017).
38. Episode 12–4, "American Nightmare" (November 3, 2016).
39. Freud, S. (1914/1957), p. 61.
40. Kihlstrom (2006), Rofé (2008).
41. Episode 6–22, "The Man Who Knew Too Much" (May 20, 2011).
42. Finzi-Dottan & Karu (2006), Vaillant (1997/1998).
43. Episode 6–4, "Weekend at Bobby's" (October 15, 2010).
44. Vaillant (1977/1998).
45. Episode 7–21, "Reading Is Fundamental" (May 4, 2012).
46. Episode 2–2, "Everybody Loves a Clown" (October 5, 2006).
47. Episode 9–14, "Captives" (February 25, 2014).
48. In episode 5–11, "Sam, Interrupted" (January 21, 2010), Dean confirms that, at that point, he has never had a long-term romantic relationship—which a therapist defines to him as meaning "more than two months."
49. Marks & Fraley (2006), Rassin (2008).
50. Casper (2014), Collins (2014), Larsen & Zubernis (2013), Wilkinson (2014).
51. Episode 5–9, "The Real Ghostbusters" (November 12, 2009).
52. Episode 11–18, "Hell's Angel" (April 6, 2016).
53. American Psychiatric Association (2013).
54. Kleiger & Khadivi (2015).
55. Episode 5–11, "Sam, Interrupted" (January 23, 2010).
56. Episode 4–9, "I Know What You Did Last Summer" (November 13, 2008).
57. In episode 7–2, "Hello, Cruel World" (September 30, 2011), Dean compares his brother to real-life mathematician and cryptographer John Forbes Nash, Jr., whose struggle with paranoid schizophrenia was depicted in the book (Nasar, 1998) and motion picture (2001) both titled *A Beautiful Mind*. "If you're gone, I swear I'm gonna strap my Beautiful Mind brother into the car."—Dean.
58. Vaillant (1977/1998), Varki & Brower (2013).
59. Episode 3–7, "Fresh Blood" (November 15, 2007).
60. Berney et al. (2014), Vaillant (1977/1998).
61. Zubernis (2016).
62. Moran (1981). Sources are inconsistent on the spelling of M'Naghten's surname; see Diamond (1964/1977).
63. Episode 7–6, "Slash Fiction" (October 28, 2011).
64. Vaillant (1977/1998), p. 383.
65. Rokeach (1964).
66. Episode 2–13, "Houses of the Holy" (February 1, 2007).
67. NPR (2014).
68. Respectively, Freud, S. (1905/1960), Freud, A. (1936).
69. Paulhus et al. (1997), Vaillant (1977/1998).
70. Langley (2014).
71. Episode 7–9, "How to Win Friends and Influence Monsters" (November 18, 2011).
72. Chatzky (2011).

# CHAPTER SEVEN

# Super-Traumatized: Managing PTSD in a Supernatural World

TRAVIS ADAMS AND
JANINA SCARLET

*"Dude, I'm okay. I'm okay, okay? I swear,
the next person who asks me if I'm okay,
I'm gonna start throwing punches."*
—Dean Winchester[1]

*"As we avoid our hurts, we can't help but undermine
our values. So, by helping clients accept their pain
and stop avoiding it, we can help them open up
to what they most deeply want in their lives."*
—clinical psychologist Steve Hayes[2]

People who experience trauma starting at a very young age[3] might learn to rely on maladaptive strategies to manage their distress—for example, some rely on alcohol and other addictive substances to help them forget their painful experiences.[4] Such coping strategies can make individuals more likely to develop posttraumatic stress disorder (PTSD) and potentially prolong their painful symptoms.[5] What, then, are the risk factors and the recovery strategies for dealing with trauma in a supernatural world?

## Know Where the Monsters Are: PTSD Risk Factors

People who develop PTSD after traumatic events, such as when Sam and Dean lose their parents, undergo torture, or face their own deaths,[6] exhibit a variety of stress-related symptoms. These symptoms vary between sufferers and may include intrusive thoughts, flashbacks, nightmares, hypervigilance, mood changes, blaming oneself or others, withdrawing from people and activities, and avoiding trauma-related reminders.[7] For instance, after he remembers his torture experiences in Hell, Sam experiences terrible flashbacks, nightmares, increased startle response, and hallucinations, and he avoids talking about his symptoms.[8] Although hallucinations are not common among trauma survivors, they can occur in as many as 20 percent of those who suffer PTSD, particularly if these individuals are experiencing high alert response (*hypervigilance*).[9]

### Avoidance

Of all the PTSD symptoms, avoidance of trauma-related reminders and emotional numbing (*experiential avoidance*) seem to pose the greatest risk for developing PTSD.[10] Dean, in particular, avoids talking about and processing his emotions. For a long time after returning from being tortured in Hell, he refuses to tell Sam any details about his traumatic experiences. He seems more hypervigilant, more irritable and impatient, and seems to be drinking more than usual.[11] His avoidance of facing his traumatic experiences might prolong his struggle with posttraumatic symptoms.

### Repeated Traumatic Experiences
Exposure to multiple traumatic experiences starting at an early age can also pose a risk for developing PTSD and other mental health disorders.[12] Children exposed to both trauma and grief at a young age are more likely to develop PTSD, anxiety, depression, or self-harm than children not exposed to trauma.

Parental neglect can also negatively affect the way the neglected individual later responds to threats. Specifically, neglect and early trauma exposure can make the individual more hypervigilant and more sensitive to responding to stressful situations.[13] After Sam and Dean lose their mother (who is killed by the yellow-eyed demon, Azazel) at an early age,[14] their father dedicates his life to hunting, leaving Dean to watch over his little brother. At one point, while their father is off tracking a *shtriga*, a kind of a witch that feeds on children's life energy, Dean briefly leaves Sam alone and Sam runs away. Their father is forced to abandon his mission and focus on tracking Sam, leading Dean to blame himself for the subsequent victims that the shtriga kills.[15]

### Addiction
A combination of PTSD and an addiction disorder can make an individual more prone to aggression.[16] Individuals who rely on experiential avoidance as a coping mechanism are also more likely to struggle with addiction.[17] Both Winchester brothers avoid sharing their pain, repeatedly saying they feel fine when they're anguished,[18] and both exhibit addictive tendencies. Dean regularly abuses alcohol and denies struggling even after his father's death,[19] and Sam becomes addicted to demon blood, despite how erratically and aggressively these behaviors can make them act.[20]

## ROAD MUSIC

### "Sympathy for the Devil" by the Rolling Stones[21]

Learning to name and understand one's thoughts is key to many therapeutic interventions[22] and can be especially important following a traumatic event, such as accidentally letting Lucifer out of Hell.[23] Cognitive
therapies examine a person's errors in thinking, called *cognitive distortions*.[24] Cognitive therapy allows individuals to examine their thoughts
in order to change the cognitive distortions (for example, "All angels
cannot be trusted") into more adaptive thoughts (e.g., "Some angels
cannot be trusted"). Through their experiences, Sam and Dean learn not
to make such generalizations about angels, monsters, demons, and even
God and Lucifer.[25]

### Lack of Social Support

The lack of social support after exposure to trauma can also
serve as a risk factor for developing PTSD.[26] In addition,
avoidance of social interactions can lead to poorer tolerance
of distress later on.[27] Long after his mother dies, Dean avoids
talking to his family members and others around him. His
father frequently leaves him alone with Sam, possibly making
it harder for Dean to process his mother's tragic death.[28] Later,
when he loses people closest to him, such as his father or his
friend Bobby, Dean displays aggressive and angry behaviors
toward those around him.[29]

### Moral Injury and Self-Blame

Moral injury occurs when a traumatic event includes "betrayal"
of the person's moral values. Moral injury can lead trauma
survivors to blame themselves or others for the witnessed or
experienced atrocity, potentially reducing the individual's ability to adaptively cope with the trauma.[30] This is what Sam

appears to be going through after freeing Lucifer from Hell. He blames himself for breaking the last seal and for failing to see through Ruby's lies. As a result, he leaves Dean, feeling guilty for his actions.[31]

## Salt and Holy Water: Posttraumatic Growth

> *"You're wrong. People can change.*
> *There is a reason for hope."*
> —Sam Winchester[32]

> *"Posttraumatic growth is an antidote to*
> *posttraumatic stress disorder"*
> —social worker Tzipi Weiss[33]

Posttraumatic growth occurs when people who have experienced trauma are able to focus on the positive aspects of their lives that stem from their struggles. The process of posttraumatic growth does not eliminate the individual's experiences but rather uses them in conjunction with specific coping tools to cultivate positivity and find meaning in the face of a traumatic experience.[34] When Dean is sent back to a world in which both his parents are still alive, he chooses to reject this world and is able to find meaning in his losses. Specifically, he chooses the reality in which he and Sam have lost their parents because it means that they will be able to save countless lives by becoming hunters.[35]

### Posttraumatic Growth Domains
Posttraumatic growth entails five key domains in which a person may experience meaningful changes: personal strength, new possibilities, relating to others, appreciation of life, and

spiritual change. While this list is not all-encompassing, these are the most common domains in which people who have experienced trauma demonstrate changes.[36]

Sam is able to display several of these domains, such as personal strength, when, despite still having hallucinations of Lucifer, he is able to focus on hunting. In addition, Sam also demonstrates appreciation for life when he runs into Amy, a kitsune who saved him when they were children. Unlike what he and Dean would normally do, Sam does not kill Amy but instead talks to her about managing her symptoms.[37]

### Facing the Trauma

Avoidance, one of the key symptoms of PTSD, can cause long-term harm in the ability to recover and may hinder a person's ability to live a fulfilling life.[38] As people begin to face traumatic memories and situations, the impact of the trauma begins to decrease and the process of healing can begin.[39]

Research shows that *exposure therapy* is one of the most effective therapies for reducing PTSD symptoms and is considered to be a "gold standard" of treatment options.[40] Exposure therapy may consist of different approaches that can be used independently or in conjunction with one another. For example, when using *imaginal exposure*, the client is asked to imagine and verbally describe the event as if it were happening in the present moment.[41] Dean does this when he finally decides to tell Sam about his experiences in Hell.[42] On the other hand, *in vivo exposure therapy*, or real-life exposure, encourages the client to physically go to locations that are associated with the traumatic event. Finally, *flooding* requires the individual to face his or her most anxiety-provoking situation for a predetermined amount of time (e.g., being around clowns for Sam[43] or flying for Dean).[44]

# THE TRAUMA ANTIDOTE: SELF-COMPASSION

One way to promote recovery is self-compassion (the practice of being kind to oneself). Self-compassion has been shown not only to reduce avoidance but to increase willingness to engage in treatment. Those who practice self-compassion are also more likely to experience a natural process of exposure to trauma, thus reducing their symptoms and increasing their overall well-being.[45]

When Dean and Castiel are sent to purgatory, Sam is left alone, wondering what happened to them.[46] Previously, when one of the Winchester brothers would vanish, the other one would attempt to search for the missing brother, but this time Sam decides to live a life that is more fulfilling to him. Sam moves in with Amelia, a veterinarian he met, allowing himself to find something he has rarely had previously: happiness.[47]

## Empathy and Compassion

When people have undergone traumatic experiences, they might feel as if no one can relate to them, or as if they were the only ones who have ever felt the way they do. They might feel alienated from themselves, the world, and their future.[48] On the other hand, when individuals experience empathy, they might feel understood and supported, such as when Dean connects with Michael after Michael explains that he is a failure for allowing his brother to get sick. Dean explains that he understands what it is like to want to be a good older brother but that there was nothing Michael could have done to prevent his brother from getting sick.[49] Studies have shown that by invoking empathy toward others, trauma survivors often experience a reduction in their own PTSD symptoms.[50]

## Maintaining Mental Health in a Supernatural World

Whether surviving a war or being tortured by demons in the fiery pit, trauma can affect a survivor's life.[51] The intrusive thoughts, memories, and painful reminders can lead survivors to want to avoid connecting with their trauma symptoms, as both Sam[52] and Dean[53] do on separate occasions. This can lead the trauma survivor to find unhealthy coping techniques, such as addictions, or lose important support systems. On the other hand, by connecting with their core values and by opening up about their traumatic experiences, survivors are more likely to recover. When Dean and Sam are sent to be actors on the show *Supernatural*, the director, Robert Singer, discusses how each episode needs to end with the brothers talking. From this we can tell that the endings of most of the episodes allow the brothers to process what they have been through and what they are going through, potentially allowing them to heal.[54]

*References*

American Psychiatric Association (2013). *Diagnostic and statistical manual of mental disorders* (5th ed.) (DSM-5). Washington, DC: American Psychiatric Association.

Asmundson, G. J., Stapleton, J. A., & Taylor, S. (2004). Are avoidance and numbing distinct PTSD symptom clusters? *Journal of Traumatic Stress, 17*(6), 467–475.

Badour, C. L., Blonigen, D. M., Boden, M. T., Feldner, M. T., & Bonn-Miller, M. O. (2012). A longitudinal test of the bi-directional relations between avoidance coping and PTSD severity during and after PTSD treatment. *Behaviour Research & Therapy, 50*(10), 610–616.

Brewin, C. R., Andrews, B., & Valentine, J. D. (2000). Meta-analysis of risk factors for posttraumatic stress disorder in trauma-exposed adults. *Journal of Consulting and Clinical Psychology, 68*(5), 748–766.

Brockman, C., Snyder, J., Gewirtz, A., Gird, S. R., Quattlebaum, J., Schmidt, N., Pauldine, M. R., Elish, K., Schrepferman, L., Hayes, C. & Zettle, R. (2016). Relationship of service members' deployment trauma, PTSD symptoms, and experiential avoidance to postdeployment family reengagement. *Journal of Family Psychology, 30*(1), 52-62.

Brown, P. J., Stout, R. L., & Mueller, T. (1999). Substance use disorder and posttraumatic stress disorder comorbidity: Addiction and psychiatric treatment rates. *Psychology of Addictive Behaviors, 13*(2), 115–122.

Calhoun, L. G., & Tedeschi, R. G. (2014). *Handbook of posttraumatic growth: Research and practice*. New York, NY: Routledge.

Currier, J. M., Holland, J. M., & Malott, J. (2015). Moral injury, meaning making, and mental health in returning veterans. *Journal of Clinical Psychology, 71*(3), 229–240.

Dulin, P. L., & Passmore, T. (2010). Avoidance of potentially traumatic stimuli mediates the relationship between accumulated lifetime trauma and late-life depression and anxiety. *Journal of Traumatic Stress, 23*(2), 296–299.

Ehlers, A., Clark, D. M., Dunmore, E., Jaycox, L., Meadows, E., & Foa, E. B. (1998). Predicting response to exposure treatment in PTSD: The role of mental defeat and alienation. *Journal of Traumatic Stress, 11*(3), 457–471.

Farrow, T. F., Hunter, M. D., Wilkinson, I. D., Gouneea, C., Fawbert, D., Smith, R., Lee, K. H., Mason S., Spence S. A., & Woodruff, P. W. (2005). Quantifiable change in functional brain response to empathic and forgivability judgments with resolution of posttraumatic stress disorder. *Psychiatry Research: Neuroimaging, 140*(1), 45–53.

Foa, E. B., Keane, T. M., Friedman, M. J., & Cohen, J. A. (Eds.). (2008). *Effective treatments for PTSD: practice guidelines from the International Society for Traumatic Stress Studies.* New York, NY: Guilford.

Guglielmo, S. S. (2014). Cognitive distortion: Propositions and possible worlds. *Journal of Rational-Emotive & Cognitive-Behavior Therapy, 33*(1), 52–53.

Hayes, S. C. (2007). Hello darkness: Discovering our values by confronting our fears. *Psychotherapy Networker, 31*(5), 46–52.

Hofmann, S. G., Asmundson, G. J. G., & Beck, A. T. (2013). The science of cognitive therapy. *Behavior Therapy, 44*(2), 199–212.

Jakupcak, M., Tull, M. T., McDermott, M. J., Kaysen, D., Hunt, S., & Simpson, T. (2010). PTSD symptom clusters in relationship to alcohol misuse among Iraq and Afghanistan war veterans seeking post-deployment VA health care. *Addictive Behaviors, 35*(9), 840–843.

Kashdan, T. B., Morina, N., & Priebe, S. (2009). Post-traumatic stress disorder, social anxiety disorder, and depression in survivors of the Kosovo War: Experiential avoidance as a contributor to distress and quality of life. *Journal of Anxiety Disorders, 23*(2), 185–196.

Kaštelan, A., Frančišković, T., Moro, L., Rončević-Gržeta, I., Grković, J., Jurcan, V., Lescia, T., Graobac, M., & Girotto, I. (2007). Psychotic symptoms in combat-related post-traumatic stress disorder. *Military Medicine, 172,* 273–277.

Laffaye, C., Cavella, S., Drescher, K., & Rosen, C. (2008). Relationships among PTSD symptoms, social support, and support source in veterans with chronic PTSD. *Journal of Traumatic Stress, 21*(4), 394–401.

Pineles, S. L., Mostoufi, S. M., Ready, C. B., Street, A. E., Griffin, M. G., & Resick, P. A. (2011). Trauma reactivity, avoidant coping, and PTSD symptoms: A moderating relationship? *Journal of Abnormal Psychology, 120*(1), 240–246.

Plumb, J. C., Orsillo, S. M., & Luterek, J. A. (2004). A preliminary test of the role of experiential avoidance in post-event functioning. *Journal of Behavior Therapy & Experimental Psychiatry, 35*(3), 245–257.

Pynoos, R. S., Steinberg, A. M., & Piacentini, J. C. (1999). A developmental psychopathology model of childhood traumatic stress and intersection with anxiety disorders. *Biological Psychiatry, 46*(11), 1542–1554.

Tarrier, N., Pilgrim, H., Sommerfield, C., Faragher, B., Reynolds, M., Graham, E., & Barrowclough, C. (1999). A randomized trial of cognitive therapy and imaginal exposure in the treatment of chronic posttraumatic stress disorder. *Journal of Consulting and Clinical Psychology, 67*(1), 13–18.

Thompson, B. L., & Waltz, J. (2008). Self-compassion and PTSD symptom severity. *Journal of Traumatic Stress, 21*(6), 556–558.

Weiss, T. (2002). Posttraumatic growth in women with breast cancer and their husbands: An intersubjective validation study. *Journal of Psychosocial Oncology, 20*(2), 65–80.

## Notes

1. Episode 2–2, "Everybody Loves a Clown" (October 5, 2006).
2. Hayes (2007).
3. Episode 1–1, "Pilot" (September 13, 2005).
4. Dulin & Passmore (2010), Pineles et al. (2011).
5. Pineles et al. (2011).
6. Parents' deaths in episodes 1–1, "Pilot" (September 13, 2005)—mother; 2–1, "In My Time of Dying" (September 28, 2006)—father. Torture, e.g., 12–2, "Mamma Mia" (October 20, 2016). Their own deaths, e.g., 2–1, "All Hell Breaks Loose," part 1—Sam; 3–16, "No Rest for the Wicked" (May 15, 2008)—Dean.
7. American Psychiatric Association (2013).
8. Episodes 7–1, "Meet the New Boss" (September 23, 2011); 7–2, "Hello, Cruel World" (September 30, 2011).
9. Kaštelan et al. (2007).
10. Plumb et al. (2004).
11. Episode 4–10, "Heaven and Hell," (November 20, 2008).
12. Pynoos et al. (1999).
13. Pynoos et al. (1999).
14. Episode 1–1, "Pilot" (September 13, 2005).
15. Episode 1–18, "Something Wicked" (April 6, 2006).
16. Brown et al. (1999).
17. Jakupcak et al. (2010).
18. Episodes 2–2, "Everybody Loves a Clown" (October 5, 2006); 4–20, "The Rapture" (April 30, 2009).
19. Episode 2–2, "Everybody Loves a Clown" (October 5, 2006).
20. Episode 4–20, "The Rapture" (April 30, 2009).
21. Written by M. Jagger & K. Richards (1968); played in episode 5–1, "Sympathy for the Devil" (September 10, 2009).
22. Hofmann et al. (2013).
23. Episode 5–1, "Sympathy for the Devil" (September 10, 2009).
24. Guglielmo (2014).
25. Episodes 5–1, "Sympathy for the Devil" (September 10, 2009); 5–9, "Changing Channels" (November 5, 2009); 5–18, "Point of No Return" (April 5, 2010).
26. Brockman et al. (2016), Laffaye et al. (2008), Pynoos et al. (1999).
27. Brockman et al. (2016).
28. Episodes 1–3, "Dead in the Water" (September 27, 2005); 1–18, "Something Wicked" (April 6, 2006).
29. Episodes 2–2, "Everybody Loves a Clown" (October 5, 2006); 7–11, "Adventures in Babysitting" (January 6, 2012).
30. Currier et al. (2015).
31. Episode 5–3, "Free to Be You and Me" (September 24, 2009).
32. Episode 5–11, "Sam, Interrupted" (January 21, 2010).
33. Weiss (2008).
34. Calhoun & Tedeschi (2014).
35. Episode 2–20, "What Is and What Should Never Be (May 20, 2007).

36. Calhoun & Tedeschi (2014).
37. Episode 7–3, "The Girl Next Door" (October 7, 2011).
38. Badour et al. (2012).
39. Asmundson et al. (2004).
40. Foa et al. (2008).
41. Tarrier et al. (1999).
42. Episode 4–10, "Heaven and Hell" (November 20, 2008).
43. Episode 7–14, "Plucky Pennywhistle's Magical Menagerie" (February 10, 2012).
44. Episode 1–4, "Phantom Traveler" (October 4, 2005).
45. Ehlers et al. (1998).
46. Episode 1–18, "Something Wicked" (April 6, 2006).
47. Farrow et al. (2008).
48. Thompson & Waltz (2008).
49. Episode 7–23, "Survival of the Fittest" (May 18, 2012).
50. Episode 8–1, "We Need to Talk about Kevin" (October 3, 2012).
51. Brewin et al. (2000).
52. Episode 7–2, "Hello, Cruel World" (September 30, 2011).
53. Episode 5–11, "Sam, Interrupted" (January 21, 2010).
54. Episode 6–15, "The French Mistake" (February 25, 2011).

# CHAPTER EIGHT

# Lifting the Veil: Effects of Childhood Trauma on the Mind, Body, and Soul

### LEANDRA PARRIS

*"You're so overcome by guilt that you can't stand to lose Dean again and he could never lose you. And so instead of choosing the world you choose each other, no matter how many innocent people die."*
—Lucifer[1]

*"While trauma can be hell on earth, trauma resolved is a gift of the gods—a heroic journey that belongs to each of us."*
—trauma therapist Peter A. Levine[2]

Young children might be ready to believe in monsters under their beds, and yet many are not ready to see all the real monsters that lurk in this world. In this sense, childhood trauma is apocalyptic. Over a life span, the veil that shields us from the ugly truths is slowly pulled back, exposing harsh realities a lesson or two at a time. But what happens if the veil is pulled back too soon, too quickly? Exploring this question through the impact of childhood trauma affords us the opportunity to gain insight into why, despite being heroes, Sam and Dean sometimes do things that are not altogether heroic. They seem willing to risk everything for the sake of the other, sometimes hitting the SELF-DESTRUCT button, even if that means burning down the world.[3]

## Understanding How and Why Trauma Occurs

Children experiencing crises with long-lasting consequences (such as the loss of a home), that are also extremely intense and unpredictable, are at risk for developing trauma-related disorders.[4] When trauma occurs, much like an apocalypse, there is shift in one's understanding of the world and things can never be the same. Because of their developmental limitations, children are particularly vulnerable to trauma. Sometimes not understanding what you see behind the veil is a good thing. But sometimes children understand just enough to conceptualize trauma without the necessary maturity or emotional resources to process the event. With this understanding of trauma, we can easily identify traumatic childhood experiences that befall the Winchester boys.

Both children, particularly Sam, are often neglected by being left alone for days with limited resources in random motel rooms.[5] The Winchester boys' daily lives are unpredictable, unstable, and often chaotic as they travel the long highways of America. There are also signs of emotional abuse, resulting from John's well-intended, but harshly delivered, tough love approach to parenthood. For example, Dean realizes a demon has taken possession of his father the minute John tells him he is proud of Dean,[6] because clearly pride is not something John

# A NEW TYPE OF TRAUMA

There are many forms of adverse childhood experiences (e.g., abuse, natural disaster) that can lead to trauma. Generally, once an experience has reached the point of being traumatic, people use the term *childhood trauma* to describe one general phenomenon. However, there are two distinct categories of trauma. The first is *acute trauma*, which develops after a single event that has a clear beginning and end, such as Dean fleeing the fire that kills his mother.[7] *Complex trauma*, on the other hand, is the result of multiple events or one long-lasting disaster with an uncertain time frame, such as the Winchesters' ongoing search for a way to stop the apocalypse (again). Complex trauma is considered the most severe type of trauma, due to the cumulative effects of ongoing trauma symptoms.[8] Children experiencing complex trauma have higher rates of dysfunction, with the effects discussed in this chapter often occurring more frequently and with greater intensity. Because Sam and Dean experience complex trauma almost continuously across their lifespan, their complex trauma becomes even more compounded. Sam and Dean's experiences might require a new trauma classification: *Winchester trauma*.

typically demonstrates toward his children. This is not to put all the blame on John. Parents with a history of childhood traumatic events, particularly those that involved being abandoned by a parent, are less likely to forge strong attachments with their children and more likely to expose them to risky situations, such as witnessing violence.[9] Grappling with the effects of war and the death of his wife,[10] John is probably doing the best he can while struggling with his own traumatic past.

Trauma can also stem from loss. The loss of their mother is crucial for both boys. Growing up, Dean remembers his mom and acutely feels her absence[11] while Sam struggles with loving someone he has never met.[12] There is another kind of loss that is unique to the Winchester boys. Through various experiences, they are provided with small opportunities to contemplate what life might be like if the world were still veiled (e.g., a teenage Sam experiencing a "normal" Thanksgiving dinner).[13] Forced to return to the hunter lifestyle, the boys experience the loss of a life that could have been. These forms of loss are overwhelming for anyone, but even more so for children.

## Outcomes of Childhood Trauma

The consequences of childhood trauma are varied, based on individual characteristics and context. However, there are outcomes that are consistent and unique to those who experienced traumatic events throughout childhood. In general, these effects manifest in the body, the mind, and the soul.

### The Body

The impact of trauma begins with biology. As humans experience stress, the body naturally prepares to fight, flee, or freeze in order to protect itself. This reaction is driven by the release of hormones, such as cortisol and adrenaline, that, with long-term activation, can overwhelm the body, causing the body to begin to burn out. Such disruptions to the body's state of homeostasis can lead to multiple concerns, such as heart problems, migraines, insomnia, and vulnerability to sickness.[14] While Sam and Dean appear physically healthy, the Winchesters' childhood trauma most likely causes them to have trouble physically relaxing in order to sleep, requiring the aide of sedatives like alcohol. Altered appetites, physical tension, and a longer response time to objects or people that evoke strong emotions are also likely present.

Further, their trauma history may have affected their neurological functioning, decreasing negative responses to violence while also increasing the rewarding properties of experiencing aggression. This could lead to behaviors that suggest indifference to hostility, increased externalizing responses to threats (e.g., fighting, throwing things), and a propensity to seek out risky situations. For example, when they experience a problem, the Winchesters often cope by seeking out new cases, which inevitably leads to attacking, fighting, killing, and destroying property,[15] perpetuating the cyclical pattern of trauma and coping with violence.

### The Mind

Bodily changes are not the only way that childhood trauma influences the way people think, feel, or behave. In terms of the mind, adverse experiences in youth can affect cognitive abilities, personality, and cognitive distortions. In terms of cognitive functioning, early childhood trauma disrupts typical development and is associated with difficulties with learning and problem solving[16] that stem from deficits in memory, processing, and general intellectual abilities.[17] Luckily, the Winchesters seem to have dodged this particular outcome.

Changes in cognitive processes can also influence the development of certain personality traits.[18] In particular, adults who have a history of childhood trauma are more likely to exhibit characteristics consistent with neuroticism, such as increased impulsivity, risk taking, and aggressive behaviors. Childhood trauma is also linked to increased openness, which can lead to the overuse of avoidant, emotion-focused strategies that hinder the healing process. These may delay recovery due to the inability to face problems head-on. The tendency to go through extreme efforts to avoid physical or emotional harm, such as the indefinite separation from your brother, is a personality trait common among adults who experienced adverse events as children. This relationship is strongest for children exposed to neglect and emotional abuse, such as Sam and Dean.

Personality influences the use of certain cognitive strategies that help people cope. Traumatized children who engage in *cognitive distortions*, such as disproportionate reactivity, negative appraisals, and self-blame, tend to experience an increase in depression, anxiety, and social stress.[19] Cognitive distortions perpetuate the thinking patterns that are detrimental to successfully moving past traumatic experiences. For example, Sam's distortions include labeling himself as "a freak"[20] and bearing a disproportionate level of guilt and self-criticism for disappointing Dean.[21]

Dean's cognitive distortions are less clear. Yet the reality of his low self-compassion and high self-blame is apparent when Sam is killed.[22] Dean tells the lifeless body of his brother, "I had one job and I screwed it up. I blew it and for that I am sorry. I guess that's what I do: I let down the people I love." In this moment Dean reveals that the anchor of his identity is his role as protector for his younger brother. Indeed, from the moment John hands four-year-old Dean his infant brother and tells him to run,[23] Dean functions as Sam's guardian. Over time he becomes more of a parent than his own father is, something John acknowledges before dying.[24] Taking on responsibilities reserved for adults can cause a child to develop issues with control and a tendency to overly invest in the protection of others.

Additional cognitive concerns relate to symptoms of depression and anxiety. Due to the loss of control and reasoning, children experiencing trauma may develop a sense of *learned helplessness*.[25] For Sam and Dean, there is no longer a reason to fight their fate as hunters and saviors of the world. All notions of a normal life are routinely abandoned after failed attempts to acclimate to a life without each other.

# ROAD MUSIC

The Winchester brothers' near-eagerness for self-sacrifice can be associated with their childhood trauma experiences, particularly incidents of emotional neglect.[27] John Winchester's inability to attend to his sons' emotional needs is, in part, responsible for Sam and Dean's continued success in saving the world through self-sacrifice because it leaves them with a lingering need to do things for others.

## The Soul

*Psyche* means *soul* in ancient Greek, which makes *psychology* literally the "study of the soul," even though the science tends not to use such a term and so the interpretation has shifted.[28] A human soul can be described as the nonmaterial essence of who each individual is, beyond body and mind. The soul can represent a person's well-being, self-concept, and relationships with others. In *Supernatural,* some people who lose their souls become increasingly emotionless and detached, eventually abandoning their value system.[29] They fundamentally lose what makes them uniquely special, despite retaining their body and mind. This makes souls—and the trading of souls—invaluable to humans and supernatural beings alike.

This detachment from emotions is similar to *alexithymia,* a condition in which someone is not able to recognize his or her own or others' emotions and therefore find it difficult to relate to other people.[30] People who have alexithymia appear to lack empathy and avoid emotional content. Those suffering from alexithymia are at greater risk for depression and feelings of indifference toward their relationships, compounding any preexisting damage of childhood trauma. This can be seen through changes in Sam when he loses his soul[31] and to some degree in Dean when his soul is trans-formed into a demon.[32]

In a way, human souls are sustained through relationships with others, flourishing as existence is validated. The need for these relationships is intensified when resources are low and demands are high (i.e., trauma). If these relationships do not exist or are dysfunctional in childhood, the person may experience some difficulty with future relationships. Children who have guardians who are unwilling to provide safety or comfort in stressful situations may develop approval- and attention-seeking behaviors that last into adulthood. Over time, they may develop a self-concept that includes fear of rejection or abandonment and an overall perception that they are unlovable. Crowley, the king of Hell, with some pretty big mommy issues, demonstrates many of these personality traits. They are highlighted when he yells, "I deserve to be loved! I just want to be loved!" as he begins to feel his humanity.[33]

When experiencing childhood trauma, if the child fears either parent yet feels the need to comfort that guardian, youth can become confused, as these feelings are counterintuitive. This state of confusion can lead to disorientation and difficulties reading emotional situations. They can begin to develop a fear of closeness, given the negative feelings associated with caring about someone after experiencing emotional abuse and neglect. They may also struggle to believe affections are reciprocated by others. For instance, Dean grows up taking care of his father and his brother, simultaneously managing the contradictory roles of son and caregiver. As an adult, he is more comfortable with surface-level, fleeting encounters, and is often unsure and distrusting of others' intentions. The one thing he is sure of is his need to protect Sam. He pours all of himself into this endeavor because, at times, it is the only thing that makes sense to him.

By contrast, Sam is more willing to develop a life and identity outside of hunting and apart from Dean. This may be associated with his experiences with John as an inconsistent, unpredictable caregiver during traumatic events. Sam cannot predict when, and to what degree, he will be safe with his father. Children with these experiences believe that relationships are not always necessary and are more likely to walk away, distancing themselves from rebuff. They are less likely to express their emotions, due to a heightened need to protect their vulnerabilities and remain independent. This can explain why Sam insists on doing things his own way and hesitates to discuss some of his more difficult experiences, such as, say, mysteriously coming back from Hell.[34]

## Trauma and Saving the World

The boys' traumatic experiences in childhood result in a combination of cognitive distortions and interpersonal difficulties that influence the Winchesters' choices when life requires sacrifice. Dean dealing with the crossroads demon,[35] Sam sacrificing himself and his half-brother (the often-forgotten Adam),[36] and the brothers choosing each other over nonfamilial love and friendship[37]—these are examples of times the brothers choose to burn their own bridges and forgo happy endings.

That said, Dean and Sam's attachment to each other as a result of their shared childhood trauma represents the most human of connections: family. Not despite of, but because of, their traumas, the brothers repeatedly win the war against the supernatural. As the prophet Chuck writes: "Up against good, evil, angels, devils, destiny, and God himself . . . they chose family."[38] Like all families, the Winchester brothers fight, rage against each other, and waiver in their support from time to time. Yet they always come back to family as the strongest—and in some ways the simplest—connection to the human world. In doing so, they find the courage, strength, and motivation required to battle forces that would otherwise be unstoppable. The Winchesters' childhood trauma produces the very weapon they need to survive the ripping of their own veil and save the world.

## Healing from Trauma

Despite the potential strength gained from experiencing childhood trauma, the idea that what kills you makes you stronger is hardly comforting. Any hope of capitalizing on the potential benefits of overcoming challenges associated with childhood trauma hinges on successful recovery, which is most likely to happen when help is provided quickly. Yet it can be difficult to assess which services will be most effective, due to variations in context, individual characteristics, and type of trauma.

However, there are some general approaches that have been found to be effective in facilitating healing and reducing future maladaptive outcomes.[39] Establishing routines, putting in place appropriate safety measures, and knowing that certain adults are consistently trustworthy are paramount to children's well-being. Throughout a traumatic event, psychological first aid (e.g., meeting basic needs) is beneficial. Once the child is ready to work toward recovery without the risk of revictimization, trauma-informed services can begin. Interventions for childhood trauma require a holistic approach that focuses on the mind (e.g., cognitive techniques), the body (e.g., mindfulness, relaxation techniques), and the soul (e.g., emotion-focused coping, building supportive relationships). Had they

# DECIDE TO BE FINE:
## A CONTRACT TO KEEP GOING

**Travis Langley**

*"Decide to be fine 'til the end of the week. Make
yourself smile because you're alive and it's your
job. And do it again the next week."*
—computer hacker Frank Devereaux[40]

*"I, _____, agree not to harm myself
or anyone else, attempt suicide, or commit
suicide for the time period from _____ to
_____ (the time of my next appointment)."*
—sample no-harm contract opening[41]

The *no-harm contract* (also called *no-suicide decision, safety agreement, suicide prevention contract*[42]) is a potentially-suicidal individual's promise to commit no self-harm for the time being. Contracting for safety in this way is a popular counseling technique even though it has been used in so many ways with so little methodical study that investigators disagree on its effectiveness.[43] One critical factor is that the individual must not feel coerced into this commitment.[44] A professional suggesting it should do so gently by pointing out its importance. Some counselors let clients write their own no-harm pledges, which might help them feel more empowered and dedicated.[45] After his family's murder, Frank Devereaux makes this choice, perhaps on his own initiative or perhaps after a professional who diagnoses him as "bipolar with delusional ideation"[46] offers the idea. However he comes to make his no-harm decision at age 24, Frank still renews it week after week in middle-age to keep going and always keep fighting.

*"There's no shame in having to fight every day;
but fighting every day—and presumably if you're
still alive to hear these words or read this . . . then
you are winning your war. You're here."*
—Always Keep Fighting founder Jared Padalecki[47]

received such services as children, it is possible that Sam and Dean would experience greater psychological adjustment as adults.

That leaves one question: Would we change the road taken by the Winchesters? If their childhood trauma, or the subsequent effects, could be erased, they would be happier, healthier, and certainly less violent as adults. Would they make better choices, maybe some that did not push the boundary of what we consider ethical? The fluidity of good and evil and their destiny to save the universe make it hard to delineate what would or would not be morally "right" in their positions. However, through the perspective of childhood trauma, factors that influence these actions and choices can be better understood. The Winchesters are willing to set themselves, and the world, on fire to avoid having to live without the other. But when they are not forgoing their lives and their happiness for the sake of brotherhood, they are sacrificing everything for humanity. They are burning for us, keeping the veil in place between this world and that of the supernatural. And, as the prophet Chuck writes, isn't that kind of the whole point?

*References*

Ashton, C. K., O'Brien-Lager, A. , Olson, K., & Silverstone, P. H. (2017). Qualitative reflections: CASA's trauma and attachment group (TAG) program for youth who have experienced early developmental trauma. *Journal of the Canadian Academy of Child & Adolescent Psychiatry, 26*(1), 12–20.

Barlow, M. R., Turow, R. E. G., & Gerhart, J. (2017). Trauma appraisals, emotion regulation difficulties, and self-compassion predict posttraumatic stress symptoms following childhood abuse. *Child Abuse & Neglect, 65*, 37–47.

Brock, S. E., Nickerson, A. B., Reeves, M. A., Conolly, C. N., Jimerson, S. R., Pesce, R. C., & Lazzaro, B. R. (2016). *School crisis prevention and intervention: The PREPaRE Model.* Bethesda, MA: National Association of School Psychologists.

Caruso, K. (n.d.). *No-suicide contracts—what they are and how you should use them.* Suicide. org: http://www.suicide.org/no-suicide-contracts.html.

Clark, D. C., & Kerkhof, J. F. M. (1997). No-suicide contracts and no-suicide decisions. *Crisis: The Journal of Crisis Intervention & Suicide Prevention, 18*(1), 2.

Drye, R., Goulding, R., & Goulding, M. (1973). No-suicide decisions: Patient monitoring of suicidal risk. *American Journal of Psychiatry, 130*(2), 171–174.

Edwards, S. J., & Sachmann, M. D. (2010). No-suicide contracts, no-suicide agreements, and no-suicide assurances: A study of their nature, utilization, perceived effectiveness, and potential to cause harm. *Crisis: The Journal of Crisis Intervention & Suicide Prevention, 31*(6), 290–302.

Eichhorn, S., Brähler, E., Franz, M., Friedrich, M., & Glaesmer, H. (2014). Traumatic experiences, alexithymia, and posttraumatic symptomatology: A cross-sectional population-based study in Germany. *European Journal of Psychotraumatology, 5*(1), 1–27.

Erozkan, A. (2016). The link between types of attachment and childhood trauma. *Universal Journal of Educational Research, 4*(5), 1071–1079.

Fidler, B. (n.d.). *No harm contract.* Brian Fidler Counseling: http://www.brianfidlercounseling.com/userfiles/569378/file/No%20Harm%20Contract.pdf.

François, A. (2008). Semantic maps and the typology of colexification: Intertwining polysemous networks across languages. In M. Vanhove (Ed.), *From polysemy to semantic change: Towards a typology of lexical semantic associations* (pp. 163–215). Amsterdam, NY: Benjamins.

Hillman, J. (1989). *A blue fire: Selected writings by James Hillman* (T. Moore, Ed.). New York, NY: HarperPerennial.

Huh, H. J., Kim, K. H., Lee, H. K., & Chae, J. H. (2017). The relationship between childhood trauma and the severity of adulthood depression and anxiety symptoms in a clinical sample: The mediating role of cognitive emotion regulation strategies. *Journal of Affective Disorders, 213*, 44–50.

Keiser, C. C., & Grossman (2016, June 1). *Do no harm!* Do No Harm: http://www.donoharm.us/.

Levine, P. (1997). *Waking the Tiger: Healing trauma.* Berkeley, CA: North Atlantic.

Malarbi, S., Abu-Rayya, H. M., Muscara, F., & Stargatt, R. (2017). Neuropsychological functioning of childhood trauma and post-traumatic stress disorder: A meta-analysis. *Neuroscience & Biobehavioral Reviews, 72*(1), 68–86.

McElroy, S., & Hevey, D. (2013). Relationship between adverse early experiences, stressors, psychosocial resources, and wellbeing. *Child Abuse & Neglect, 38*(1), 65–75.

McMyler, C., & Pryjmachuk, S. (2008). Do "no-suicide" contracts work? *Journal of Psychiatric & Mental Health Nursing, 15*(6), 512–522.

Miller, M. (1999). Suicide-prevention contracts: Advantages, disadvantages, and an alternative approach. In D. J. Jacobs (ed.), *The Harvard Medical School guide to suicide assessment and intervention* (pp. 463–481). San Francisco, CA: Jossey-Bass.

Misiak, B., Krefft, M., Bielawski, T., Moustafa, A. A., Sąsiadek, M. M., & Frydecka, D. (2017). Toward a unified theory of childhood trauma and psychosis: A comprehensive review of epidemiological, clinical, neuropsychological and biological findings. *Neuroscience & Biobehavioral Reviews, 75*(1), 393–406.

Murphy, A., Steele., M., Dube, S. R., Bate, J., Bonuck, K., Meissner, P., Goldman, H., & Steele, H. (2014). Adverse Childhood Experiences (ACEs) Questionnaire and Adult Attachment Interview (AAI): Implications for parent child relationships. *Child Abuse & Neglect, 38*(2), 224–233.

Nolen-Hoeksema, S., Girgus, J. S., & Seligman, M. E. P., (1986). Learned helplessness in children: A longitudinal study of depression, achievement, and explanatory style. *Journal of Personality & Social Psychology, 51*(2), 435–442.

Pfeiffer, K. L., (n.d.). *Creating a safety plan.* The Sunny Shadow: https://thesunny-shadow.com/creating-a-safety-plan/.

Potter, M., & Dawson, A. (2001). From safety contract to safety agreement. *Journal of Psychosocial Nursing, 39*(1), 38-46.

Prudom, L. (2015, March 12). *"Supernatural" star Jared Padalecki talks depression and why you should "Always Keep Fighting."* Variety: http://variety.com/2015/tv/people-news/jared-padalecki-always-keep-fighting-depression-suicide-twloha-120145 1708/.

Purnell, C. (2010). Childhood trauma and adult attachment. *Healthcare Counseling & Psychotherapy Journal, 10*(2), 9-13.

Seligman, M. E. P. (1975). *On depression, development, and death.* San Francisco, CA: Freeman.

Szentágotai-Tătar, A., & Miu, A. C. (2016). Individual differences in emotion regulation, childhood trauma and proneness to shame and guilt in adolescence. *PLoS ONE, 11*, e0167299.

TheraNest (n.d.). *Free downloadable forms & templates for counselors & psychtherapists.* TheraNest: https://www.theranest.com/free-counseling-note-templates/.

Wallace, D. (2016, January 10). *Anger management.* Cashman Center: http://cashman-centermn.com/1591-2/.

Yuen, C. (2016, March 15). *Psychologists support Education Bureau's "no suicide" student contracts.* Hong Kong Free Press: https://www.hongkongfp.com/2016/03/15/psychologists-support-education-bureaus-no-suicide-student-contracts/.

Zilberstein, K. (2014). Neurocognitive considerations in the treatment of attachment and complex trauma in children. *Clinical Child Psychology & Psychiatry, 19*(3), 336-345.

Zlotnick, C., Mattia, J. I., & Zimmerman, M. (2001). The relationship between posttraumatic stress disorder, childhood trauma and alexithymia in an outpatient sample. *Journal of Traumatic Stress, 14*(1), 177-188.

## Notes

1. Episode 11–10, "The Devil in the Details" (January 20, 2016).
2. Levine (1997), p. 12.
3. e.g., episode 10–23, "My Brother's Keeper" (May 20, 2015).
4. Brock et al. (2016).
5. e.g., episode 1–18, "Something Wicked" (April 6, 2006).
6. Episode 1–22, "Devil's Trap" (May 4, 2006).
7. Episode 1–1, "Pilot" (September 13, 2005).
8. Brock et al. (2016), Misiak et al. (2017).
9. Murphy et al. (2014).
10. Episodes 1–1, "Pilot" (September 13, 2005); 8–12, "As Time Goes By" (January 30, 2013).
11. Episode 5–16, "Dark Side of the Moon" (April 1, 2010)
12. Episode 2–4, "Children Shouldn't Play with Dead Things" (October 9, 2006).
13. Episode 5–16, "Dark Side of the Moon" (April 1, 2010).
14. e.g., Misiak et al. (2017).
15. e.g., Episode 10–13, "Halt & Catch Fire" (February 10, 2015).
16. See Zilberstein (2014) for a review.
17. Malarbi et al. (2017)
18. McElroy & Hevey (2014), Misiak et al. (2017).

19. Huh et al. (2017).

20. Episode 4–4, "Metamorphosis" (October 9, 2008).

21. Episode 8–23, "Sacrifice" (May 15, 2013).

22. Episode 2–22, "All Hell Breaks Loose," part 2 (May 17, 2007).

23. Episode 1–1, "Pilot" (September 13, 2005).

24. Episode 2–1, "In My Time of Dying" (September 28, 2006).

25. Nolen-Hoeksema et al. (1986); Selgiman (1975).

26. Written by Donald Roeser & Richard Meltzer (1981); played in episode 1–17, "Hell House" (March 20, 2006).

27. Huh et al. (2017).

28. François (2008), Hillman (1989).

29. Episodes 6–5, "Live Free or Twihard" (October 22, 2010); 11–5, "Thin Lizzie" (November 4, 2015).

30. Eichhorn et al. (2014), Zlotnick et al. (2001).

31. e.g., episode 6–5, "Life Free or Twihard" (October 22, 2010).

32. Episode 10–1, "Black" (October 7, 2014).

33. Episode 8–23, "Sacrifice" (May 15, 2013).

34. Episode 6–1, "Exile on Main St." (September 24, 2010).

35. Episode 2–22, "All Hell Breaks Loose," part 2 (May 17, 2007).

36. Episode 5–22, "Swan Song" (May 13, 2010).

37. Episode 8–10, "Torn and Frayed" (January 16, 2013).

38. Episode 5–22, "Swan Song" (May 13, 2010).

39. e.g., Ashton et al. (2017), Brock et al. (2016).

40. Episode 7–11, "Adventures in Babysitting" (January 6, 2012).

41. Based on Fidler (n.d.); TheraNest (n.d.); Yuen (2016).

42. Respectively Drye et al. (1973); Potter & Dawson (2001); Miller (1999).

43. Clark & Kerkhof (1997); Edwards & Sachmann (2010).

44. Caruso (n.d.); McMyler & Pryjmachuk (2008).

45. Keiser & Grossman (2016); Pfeiffer (n.d.); see also Wallace (2016).

46. Episode 7–11, "Adventures in Babysitting" (January 6, 2012).

47. Prudom (2015); see also *Ecclesiastes* 9:4.

# CHAPTER NINE

# Hunting for Identity

## MELANIE BOYSEN
## AND WIND GOODFRIEND

*"Nothing's unbreakable, really. Nothing's
safe if you poke at it long enough."*
—Charlie Bradbury[1]

*"When established identities become outworn . . . special
crises compel men to wage holy wars, by the cruelest
means, against those who seem to question or
threaten their unsafe ideological bases."*
—developmental psychologist Erik Erikson[2]

The choices we make in each major stage of life are what
define us. At each stage, we are faced with a crucial decision
that may determine the path we follow and the type of person
we become. For most of us, while these choices are instrumental and essential to happiness, they are relatively banal or even
stereotypical. We choose between a job we will enjoy and one

that will pay more, or perhaps we choose to remain faithful rather than have an affair. For Sam and Dean Winchester, by contrast, most choices are critical not only to their own day-to-day existence but also to the entire world's existence. Their sardonic motto, "Saving people, hunting things—the family business,"[3] masks how important each choice is. Stages of development and the choices we make at all the psychological forks in life's road figure into the central theme of arguably the most comprehensive theory within developmental psychology: Erik Erikson's psychosocial stages of development.

## Erikson's Psychosocial Stages of Development

Most people in Western cultures are familiar with the idea of a "midlife crisis."[4] As people realize half of their life has passed, they may react negatively by trying to recapture their youth or by questioning the lifestyle they have (perhaps inadvertently) created for themselves. However, many of us actually experience several such "crises" throughout our entire lives, not just upon reaching middle age. *Developmental psychology* studies how people grow and change as they proceed through the life cycle, based on their choices. As shown throughout the series, Sam and Dean Winchester continually have to make choices, including everything from whether to sacrifice their soul for a brother[5] or staying in the hunter lifestyle.[6] Turning into a demon, a vampire, a corpse, or a corporate executive[7] can make either Winchester brother's crises of identity more complicated than most people's.

While many theories and individual studies within developmental psychology will focus on a particular age (such as adolescence) or a particular outcome (such as views of morality), one theory attempted to create a template for how our identities and choices continue to develop from birth to death: developmental psychologist Erik Erikson's *theory of psychosocial stages of development*.[8] During each of the eight stages Erikson said people experience over the course of the average life span, we make a critical choice that will lead to a healthy or unhealthy expression of self and identity.[9] Starting in infancy, our identity is ever-changing, evolving, and building off the previous choices we've made. Happily, Erikson notes that we can change our path to overcome unhealthy or negative mistakes; nothing is set in stone. What choices have the Winchesters made at each crucial psychological stage, according to Erikson's paradigm?

### Stage 1: Trust versus Mistrust [Infancy]

The first major crisis occurs during the first year of life. If a baby's needs are met with consistent love, the baby develops basic trust in others. The main question here is simple: Will others fulfill my needs or do I have to do it myself? If children learn to trust others, especially their parents, they will have better social skills and happier relationships throughout life. Without trust, individuals avoid intimacy, feel suspicious, and have poor relationships in general.[10]

While Sam appears to have fairly normal trust levels, Dean is a paragon of mistrust. Dean rarely trusts anyone outside close family. While some might argue that his reluctance to engage in close relationships leads to a self-fulfilling prophecy that causes people to eventually leave him, even his closest relationships teach him not to rely on others. His parents leave him, his brother leaves him, and so does the one lover he allows past his guarded self.[11] Throughout the series, Dean refuses to accept help from others unless it is absolutely necessary, and even then he hates to do it.

### Stage 2: Autonomy versus Shame and Doubt [Early Childhood]

As toddlers pass through the second stage, they struggle to define themselves through their own independence. Developing *autonomy* indicates children who are able to depend on themselves as well as stand up for themselves. On the other hand, when a child has trouble becoming his or her own person, that leads to feelings of *shame and doubt*. The child low in autonomy will be easily influenced, less able to make decisions without input from others.[12]

Sam and Dean struggle with defining themselves, especially in such a strong family dynamic. Dean usually takes the role of a troubled son who blindly follows in their father's footsteps without question, defending him no matter what.[13] Sam, on the other hand, is not happy about being in his father's or his brother's shadow; he strikes out on his own whenever possible and stands up for those in trouble regardless of any price it might cost him.[14] While Sam shows clear signs of choosing autonomy, Dean in contrast shows greater inclination toward shame and doubt, frequently questioning himself and his choices and overcompensating by projecting overconfidence.

### Stage 3: Initiative versus Guilt [Roughly 3–5 Years of Age]

At this age, life forces many children into a larger social world of other children in preschool or child-care settings. During Erikson's third stage, children choose whether to take initiative in their life and struggle with self-control. A child who develops *initiative* learns self-discipline, leadership, confidence, and goal-setting, whereas a child who struggles will feel self-deprecating *guilt*, resulting in poor social skills as indicated by poor eye contact, sarcastic humor, or other efforts to avoid real interactions.[15]

Both Sam and Dean have difficulty operating independently and make decisions in their lives that tend to lean toward guilt.

Dean feels guilt for not always being successful as Sam's protector, failing in his first social expectation.[16] Sam continues to feel deep guilt for disappointing his father and for attempting to leave the hunter tradition.[17] Both struggle to display self-discipline and exhibit this guilt in unhealthy behaviors, such as a steady diet of cheeseburgers,[18] drinking alcohol,[19] or even experimenting with injections of demon blood as a drug substitute.[20]

### Stage 4: Industry versus Inferiority (Roughly 6–12 Years of Age)

As our individual identities truly begin to solidify, Erikson suggests that we decide whether or not to believe in ourselves. A tendency toward *industry* indicates that we believe we are capable of learning knowledge and/or skills we can use to eventually embark on a career. This leads to good use of technology, a sense of playfulness and exploration, self-efficacy, and the belief that we have mastered something important in spite of challenges. Inferiority, on the other hand, leads to low self-esteem, timidity, and submissiveness.[21]

In this area, the brothers are at opposite ends of the spectrum. From childhood, Dean tends to obey his father without question. Instead of choosing a path of independence, Dean takes this role to the extreme and perceives his main responsibility to be watching over Sam, regardless of the cost to himself.[22] Dean's subsequent darker, biting sense of humor and his tendency toward unquestioning conformity to a path chosen for him reflect his lack of industry. Sam, on the other hand, chooses the independent path of industry when he leaves for college to prepare for a career in law, in an explicit attempt to escape the family's controlling ways.[23]

### Stage 5: Identity versus Role Confusion (Adolescence)

In puberty, teenagers are in the purgatory between childhood and adulthood. At this stage, according to Erikson, we truly explore our own identity. A solid sense of *identity* indicates that we have experimented with different roles for ourselves, chosen one we prefer, and started a journey we believe matches our passions and talents. Part of this path is challenging authority and questioning the status quo; this rebellion promotes an empowered and independent self. The choice to simply accept without question the identity foisted upon you by family or society indicates a state of *role confusion*: a lack of true identity, which Erikson notes can lead to self-doubt, submissiveness, and lack of confidence.[24]

As already mentioned, Sam explores an independent identity more than Dean does, which may be the key to Sam's relatively healthier demeanor and more satisfied outlook on life. However, even Sam feels pulled in two directions, struggling between accompanying Dean as a hunter[25] and continuing his education in a path he has chosen for himself.[26] Sam's two, mutually exclusive dreams clash frequently, causing him to struggle with identity confusion. While Dean does make unhealthy choices quite often, his identity appears to be solid and self-assured; at least in this stage, Dean may have more personal closure and feel more confident than his brother in this aspect of identity.

### Stage 6: Intimacy versus Isolation (Young Adulthood)

We have all felt the nervous anticipation of potentially starting a new relationship. In Erikson's theory of psychosocial stages of development, one of the most anxiety-provoking stages or life crises revolves around our ability to make sincere, lasting connections with other people. Often, this comes in the form of a monogamous, intimate relationship with a romantic part-

## MORAL DEVELOPMENT

At the start of the series, Sam seems to be on a healthier path—at least according to Erikson's theory—but sometimes Dean takes on the role of moral compass. Another theory in developmental psychology comes from psychologist Lawrence Kohlberg, who suggested that people go through three stages of moral development.[27] The three stages include *pre-conventional*, when decisions are made based on a selfish perspective, *conventional*, in which decisions are based on following rules or laws, and *post-conventional*, the highest level of morality in which decisions are based on abstract conceptions of justice and what is best for the most people or for the larger community.

When Sam wants to save a woman who is a werewolf because he finds her appealing (a pre-conventional decision), Dean says she needs to be killed while Sam tries to find an alternative. When it comes down to it, Sam comes to agree that there is no other way and kills her himself because of the danger she poses to others (a conventional or post-conventional decision).[28] Years later, though, Dean acts similarly when he befriends vampire, Benny. In this case, Sam steps in with the mantra of killing a vampire who could go rogue while Dean tries to justify keeping him alive.[29] At the end of this friendship, Dean makes a conventional decision to let the vampire live due to his good behavior, causing tension between Sam and himself.[30]

ner. Intimacy may be frightening, but Erikson believed that a healthy identity requires the ability to make this connection both emotionally and sexually. Without the willingness to truly share our life with a significant other, we will become isolated, withdrawn, and will sabotage potential relationships out of fear.[31]

Throughout the series, Sam and Dean struggle to form meaningful relationships outside of their own family. In college, Sam has a promising relationship with a girlfriend, but he never really recovers after she died.[32] Still, Sam shows more intimacy than Dean in that he demonstrates the ability to share both emotional and sexual intimacy with women.[33] Dean, on the other hand, appears to mostly live in psychological *isolation* because he avoids opening up and developing greater intimacy with others. He enjoys thinking of himself as a playboy with no real attachments. This identity is challenged by a woman named Cassie, to whom he opens up and shares his secrets no matter how unbelievable they seem.[34] After she breaks up with him, Dean refuses to be anything but physical with women; his choice of isolation becomes even more solidified.

### Stage 7: Generativity versus Stagnation [Middle Adulthood]

Throughout middle adulthood, we face a crisis called generativity versus stagnation. Here, we hope to contribute to the world in a truly meaningful way, leaving a legacy of which we can be proud. Accomplishing *generativity* means we are successfully productive and honestly feel we are leaving the next generation in a better place than our own. Failure to accomplish this leaves us with a sense of *stagnation* which involves self-indulgence and general apathy toward others.[35] Psychologically stagnant indidividuals become resentful and blame others for their own fates.

For both Winchester brothers, generativity is focused on eliminating evil and on furthering the tradition of hunting to save humanity even after they die. They train other hunters;[36] they want the world to have a fighting chance. Perhaps they are both able to make the healthier choice in this particular crisis because of the role model they find in Bobby, an older hunter who mentors them.[37] No matter how much the Winchesters profess a lack of faith in humanity, they are always the first to help those in need, displaying that they are on the healthy side of this crisis of identity.

# ROAD MUSIC

### "Simple Man" by Lynyrd Skynyrd[38]

According to Erikson, we struggle to make healthy choices at major life crossroads, including our career path. People who frequently change jobs may have a low level of career maturity, which can lead to a life of confusion and second guesses.[39] After dealing with so much darkness, Sam decides to walk away from the hunter lifestyle. Leaving Dean to continue on by himself,[40] he tries to forge a normal, more conventional life. Sometimes, stress in life—something the Winchesters have in spades—leads to *narrow limits*, or a motivation to be content with a small and humble piece of the world.[41]

### Stage 8: Integrity versus Despair (Older Adulthood)

The end of life must come for us all. Erikson's final crisis of identity is the inner struggle over whether we can die with integrity, due to a sense of pride in our personal history, or die with *despair* over years of wasted opportunity. People who develop a sense of *integrity* can face death with a sense of overall satisfaction and contentment, while despair leads to regret and a desperate attempt to change things—perhaps too late. Despair can lead to anger and resentment, as well as a feeling that the entire struggle of humanity is inevitably going to fail. In this way, personal failure is generalized to failure for all.[42]

In the life of a hunter, death is always around the next corner. Even though they are not chronologically old, the Winchester brothers have lived a very hard life. Even without considering their time in other realms where time passes differently, they know that death is a real possibility, which could make them experience Erikson's stage earlier than most people. Sam and Dean know that hunters have short lifespans compared to most, and at times they seem genuinely interested in the opportunity to die in a moment of relative peace.[43] Both brothers are willing to sacrifice themselves over and over if it means they can make death worthwhile.[44] In this final stage of life, when sacrifices and hardships can be seen as choices leading toward a path of integrity, individuals with integrity will want to make the healthy choice.

## The Ultimate Crisis

From the psychological perspective, the hunter lifestyle accelerates Erikson's psychosocial stages of development. Typically, the eight stages progress in a set order and build upon themselves, leading to a reflection upon life in the final stage before death. But in Sam and Dean's case, morality is salient. While many observers of the Winchesters' adventures might identify their encounters with supernatural beings as their most crucial crises, a psychological perspective indicates that their most essential struggle is actually within themselves. Facing life—and death—while maintaining independence, intimacy with others, and personal integrity is what the struggle may really be about. Perhaps the fight against demons from Hell throughout the entire series is a metaphor, representing the struggle against our inner demons of mistrust, guilt, doubt, and despair.

*References*

Erikson, E. H. (1950/1993). *Childhood and society.* New York, NY: Norton.
Erikson, E. H. (1956). The problem of ego identity. *Journal of the American Psychoanalytic Association, 4*(1), 56–121.
Erikson, E. H. (1959/1980). *Identity and the life cycle.* New York, NY: Norton.
Horney, K. (1945). *Our inner conflicts.* New York, NY: Norton.
Kohlberg, L. (1968). The child as a moral philosopher. *Psychology Today, 2*(4), 25–30.
Munley, P. H. (1975). Erik Erikson's theory of psychosocial development and vocational behavior. *Journal of Counseling Psychology, 22*(4), 314–319.
O'Connor, D., & Wolfe, D. M. (1991). From crisis to growth at midlife: Changes in personal paradigm. *Journal of Organizational Behavior, 12*(4), 323–340.

## Notes

1. Episode 7–20, "The Girl with the Dungeons and Dragons Tattoo" (April 27, 2012)
2. Erikson (1956).
3. First said by Dean in episode 1–2, "Wendigo" (September 20, 2005).
4. O'Conner & Wolfe (1991).
5. Episode 3–16, "Ain't No Rest for the Wicked" (May 15, 2008).
6. Episode 1–16, "Shadows" (February 28, 2006).
7. Demon—Dean starting in episode 9–23, "Do You Believe in Miracles?" (May 20, 2014); vampire—Dean in episode 6–5, "Live Free or Twihard" (October 22, 2010); corpse—either brother many times staring with Dean in episode 2–1, "In My Time of Dying" (September 28, 2006), followed by Sam in 2–21, "All Hell Breaks Loose," part 1 (May 10, 2007); corporate executive—Dean in episode 4–17, "It's a Terrible Life" (March 26, 2009).
8. Erikson (1950/1993, 1959/1980).
9. Erikson (1950/1993, 1959/1980).
10. Erikson (1950/1993).
11. Mother dies, father vanishes, and brother is in college at the beginning of episode 1–1, "Pilot" (September 12, 2005); girlfriend breaks up with him in 5–16, "Dark Side of the Moon" (April 1, 2010).
12. Erikson (1959/1980).
13. Episodes 1–1, "Pilot" (September 13, 2005); 1–18, "Something Wicked" (April 6, 2006); 4–13, "After School Special" (January 29, 2009).
14. Episode 4–13, "After School Special" (January 29, 2009).
15. Erikson (1959/1980).
16. Episode 1–18, "Something Wicked" (April 6, 2006).
17. Episode 1–20, "Dead Man's Blood" (April 20, 2006).
18. Episode 3–15, "Time Is On My Side" (May 8, 2008).
19. Episode 7–4, "Defend Your Life" (October 14, 2011).
20. Episode 4–20, "The Rapture" (April 30, 2009).
21. Erikson (1959/1980).
22. Episodes 1–9, "Home" (November 15, 2005); 1–15, "The Benders" (February 14, 2006).
23. Episode 1–1, "Pilot" (September 13, 2005).
24. Erikson (1959/1980).
25. Episode 1–1, "Pilot" (September 13, 2005).
26. Episode 1–16, "Shadows" (February 28, 2006).
27. Kohlberg (1968).
28. Episode 2–17, "Heart" (March 22, 2007).
29. Episodes 8–5, "Blood Brother" (October 31, 2012); 8–9, "Citizen Fang" (December 5, 2012).
30. Episode 8–10, "Torn and Frayed" (January 16, 2013).
31. Erikson (1950/1993, 1959/1980).
32. Episode 1–1, "Pilot" (September 13, 2005).
33. Episode 2–17, "Heart" (March 22, 2007).
34. Episode 1–13, "Route 666" (January 31, 2006).
35. Erikson (1959/1980).
36. Episode 7–11, "Adventures in Babysitting" (January 6, 2012).
37. Episodes 4–1, "Lazarus Rising" (September 18, 2008); 6–4, "Weekend at Bobby's" (October 15, 2010).

38. Written by R. Van Zant & G. Rossington (1973); played in episode 5–3, "Free to Be You and Me" (September 24, 2009).
39. Munley (1975).
40. Episode 5–3, "Free to Be You and Me" (September 24, 2009).
41. Horney (1945).
42. Erikson (1950/1993, 1959/1980).
43. Episode 1–12, "Faith" (January 17, 2006).
44. Episodes 8–23, "Sacrifice" (May 15, 2013); 5–22, "Swan Song" (May 13, 2010).

# Anger

## TRAVIS LANGLEY

*"Let's face it. You're not exactly Mr. Anger Management."*
—Bobby to Sam[1]

*"In the days that follow, I discover that anger is
easier to handle than grief."*
—author Emily Giffin[2]

Anger arises from a sense that the situation is not what we feel or believe it should be[3] and bolsters us to do something about it.[4] It is the "red hot" emotion that can be more dangerous than other emotions but also carries great potential. While anger may be destructive, hurting the angry person inside while the feeling simmers and stews or prompting aggression more readily than other emotions do, it can also be constructive when it energizes our efforts to stand up for what's right in productive ways.[5]

A person who never shows anger, or one who does not show it in situations where it seems fitting, can be seen as lacking passion.[6] When Dean seems resigned to his terminal diagnosis after electric shock injures his heart, and again later when his time is running out before hellhounds will come to claim his soul, his lack of urgency over his heart and soul predicaments frustrates his brother, who wants Dean to get angry.[7] Sam wants him to get fired up. Anger can cause many problems, to be sure, but it can also serve a purpose.

When this anger does arise, though, it is not always adaptive. Kübler-Ross noted that it "is very difficult to cope with from the point of view of family and staff [because] this anger is displaced in all directions and projected onto the environment at times almost random."[8] (Chapter 6, "A Trunk Full of Defense Mechanisms," explains displacement and projection.) In other words, people take it out on others around them. Even though Layla Rourke faces her looming death by brain tumor with peace and faith, her mother gets irate with Dean and others whose terminal conditions get healed.[9]

Vengeful spirits are the *Supernatural* characters who show the greatest anger over their own deaths and the ones whose actions, though admittedly more extreme, may be most analogous to how some people act when angry about terminal conditions. Some of the ghosts seek revenge, but plenty of them displace their anger onto anybody, taking it out on people who had nothing to do with causing their deaths.[10] Despite the potential for expressions of anger to feel empowering, they can simply be destructive when no constructive purpose seems readily available or appealing to the angry individual.

Destructive behavior can become more likely than constructive behavior when hatred or a desire for retribution plays a role in the person's anger,[11] and it's hard not to hate someone who would kill you. As a ghost, Bobby Singer tries to be a helpful spirit but begins to endanger others in his pursuit of revenge against his murderer, Dick Roman.[12] Pursuing justice is good. People who believe we can make justice happen are more often active, take-charge folks, ready to set aside short-term self-interests and able to stay motivated while laboring to fulfill long-term goals,[13] but single-minded, shortsighted drive for revenge is not so sweet. Revenge can make people feel worse and leave them dissatisfied, especially when directed at innocent targets.[14] Among the reasons that revenge might fail to satisfy is the same problem that can leave many terminally ill individuals frustrated: the inability to lash out at anybody responsible for their fates. For some, including Elizabeth Kübler-Ross herself during her final years,[15] longing to feel angry for problems that no human being caused can result in feeling anger toward God.[16]

The inability to express, rechannel, or otherwise defuse anger in healthy ways is frustrating. Frustration may intensify and create growing feelings of bitterness, or the individual might simply give up. Some, though, transform it into action as they try to do something to change their fate.[17] For others, it's time to bargain.

*"We need to talk about your anger management issues."*
—Crowley to Dean[18]


*"Usually when people are sad, they don't do anything.*
*They just cry over their condition. But when they get*
*angry, they bring about a change."*
—Malcolm X[19]


## References

Bohm, T., & Kaplan, S. (2011). *Revenger: On the dynamics of a frightening urge and its taming.* London, UK: Karnac.

Brandt, A. (2014). *Mindful anger: A pathway to emotional freedom.* New York, NY: Norton.

Breitbart, G. (Ed.). (1965). *Malcolm X speaks: Selected speeches and statements.* New York, NY: Grove.

De Rivera, J. (1981). The structure of anger. In J. de Rivera (Ed.), *Conceptual encounter: A method for the exploration of human experience* (pp. 35–81). Washington, DC: University Press of America.

Eadeh, F. R., Peak, S. A., & Lambert, A. J. (2017). The bittersweet taste of revenge: On the negative and positive consequences of retaliation. *Journal of Experimental Social Psychology, 68,* 27–39.

Exline, J. J., Grubbs, J. B., & Homolka, S. J. (2015). Seeing God as cruel or distant: Links with divine struggles involving anger, doubt, and fear of God's disapproval. *International Journal for the Psychology of Religion, 25*(1), 29–41.

Exline, J. J., Prince-Paul, M., Root, B. L., & Peereboom, K. S. (2013). The spiritual struggle of anger toward God: A study with family members of hospice patients. *Journal of Palliative Medicine, 16*(4), 369–375.

Giffin, E. (2010). *Heart of the matter.* New York, NY: St. Martin's.

Gower, M. (2013). Revenge: Interplay of creative and destructive forces. *Clinical Social Work Journal, 41*(1), 112–118.

Grubbs, J. B., & Exline, J. J. (2014). Why did God make me this way? Anger at God in the context of personal transgressions. *Journal of Psychology & Theology, 42*(4), 315–325.

Halperin, E., Russell, A. G., Dweck, C. S., & Gross, J. J. (2011). Anger, hatred, and the quest for peace: Anger can be constructive in the absence of hatred. *Journal of Conflict Resolution, 55*(2), 274–291.

Haner, C. F., & Brown, P. A. (1955). Clarification of the instigation to action in the frustration-aggression hypothesis. *Journal of Abnormal & Social Psychology, 51*(2), 204–206.

Keltner, D., Ellsworth, P. C., & Edwards, K. (1993). Beyond simple pessimism: Effects of sadness and anger on social perception. *Journal of Personality & Social Psychology, 64*(5), 740–752.

Kübler-Ross, E. (1969). *On death and dying: What the dying have to teach doctors, nurses, clergy, & their own families [Kindle version].* London, UK: Routledge.

Kübler-Ross, E. (1997). *The wheel of life: A memoir of living and dying.* New York, NY: Scribner.

Kübler-Ross, E., & Kessler, D. (2005/2014). *On grief and grieving: Finding the meaning of grief through the five stages of loss.* New York, NY: Simon & Schuster.

Lattin, D. (1997, May 31). *Expert on death faces her own death: Kübler-Ross now questions her life's work.* SFGate: http://www.sfgate.com/news/article/Expert-On-Death-Faces-Her-Own-Death-Kubler-Ross-2837216.php.

Lipkus, I. M. (1991). The construction and preliminary validation of a global belief in a Just World Scale and the exploratory analysis of the multidimensional belief in a Just World Scale. *Personality & Individual Differences, 12*(11), 1171–1178.

Saussy, C. (1995). *The gift of anger: A call to faithful action.* Louisville, KY: Westminster John Knox.

Schreiber, J. A. (2012). Psychometric properties of the Image of God Scale in breast cancer survivors. *Oncology Nursing Forum, 39*(4), E346–E352.

Sjöström, A., & Gollwitzer, M. (2015). Displaced revenge: Can revenge taste "sweet" if it aims at the wrong target? *Journal of Experimental Social Psychology, 56*, 191–202.

Sullman, M. J. M. (2015). The expression of anger on the road. *Safety Science, 72*, 153–159.

Tangney, J. P., Hill-Barlow, D., Wagner, P. E., Marschall, D. E., Borenstein, J. K., Sanftner, J., Mohr, T., & Gramzow, R. (1996). Assessing individual differences in constructive versus destructive responses to anger across the lifespan. *Journal of Personality & Social Psychology, 70*(4), 780–796.

Tavris, C. (1989). *Anger: The misunderstood emotion.* New York, NY: Simon & Schuster.

Tiedens, L. Z., & Linton, S. (2001). Judgment under emotional certainty and uncertainty: The effects of specific emotions on information processing. *Journal of Personality & Social Psychology, 81*(6), 973–988.

Zuckerman, M., & Gerbasi, K. C. (1977). Belief in a just world and trust. *Journal of Research in Personality, 11*(3), 306–317.

## Notes

1. Episode 5–20, "The Devil You Know" (April 29, 2010).
2. Giffin (2010), p. 336.
3. De Rivera (1981).
4. Keltner et al. (1993), Tavris (1989).
5. Brandt (2014), Sullman (2015), Tangney et al. (1996).
6. Saussy (1995), Tiedens & Linton (2001).
7. Heart—episode 1–12, "Faith" (January 17, 2006); soul—3–1, "The Magnificent Seven" (October 4, 2007); body, too, when the archangel Michael plans to inhabit it for eternity—4–16, "On the Head of a Pin" (March 19, 2009).
8. Kübler-Ross (1969), p. 63.
9. Episode 1–12, "Faith" (January 17, 2006).
10. e.g., episodes 1–1, "Pilot" (September 13, 2005); 5–12, "Swap Meat" (January 28, 2010); 7–7, "The Mentalists" (November 4, 2011); and many more.
11. Bohm & Kaplan (2011), Gower (2013), Halperin et al. (2011).
12. Episode 7–23, "Survival of the Fittest" (May 18, 2012).
13. Lipkus (1991), Zuckerman & Gerbasi (1977).
14. Eadeh et al. (2017), Schreiber (2012), Sjöström & Gollwitzer (2015).
15. Lattin (1997), Kübler-Ross (1997), Kübler-Ross & Kessler (2005/2014.
16. Exline et al. (2013, 2015), Grubbs & Exline (2014).
17. Haner & Brown (1955).
18. Episode 10–2, "Reichenbach" (October 14, 2014).
19. Breitbart (1965), p. 107.

# PART III

# SECRETS AND LIES

## CHAPTER TEN

# Bro Moments: Communication Between Men

BILLY SAN JUAN AND
PAUL VANPORTFLIET

*". . . drinking a beer, sharing their feelings. The two
of them. Alone, but together. Bonded. United."*
—*Supernatural: The Musical* director Marie[1]

*"Some men believe that tear ducts on men are like nipples—
we only have them through a biological accident."*
—psychologist Christopher Kilmartin[2]

Young boys are often raised to suppress expressions of
emotion as a way to guard against vulnerability, a phenomenon that carries through to adulthood.[3] This, along with other
stereotypical male traits, creates a role for the gender of "male,"
nonconformity to which may lead to negative social or even
mental consequences.[4] Sam and Dean exhibit a brotherhood
that can be explored through the lens of a concept called *gender
role strain,* in that their adherence to masculine narratives causes

dysfunction in their relationship due to the unrealistic expectations they entail. However, the brothers' masculine identities also embody healthy and positive traits that may help them in their war against the forces of Heaven and Hell. Sam and Dean Winchester argue and fight. They also protect each other and share moments no one else could understand. You see, Sam and Dean Winchester are not just brothers. Sam and Dean are men.

## Communication Between Brothers

The Winchester boys are tough, and yet, they struggle with a basic human skill: communication. Communication, especially self-disclosure about emotional events, may trigger several biological processes, including "striking reductions in blood pressure, muscle tension, and skin conductance during or immediately after the disclosure."[5] Despite the benefits of communication, the brothers are often reluctant to communicate readily. For example, Dean has chastised Sam and told him, "Just back off, okay? Just because I'm not sharing and caring like you want me to."[6]

Communication does more than just enhance health. Communication, and the vulnerability that comes with it, allows for self-expression, emotional growth and regulation, strengthening of relationships, seeking out social support, feelings of connection, and feelings of being understood.[7] Unfortunately, these perks are rarely compelling enough to override the Winchesters' adherence to the masculine narrative to be strong and invulnerable. They engage in a series-long struggle to protect each other. Furthermore, Sam's modern communication style involves upfront discussion of emotions and a lack of regard for the stoic anti-vulnerability that Dean exudes. Conversely, Dean exhibits a bravado that is in line with traditional masculinity narratives. He refuses to speak about feelings, and the mere mention of his weaknesses may prompt either a playful dismissal of the topic or outright irritation.

However, the brothers also communicate well in a pro-masculine manner. They bond in a way considered socially appropriate for men. This includes ogling women, teasing each other, and reminiscing fondly. When Sam attempts to express his mourning over Dean's impending death by hellhound, Dean counters, "You're not gonna bust out the misty goodbye speech, okay? I mean, if this is my last day on Earth, I don't want it to be socially awkward."[8] He then turns on the radio, and the Winchester boys bond by singing rock together. Though this may be viewed as a strategy to avoid these feelings, it can also be viewed as a socially appropriate moment of intimacy between the two brothers. Stereotypically, it is forbidden for men to directly express their feelings. However, implied feelings are normalized through shared active experiences, such as singing. Or hunting demons.

## Gender Role Strain

The Winchester boys' intersibling communication is moderated by how they subconsciously weigh the breaking of normative male behaviors and expressions of emotions against the cost of breaking those norms. *Gender role strain* is an umbrella term for situations wherein people's attempted adherence to their beliefs about their gender may cause negative consequences. These may include "stress, conflict, and other problems in situations that make them seem inadequate.[9] The gender role strain model consists of a number of tenets, each of which are seen in the Winchester brothers' relationship.[10]

*People define gender roles by gender.* Sam and Dean identify as men, exhibit typical male behaviors and beliefs, and abide by basic narratives of masculinity. These include beliefs that may define the social narrative for masculinity: anti-femininity, physical toughness, emotional stoicism, identity as providers and protectors, aggression, and a value on social status.[11] These four beliefs can serve as the basis for examining the rest of the gender role strain tenets. These beliefs are expressed by characters in the *Supernatural* universe. For example, Bobby admonishes Dean by exclaiming, "I am so sorry your feelings are hurt, princess!"[12] The implications that Dean has feelings, that his feelings are hurt, and that he is acting like a princess all serve to undermine these masculine tenets.

*Masculinity narratives are contradictory.* Sam and Dean want to take care of each other, in adherence to the masculine role of "protector." However, their method of protecting the other's psychological health is frequently contradictory. Sam often attempts to speak to Dean about his feelings. For example, he pleads, "You're tail-spinning, man. And you refuse to talk about it. . . . You don't have to handle this on your own. No one can."[13] Dean often hides his thoughts and feelings from Sam. This dissonance, though adhering to a masculine narrative, is a key source of conflict for the brothers. It takes a large amount of effort, a significant situation, or a near-death experience for Dean to overcome his hesitation to express feelings.

*Norms are regularly violated.* Traditional gender roles are routinely violated, due to the nature of reality. On the one hand, Dean fits his stereotypical masculine role, as exemplified by his single-handed repair of his totaled Impala on more than one occasion as well as when he is portrayed as a professional mechanic in an elaborate hallucination created by a djinn that captures him.[14] On the other, Dean also violates the traditionally masculine role when viewers learn that he has developed a great deal of culinary expertise in the absence of caregivers to provide food for him and his brother. In fact, his delicious creations are well known by those who have sampled his cooking; Sam and Death have both complimented Dean's food.[15]

*Violation of masculine narratives are often socially condemned.* Sam and Dean experience these condemnations in both explicit and implicit ways. Sam and Dean will often tease each other, become frustrated, or even express outright anger at violations of their masculine narrative. On one occasion, Sam earnestly tells Dean, "You and me, we're all that's left. So, uh, if we're gonna see this through, we're gonna do it together." In response, Dean mocks Sam, saying, "Hold me, Sam. That was beautiful."[16] In true Winchester fashion, a heartfelt moment that violates the hypermasculine narrative of a male hunter is socially condemned and met with sarcastic humor.

*Masculine narrative beliefs can lead to negative mental consequences.* Sam and Dean identify strongly in their brotherhood, and they bond as mutual protectors and providers. When unable to protect each other, they suffer mental anguish. Dean even goes so far as to make a deal with a crossroads demon to resurrect Sam.[17]

*Masculine roles can lead to overconformity, due to fear of violations.* Dean is often teased, both by Sam and by demons, about his tendency to overconform to masculine tropes. Sam even teases Dean when they are mistaken for a romantic couple, and he tells Dean, "Well, you are kind of butch. They probably think you are overcompensating."[18]

*Gender roles are dysfunctional in many ways.* Traditional characteristics of masculinity are highly dysfunctional for a modern age. Sam and Dean's brotherly bond, though strong through their commitment to protect each other, also suffers because of their difficulty in effectively communicating their feelings. Staying silent, denying hurt or fear, and acting "tough" only accentuate the energy spent hiding their vulnerable emotions. The demon Ruby once even calls them out on it, and states, "Look at you, trying to be all stoic. My God, it's heartbreaking."[19]

*Gender roles are also experienced in work and family roles.* Dean's role as protector of his younger brother began at a very young age, from the moment he ran out of his home while his mother burned on the ceiling. Dean identifies as his brother's guardian. This point is made in a flashback when Dean gives Sam holiday gifts and lies about their father visiting for Christmas, which shows Dean's adopted role as Sam's guardian by being a provider of gifts and merriment.[20]

*Historical change causes gender role strain.* Changes in social values can cause role strain due to beliefs passed down through family generations and shifting modern times. The difference between generations is observable when contrasting Sam and Dean to their hunter grandfather, Samuel Campbell.[21] Campbell appears as a hypermasculine, gruff, and suspicious individual. He does not "play well with others" and struggles to bring himself to tolerate others as necessary. By contrast, even Dean's hard-line masculinity is adapted to allow for greater expression of emotion and vulnerability.

## Positives of Masculinity

Even though the Winchester brothers have problems communicating with each other, there are ways in which their adherence to masculinity narratives are positive, healthy, and adaptive. Examples of positive masculinity narratives include intimacy development, caring styles, provision of social welfare, and use of humor for intimacy.[22]

### Intimacy Development

Men tend to develop intimate relationships with each other through high-action activities. Dean calls upon Sam to discuss the terms by which Sam must die, leading to a physical fight between the brothers. However, Dean opts instead to kill Death when remembering his family memories. In this high-octane moment, Dean and Sam's relationship strengthens as a direct result of the action they were both part of.

### Caring Styles

Men are often taught to be responsible for loved ones and friends. Dean learns this from an early age, when his father (whom he admires) places Sam in his arms as their mother dies. He is told to "take his brother outside" and "don't look back." Dean is given the responsibility to care for his brother, a responsibility he carries out throughout his life. As they grow up, the boys continue this style of caring, and their relationship grows in its identity as caregivers and protectors for each other.

### Provision of Social Welfare

Masculinity narratives often involve the idea that men have a duty to contribute to the well-being of a society through either the creation of organizations or through mentorships. Sam and Dean assume the traditional masculine identities of "protector" and "avenger" during their adventures.

A prime example of this phenomenon is when Dean assumes the role of protector. This occurs in their efforts to aid God in sealing the Darkness, where she can do no harm to the world. Dean takes up the role of protector by volunteering to carry a spirit bomb within himself to Amara.

### Use of Humor for Intimacy

Men are taught to use humor as a foundation for friendship, as well as a method for healing and coping. This is seen in the brotherly teasing between the Winchester boys. At times, they will tease each other. At times, they will engage in oddly timed nonsequiturs or sarcasm. Dean often relies on hyperbole and sardonicism, such as softening his voice and saying, "Hold me, Sam. That was beautiful."[23] At one point, they even play pranks on each other. With each smile and laugh, the boys' bond grows stronger in a manner of intimacy that is deemed socially appropriate for men.

## ROAD MUSIC

### "Eye of the Tiger" by Survivor[24]

A common feature of traditional conceptions of masculinity is aggression.[25] Cultural stereotypes normalize the solution of male-male arguments through the use of fisticuffs, rather than conversation. Sam and Dean have sometimes settled their arguments by physically fighting each other.[26] However, as their bond grows throughout the series, we see that expressing their emotions becomes easier for them. It's important to note that they also playfully slap or punch each other at times, which is a socially accepted way for men to show affection for each other.

## Brothers in Arms

Sam and Dean Winchester are not your typical men. They have endured loss and pain beyond what any mortal should experience. Though they are warriors in a battle between Heaven and Hell, they are also prone to the same masculine gender role narratives that prompt discord in their brotherhood. The conflict causes poor communication between them, though they are still able to bond in ways that the culture deems appropriate. Despite the challenges imposed by their masculine gender roles, the brothers are also able to use positive aspects of their gender roles to communicate in a healthy manner. And it works quite well, because Sam and Dean Winchester are not just men. They are brothers.

### References

Fischer, A. R., Tokar, D. M., Good, G. E., & Snell, A. F. (1998). More on the structure of male role norms: Exploratory and multiple sample confirmatory analyses. *Psychology of Women Quarterly, 22*, 135–155.

Kilmartin, C. (2010). *The masculine self.* Cornwall-on-Hudson, NY: Sloan.

Levant, R. F., Wong, Y. J., Karkis, E. N., & Welsh, M. M. (2015). Mediated moderation of the relationship between the endorsement of restrictive emotionality and alexithymia. *Psychology of Men & Masculinity, 16*(4), 459–467.

Kiselica, M. S., Benton-Wright, S., & Englar-Carlson, M. (2016). Accentuating positive masculinity: A new foundation for the psychology of boys, men, and masculinity. In Y. J. Wong & S. R. Wester (Eds.), *APA handbook of men and masculinities* (pp. 123–143). Washington, DC: American Psychological Association.

Pennebaker, J. W. (1995). Emotion, disclosure, and health: An overview. In J. W. Pennebaker (Ed.), *Emotion, disclosure, and health* (pp. 3–10). Washington, DC: American Psychological Association.

Pleck, Joseph. (1995). The gender role strain paradigm: An update. In R. F. Levant & W. S. Pollack (Eds.), *A new psychology of men* (pp. 11–32). New York, NY: Basic.

Smith, R. M., Parrott, D. J., Swartout, K. M., & Tharp, A. T. (2015). Deconstructing hegemonic masculinity: The roles of antifemininity, subordination to women, and sexual dominance in men's perpetration of sexual aggression. *Psychology of Men & Masculinity, 16*(2), 160–169.

## Notes

1. Episode 10–5, "Fan Fiction" (November 11, 2014).
2. Kilmartin (2010), p. 157.
3. Levant et al. (2015).
4. Pleck (1995).
5. Pennebaker (1995), p. 5.
6. Episode 2–2, "Everybody Loves a Clown" (October 5, 2006).
7. Kilmartin (2010)
8. Episode 3–16, "No Rest for the Wicked" (May 15, 2008).
9. Kilmartin (2010), p. 46.
10. Pleck (1995), Kilmartin (2010), Smith et al. (2015).
11. Fischer et al. (1998), Kilmartin (2010).
12. Episode 4–22, "Lucifer Rising" (May 14, 2009).
13. Episode 2–4, "Children Shouldn't Play with Dead Things" (October 19, 2006).
14. Episode 2–20, "What Is and What Should Never Be" (May 3, 2007).
15. Episodes 8–14, "Trial and Error" (February 13, 2013); 10–23, "Brother's Keeper" (May 20, 2015).
16. Episode 1–11, "Scarecrow" (January 10, 2006).
17. Episode 2–22, "All Hell Breaks Loose," part 2 (May 17, 2002).
18. Episode 2–11, "Playthings" (January 18, 2007).
19. Episode 3–9, "Malleus Maleficarum" (January 31, 2008).
20. Episode 3–8, "A Very Supernatural Christmas" (December 13, 2007).
21. Episode 4–3, "In the Beginning" (October 2, 2008).
22. Kiselica et al. (2016).
23. Episode 1–11, "Scarecrow" (January 10, 2006).
24. Written by F. Sulliven & J. Peterek (1982); sung by J. Ackles as Dean in episode 4–6, "Yellow Fever."
25. Kilmartin (2010), p. 7.
26. Episode 1–10, "Asylum" (November 22, 2005).

## CHAPTER ELEVEN

# The Family Addiction:
# Saving People, Hunting Things

## JUSTINE MASTIN AND
## WILLIAM BLAKE ERICKSON

*"Face it, darling, you're an addict. Death is*
*your drug. And you're going to spend the*
*rest of your life chasing that dragon."*
—Crowley[1]

*"Addictions always originate in pain, whether felt openly or*
*hidden in the unconscious. They are emotional anesthetics."*
—physician Gabor Maté[2]

Sometimes, people can be so controlled by outside forces
that they act in ways contrary to their nature. Drugs, alcohol, and certain activities can have a powerful effect on reward circuitry in the brain, affecting learning, memory, and even social behaviors. Such overactivation of these circuits can give rise to compulsive, potentially life-threatening behaviors, better known as addictions.[3] People who become addicted

suffer themselves, but their addiction also impacts families and communities on emotional, psychological, and financial levels.[4] Whether it's stashing a flask of Hunter's Helper in the pocket of a leather jacket, sucking demon blood from its source, or perhaps even hunting itself, addiction is an ever-present facet of the *Supernatural* landscape.

## Understanding Addiction

To discover if people are facing addiction, we focus on their relationship with a substance or behavior and whether (or how much) that relationship is damaging to them.[5] Just like any relationship, sometimes another person or a substance (or a super-power or demon's blood) has a deleterious impact on life, causing distress.[6] Some people are able to continue to have a relationship with that entity (by means such as casual social drinking) and some are not; some must cut it out of their lives completely as an act of self-preservation. Eventually, Sam must give up drinking demon blood because, in spite of the incredible demon-vanquishing powers it gives him, it weakens his physical body and nearly destroys his most important personal relationships.[7]

### Causes of Addiction

Research indicates that addiction has a genetic basis but is also influenced by people's environment.[8] Not only does an addiction impact the people who have the addiction, but it impacts everyone with whom they have contact, especially their family.[9] This is one of the reasons that addiction is often referred to as a *family disease*. As the angel Castiel gains power from the souls from Purgatory and begins to become "drunk with power," it drastically changes his relationship with his chosen family, to the point that he tells them, "You will bow down and profess your love unto me, your Lord, or I shall destroy you."[10] His actions and the Winchesters' reactions are consistent with common characteristics seen among families dealing with addiction: difficulty forming functional relationships with family members, emotional or physical abuse within the family, and instability in important areas of life.[11]

## Alcoholic Family Systems

Oftentimes, families can facilitate and perpetuate addiction to their own detriment. In the *Supernatural* universe, much of Bobby Singer's family structure revolves around alcohol consumption, making it emblematic of an *alcoholic family system*. Not only is Bobby's father a "mean drunk," but his mother reinforces the man's addiction by being careful not to anger him.[12] This works to preserve the old man's addiction at the expense of protecting her son from harm. Alcoholic family systems often perpetuate addiction across generations,[13] thanks in large part to their practice of secret-keeping. The Singer household is a classic example of how secret-keeping and complacency maintain alcoholism within alcoholic families. Bobby was both a witness to and a victim of his father's physical expressions of anger, and feared that he would turn out the same way. Adult children of alcoholics have shared similar stories of fear in that "basically, the child is taught repeatedly, overtly and covertly, not to trust anyone, including him or herself."[14]

Because of a parent's substance use, he or she is often absent physically and/or emotionally from the home. This can impact attachment in families and lead to a greater chance of children developing their own personality dysfunctions as adults.[15] John's absences place Dean in the role of adult at a young age, forcing him to act as a parent to young Sam. Children who live in homes with an addict can develop into "parentified children," a state of role reversal in which a child feels obliged to act like a parent to that child's parent or parental figure or to other children in the home.[16] (For more on parentification, see chapter 4, "Carrying on after Parental Loss.") John neglects his children in order to pursue "the job," causing their nutritional, educational, and nurturance needs to go largely unmet,[17] and Dean often must play the parental role to a brother only four years younger than he is. Having another parental figure around can help fill the void in the family structure. By helping the boys meet some of their needs as they're growing up, surrogate father Bobby helps foster their resilience.[18]

### Self-Medication

Some who become addicted initially pick up drugs or alcohol to *self-medicate*, or rather to defeat some metaphorical "demon" that they are fighting. Although those who abuse chemicals may experience some relief, the drug quickly begins to cause its own problems.[19] In *Supernatural*, addictive substances are often as otherworldly as the entities hunters face. Sam starts drinking literal demon blood as a way to get stronger so that he can fight a still greater demon. This "drug" interacts with, and exacerbates, powers already inside him, causing him to crave ever greater amounts of demon blood. Such a situation is reminiscent of those who have a genetic predisposition to addiction: That marker is already within them. Those who come from families with a history of substance abuse and are aware of their predisposition may choose to never pick up a drink or try a drug, because they fear even the possibility that they might become addicted. These may be conscious choices, but they are still operating out of fear of who—or what—they might become.

### Compulsive Habits

Addictions do not always involve foreign chemicals. They can be entirely behavioral, while nevertheless producing similar changes in the brain.[20] (Some professionals refer to *addictive behavior* to identify addict-like actions, regardless of whether physiological addiction is known to be involved.[21]) The motivations, however, are the same as substance-related addictions. John begins hunting for the same reasons that many people start abusing drugs: the pain of loss and the inability to move past it. Hunting may be the natural calling of the Winchesters, but it is also at times a coping mechanism. Emotionally, John remains stuck in that moment when he first picks up a shotgun to hunt until his dying day. The boys have a bit more awareness about their "use" of hunting. They recognize the importance of other aspects of life, such as friends, even if most of their friends are supernatural or dead, and hobbies—the boys love movies and Dean has an excellently curated collection of *Busty Asian Beauties* magazines. They do not have the luxury of a normal childhood because of their father's "hunting problem," so these passions help them cope with life's challenges. Even with the boys' insight into the addictive nature of hunting, they are still constantly working in a high-stakes, high-pressure situation that is likely to end in another death for one or both of them. Instead of dealing with their feelings, it seems easier, as Dean says to "shove it down and . . . let it come out in spurts of violence and alcoholism."[22]

## Living with Addiction

Almost by definition, an addiction weaves itself into the sufferer's life. Individuals work to find ways to remain high-functioning, which often masks the severity of their affliction. Despite initially leading a successful double life with an addiction, the chemical, emotional, and interpersonal side effects begin to take their toll.

### Shame

Shame is a quintessential aspect of addiction.[23] *Shame* is defined as "the intensely painful feeling or experience of believing that we are flawed and therefore unworthy of love and belonging—

something we've experienced, done, or failed to do makes us unworthy of connection."[24] Whether one is in active addiction, recovery, or living in an alcoholic household, there is a level of shame inherent to every relationship with addiction. This shame emerges from constant secret-keeping and protecting the addicted person, the family, and/or the addiction itself. This journey looks similar whether the demons are literal, metaphorical, or, in the case of the Winchesters, both. Even when Dean was literally "raised from perdition" by an angel of the Lord, he didn't feel deserving.[25] For all his bravado, Dean does not feel worthy of love and respect. As a result, he shows little to no compassion for himself, despite feeling it for others. Thus, shame both shapes and warps his life. As Crowley says, "Your problem, mate, is that nobody hates you more than you do. Believe me, I've tried."[26]

### Withdrawal

Families often contribute to the maintenance and upkeep of addiction. Not only are those with addictions desperate for the reinforcing effects of their chosen chemical, the biological impact of abstaining can bring about life-threatening side effects of withdrawal. For hunters, the dangerous pursuit produces both a high and a sense of relief once the drug hits their system. When the boys are not able to hunt for long periods, Dean especially feels a sort of "withdrawal" effect: "Come on, give me something to punch already."[27] Hunting is not yet classified as a behavioral addiction but it shares some qualities of gambling disorder,[28] a recognized addictive disorder.

## Treatment and Recovery: Motivation for Change

No matter what sort of addiction people have, successfully overcoming it requires them to want to seek treatment in the first place. In the high-stakes job of hunting, every single day

# ROAD MUSIC

### "Heroin" by Velvet Underground[29]

The song "Heroin" by Velvet Underground has been an ode to living with substance abuse since it was released in 1967.[30] Heroin is a highly addictive, opioid drug. Opioid addiction—including both legal and illegal opioid use—is widespread. In 2015 alone, 33,000 US deaths were attributed to opioid overdose, the most of any year on record.[31] Few scenes encapsulate both the rapture and desolation of substance abuse as well as the scene showing a desperate Crowley injecting himself with human blood, set to this song.[32]

could be their last. The brothers have already died before and, whether it's Hell or Purgatory, they know what lies beyond the veil. In their experience, even the afterlife is bloody. It makes sense that they would turn to anything they could get their hands on to cope with the fear, anger, and pain caused by such a life. Hunting is rooted in their desire to do good. But shame prevents them from seeing themselves as worthy of the same health and protection they provide to others.

## Intervention: How Family Helps and Hurts

At times it is necessary for family and friends to step in and let their loved one know that their use is a problem.[33] Many people living with addiction do not realize the toll it has taken on them, but those around them do. This might look like the family getting together and asking their loved ones to get help, or, in the case of people being a danger to themselves or others, checking them into a hospital. Since most hospitals are not equipped to help hunters with supernatural maladies, interventions for our heroes usually look different from what would typically be prescribed by a psychiatrist: When Sam needs to detox from his demon blood use, Bobby and Dean lock him in a bunker covered in sigils.[34]

One of the most challenging aspects of healing, however, is that the family must realize that it is not just the person with the addiction who has a "problem," but that the whole family system is "sick." Often, families do not want to face this and prefer their loved one to stay ill so that they do not have to confront what else is going on. Sometimes, though they are generally loath to admit it to themselves, they may even prefer their loved ones in a using state and do not want them to change. As long as he's functional, Crowley on human blood is a more agreeable and sensitive Crowley. Knowing that Crowley is experiencing cravings, Dean offers him his own blood in exchange for information.[35] For Dean, this is both a selfish and a manipulative act: He needs the information and would likely also prefer a more "human" Crowley as his prisoner in the bunker. Others, who pretend to be friends, want the addicted person to stay ill as well, often because they are gaining something from that person's vulnerability. For example, the demon Lola's reason for providing Crowley with the human blood that he craves is to weaken him, not to help him.[36] In the clinical context, the addicted person's family members may have both selfish and selfless reasons for maintaining the addiction. Like human blood for Crowley, the addiction has both pacifying and dangerous effects. While it can be difficult for family members to recognize the ways that they have welcomed addiction into their lives, such a realization is crucial for both the addicted person and the family to recover.

## Change Comes from Within

As any psychotherapist can attest, change is hard under the best of circumstances. But when one is battling the demons

## GAMBLING DISORDER USED AS TEMPLATE FOR "HUNTING DISORDER"

Four (or more) in 12-month period:

- Needing to hunt greater threats to achieve the same fulfillment.
- Restless or irritable when trying to cut down on or stop hunting entirely.
- Making repeated unsuccessful attempts to stop hunting or to cut back/control it.
- Preoccupied with hunting.
- Hunting when feeling distressed.
- After losing a hunt, returning to get even.
- Telling lies to conceal the extent of involvement with hunting.
- Jeopardizing/losing a significant relationship or career due to hunting.
- Relying on others to provide money due to hunting.[37]

of addiction, change can feel almost impossible. Bobby Singer swung between alcoholism and hunting obsession for his entire adult life. Not even his healthiest motivations—commitment to his adopted sons, Sam and Dean, and his desire to help save the world—were enough to motivate him to overcome his addictions. So where does this leave brothers Sam and Dean?

Ultimately, no matter what help or hurt comes from the outside, change is unlikely unless we decide to make that change ourselves. Despite all their challenges, the family of choice that Sam and Dean have created is committed to doing good for the world and for each other. While their shared addictions arise from factors beyond their control, they become a means to cope with their dangerous lives. They hunt because of their deep love and commitment to the world. If they could channel this commitment toward making healthier choices related to their own well-being, they could possibly defeat all their demons—those in the world and those within themselves.

## References

American Psychiatric Association. (2013). *Diagnostic and statistical manual of mental disorders* (5th ed.) (DSM-5). Washington, DC: American Psychiatric Association.

American Society of Addiction Medication (2011, April 19). *Definition of addiction.* ASAM: http://www.asam.org/quality-practice/definition-of-addiction.

Brown, B. (2013, January 14) *Shame v. guilt.* Brené Brown: http://brenebrown.com/2013/01/14/2013114shame-v-guilt-html/.

Centers for Disease Control & Prevention (n.d.). *Opioid overdose.* CDC: https://www.cdc.gov/drugoverdose/index.html.

Clark, L. (2014). Disordered gambling: The evolving concept of behavioral addiction. *Annals of the New York Academy of Sciences, 1327*(1), 46–61.

Ertl, V., Saile, R., Neuner, F., & Catani, C. (2016). Drinking to ease the burden: A cross-sectional study on trauma, alcohol abuse and psychopathology in a post-conflict context. *BMC Psychiatry, 16*(1), 2–13.

Fergus, S., & Zimmerman, M. A. (2005). Adolescent resilience: A framework for understanding healthy development in the face of risk. *Annual Review of Public Health, 26*, 399–419.

Hall, C. W., & Webster, R. E. (2007). Risk factors among adult children of alcoholics. *International Journal of Behavioral Consultation and Therapy, 3*(4), 494–511.

Harvard, J. (2004). *The Velvet Underground & Nico (33).* New York, NY: Continuum.

Kober, H., Lacadie, C. M., Wexler, B. E., Malison, R. T., Sinha, R., & Potenza, M. N. (2016). Brain activity during cocaine craving and gambling urges: An fMRI study. *Neuropsychopharmacology, 41*(2), 628-637.

Lander, L., Howsare, J., & Byrne, M. (2013). The impact of substance use disorders on families and children: From theory to practice. *Social Work in Public Health, 28*(3–4), 194–205.

Luoma, J. B., Kohlenberg, B. S., Hayes, S. C., & Fletcher, L. (2012). Slow and steady wins the race: a randomized clinical trial of acceptance and commitment therapy targeting shame in substance use disorders. *Journal of Consulting & Clinical Psychology, 80*(1), 43–53.

National Council on Alcoholism and Drug Dependence. (2015, July 25). *Intervention: Tips and Guidelines.* NCADD: https://www.ncadd.org/family-friends/there-is-help/intervention-tips-and-guidelines.

National Institute on Drug Abuse. (2017). *Drug abuse is costly.* National Institutes of Health: https://archives.drugabuse.gov/about/welcome/aboutdrugabuse/magnitude/.

Nestler, E. J. (2014). Epigenetic Mechanisms of Drug Addiction. *Neuropharmacology, 76*, 259–268.

Prakash, O., Avasthi, A., & Benegal, V. (2012). Should pathological gambling be consider an addictive behavior? *Asian Journal of Psychiatry, 5*(3), 211–214.

US Department of Health and Human Services, Children's Bureau (2003). *Child welfare information gateway: A bulletin for professionals.* Washington, DC: US Government Printing Office.

Velleman, R., & Templeton, L. (2007). Understanding and modifying the impact of parents' substance misuse on children. *Advances in Psychiatric Treatment, 13*(2), 79–89.

## Notes

1. Episode 10–2, "Reichenbach" (October 14, 2014).
2. Maté (2010) p. 36.
3. American Society of Addiction Medication (2011).
4. National Institute on Drug Abuse (2017).
5. American Psychiatric Association (2013).
6. American Psychiatric Association (2013).
7. Episode 4–20, "The Rapture" (April 30, 2009).
8. Nestler (2014).
9. Lander et al. (2013).
10. Episode 6–22, "The Man Who Knew Too Much" (May 20, 2011).
11. Velleman & Templeton (2007).
12. Episode 7–10, "Death's Door" (December 2, 2011).
13. Velleman & Templeton (2007).
14. Fergus & Zimmerman (2005), p. 496.
15. Fergus & Zimmerman (2005).
16. Lander et al. (2013).
17. US Department of Health and Human Services (2003).
18. Ertl et al. (2016).
19. Hall & Webster (2007).
20. Kober et al. (2016).
21. Marlatt et al. (1988), Prakash et al. (2012).
22. Episode 6–14, "Mannequin 3: The Reckoning" (February 18, 2011).
23. Luoma et al. (2012).
24. Brown (2013).
25. Episode 4–1, "Lazarus Rising" (September 18, 2008).
26. Episode 9–11, "First Born" (January 21, 2014)
27. Episode 10–20, "Angel Heart" (April 29, 2015).
28. Clark (2014).
29. Written by L. Reed (1967); played in episode 9–16, "Blade Runners" (March 18, 2014).
30. Harvard (2004).
31. Centers for Disease Control & Prevention (n.d.).
32. Episode 9–16, "Blade Runners" (March 18, 2014).
33. National Council on Alcoholism and Drug Dependence (2015).
34. Episode 4–21, "When the Levee Breaks" (May 7, 2009).
35. Episode 9–10, "Road Trip" (January 14, 2014).
36. Episode 9–16, "Blade Runners" (March 18, 2014).
37. Adapted from American Psychiatric Association (2013), pp. 490, 491, 585.

## CHAPTER TWELVE

# Crossroads and a River of Crap:
# How Killing Affects Those Who Kill

### STEPHAN SCHAFFRATH
### AND COLT J. BLUNT

*"The violence of combat assaults psyches, confuses ethics,*
*and tests souls. This is not only a result of the violence*
*suffered. It is also a result of the violence inflicted."*
—author Karl Marlantes[2]

*"I think the Dean and Sam story sucks. It is not fun.*
*It's not entertaining. It is a river of crap that would*
*send most people howling to the nuthouse!"*
—Dean to fans of novels about his life[1]

Narratives that intelligently deal with violence can help us better understand our species and its propensity toward the ultimate act of destruction. Despite the immense metaphysical parameters to which the viewers' imaginations are stretched, realistic portrayal and treatment of how characters like Sam and Dean react as human beings and deal with the effects of violence, both as recipients and purveyors of it, keep the narrative grounded in something that resembles a plausible reality.[3] Heroes fictional or factual can carry with them unimaginable psychological baggage, both in terms of traumas that happen to them (such as repeated losses of loved ones[4]) and things they do both with and without *volition* (perceived choice or free will[5]). Nevertheless, many heroic individuals such as the Winchesters strive to hold on to their humanity and counteract their acquired *desensitization* (reduced sensitivity through repeated exposure) to violence.[6] The ongoing story line focuses on how—and at what cost—this happens.

How deeply does the act of killing affect the person who kills?

## The Toll on the Hunter

Trauma from killing can manifest in the form of *posttraumatic stress disorder* (PTSD). Indeed, research has shown that the act of killing significantly increases the likelihood of developing PTSD among soldiers—a phenomenon that has been called *perpetration-induced traumatic stress* (PITS).[7] Signs and symptoms of this disorder can be seen in the hunters in *Supernatural*, including detachment from reality, hypervigilance against potential threats, avoidance behavior, and difficulty experiencing positive mood. Furthermore, such trauma, if left untreated, can result in further psychological dysfunction, including depression, substance abuse, psychosis, and suicide. Sam and Dean both struggle with maladaptive coping strategies throughout their never-ending war, dabbling in alcohol use, unnecessary risk-taking, and self-destructive behaviors. Out of necessity, they become jumpy and untrusting—ever-vigilant and on guard. Yet, the brothers anchor each other, each keeping the other from teetering off into oblivion or becoming the very monsters they hunt. This is perhaps the best they can hope for, as the effects of their trauma are unlikely to abate on their own.

Dean and Sam are by no means immune to the effects of their frequent need to end the infernal existence of their adversaries. Though they may be able to more easily justify their slaying of Hell's more bestial denizens, research suggests that it is impossible to avoid at least some empathic response to seeing the results of foes one has vanquished, even if one has been conditioned to dehumanize them.[8] Bringing about the death of the possessed (those unfortunate innocents inhabited by demons) is undoubtedly a different story, akin to causing civilian (noncombatant) casualties in the course of combat.[9] Taking a life is consistently identified as the most traumatic experience for those in law enforcement, even ranking above witnessing another officer die in the line of duty.[10] The taking of life may be the most extreme trauma for many soldiers as well.[11]

## Making a Hunter

People in roles of authority hold power over those under them, power that makes those in the subordinate position more likely to obey or comply with a variety of instructions and orders. As a father to two boys growing up in cheap hotel rooms, John Winchester is often more of a commanding officer than their nurturer. Admitting as much to Sam, John says outright that somewhere along the line, he "stopped being your father and I-I became your—your drill sergeant."[12]

In what may be the most famous research on obedient aggression, psychologist Stanley Milgram conducted a study in which an authority figure ordered participants to deliver supposedly dangerous electric shock to someone for providing incorrect responses to a learning task.[13] A social psychologist of Jewish descent, Milgram became interested in the subject of obedience following the trial of Adolf Eichmann, a Nazi member of the *Schutzstaffel* (SS) who was a primary organizer of the Holocaust.[14] Milgram wanted to understand all those soldiers who had followed the orders that killed millions, and to find out if the potential for such murderous obedience was widespread. No one was really given electric shocks in his original, most famous study or in his numerous follow-up studies,[15] but his volunteer participants did not know that. As far they knew, they might be killing someone, and about two-thirds were willing to administer what they believed was a dangerous level of shock when ordered to by the researcher.

Beyond responding to the mere authority of their father as they learn to become killers, the Winchester boys also become initiated into a larger population of killers, the community of hunters. When people become members of a group of killers, killing becomes an acceptable thing to do, since the killer acts as part and on behalf of the group. David Grossman—a retired US Army lieutenant colonel, former professor of psychology at the US Military Academy at West Point, and perhaps the foremost expert on the psychological study of killing (known as *killology*)—refers to this as *group absolution*.[16] Another researcher's study involving interviews with Israeli combat soldiers completing mandatory service indicated that the combination of training and the involuntary nature of service resulted in two seemingly conflicting themes: self-control and thrill. That is, soldiers internally justified their mandatory service by interpreting it as contributing to a sense of *self-actualization* (a drive for self-fulfillment and achieving one's full potential) and thus in line with a choice they would have consciously made, and enjoyed the thrill of risk-taking.[17] If such soldiers experience increased perceived agency and empowerment the more training they receive and the more obedience they develop, does this explain Sam and Dean's comfort with the hunter life and all that comes with it? Like the soldiers in the aforementioned study, they certainly do not choose the lifestyle but rather are conscripted. And, like those soldiers, they may come to see it as a calling.[18] Further, research suggests that experiences with killing make future instances of killing easier.[19] Yet, Sam and Dean do not romanticize their roles, telling wannabe hunters that a life such as theirs resembles "a river of crap that would send most people howling to the nuthouse."[20]

Despite their difficult upbringing, Sam and Dean earnestly pursue a warrior code that includes the virtue of empathy and respect for one's adversary (which, in their case, often includes reminding themselves that many monsters have been victims themselves [21]). Such codes have popped up throughout history, such as the samurai's bushido and the European knight's code of chivalry, as well as in fiction. According to one author who is a real-life combat veteran, "The ideal response to killing in war should be one similar to a mercy killing, sadness mingled with respect."[22] Despite occasionally dabbling in torture, the Winchester boys strive to hang on to what little decency they can find.

## If You're Not One of Us, You're One of Them

Much of *Supernatural*'s narrative is dominated by a discourse of *us* versus *them*. Feeling part of the good side facilitates violence against those who are perceived to be on the bad or wrong side.[23] Research has consistently demonstrated the tendency to experience bias toward people outside of our own groups, and these biases tend to become amplified when paired with negative emotions.[24] The monstrous nature of adversaries in the show serves as a valuable commentary for what happens in real-life combat, where human nature dictates that one objectifies one's enemy into something less than human. The Nazis are perhaps the most salient example of this practice, though

even the US military makes efforts to distance its soldiers and
to dehumanize enemy combatants. Of course, in *Supernatural*, one does not even need to engage in pseudospeciation, as
Sam and Dean hunt real monsters, or at least people who have
taken on a monstrous aspect such as the Bender[25] and Styne
families.[26]

## Transformation and Community among Killers

The biggest cost of living a life immersed in violence is what it
does to oneself. As Sam and Dean slay monster after monster,
they seem to become more monstrous themselves. When they
first hunt a Wendigo, they glimpse the horrors of transformation they will face frequently on their journey.[27] In Native
American lore, Wendigos start out as human beings who, as a
result of succumbing to cannibalism, gradually grow more and
more powerful. As Wendigos become more powerful, they
progressively lose their humanity until there is nothing left.[28]

Sam and Dean are imbued with increasing degrees of supernatural characteristics as they kill their way through the realms
of monstrous beings and become increasingly at risk of becoming more and more like what they hunt. Most notably are Sam's
erstwhile addiction to demon blood, which gives him supernatural powers,[29] and Dean's trading places with Cain as the
bearer of the Mark,[30] which makes him temporarily immortal
and transforms him into a powerful demon.[31]

Dean, who enjoys playing the tough guy who rarely gives
a damn, is ironically more in touch with his feelings about
himself than his brother is. After Sam and Dean annihilate a
murderous shapeshifter, Dean explains to Sam that they themselves are "freaks" as well, not unlike the shapeshifter they just
killed.[32] Dean feels that they are not fit to live among regular

people, just like the monsters that they slay. The Winchesters inhabit a world of otherness, a world apart from what the vast majority of people know to be normal or even real.

Those who have been initiated into such a culture of violence are not like the rest. Dean realizes this early on. Sam's recognition of this point takes longer. It is not coincidental that deadly violence is sometimes likened to sex.[33] Psychological effects of violence on the aggressor may depend upon the distance and method in which the killing takes place, with closer, more intimate methods resulting in greater trauma. As such, those in charge of long-range weapons, such as intercontinental ballistic missiles (ICBMs) would be expected to experience the least amount of trauma, those using firearms to experience more trauma, and those killing at close range with bladed weapons or their bare hands—(*the sexual range*[34]) to experience the most trauma. Both killing and sex are threshold experiences that catapult one into another realm. Once that curtain is pulled, there is no return. And just as in sex, there are better and worse ways to be introduced to killing. The Winchester brothers are introduced to killing at a prepubescent age, which may explain why they struggle to maintain meaningful intimate relationships.

Like combat soldiers, who gravitate toward the company of other combat soldiers,[35] the Winchesters connect with other hunters for community. The hunter community and identity keep drawing the brothers, despite the physical and mental hardships involved in it; in fact, they yearn to learn more.[36] This can conceivably reflect a desire for some sense of community, stability, and surrogate family, a desire for some degree of normality even in the midst of their far-from-normal lives. *Supernatural* is riddled with references to the normal "apple pie" life that eludes the brothers.[37] But once one is initiated into the realm of deadly violence, it is difficult to escape. Not unlike

## ROAD MUSIC

### "Rooster" by Alice in Chains[38]

"Rooster" by Alice in Chains plays as the Winchesters salt and burn the body of Nurse Glockner, whose ghost they have been asked to stop by a Marine Corps buddy of their father's.[39] In the context of the scene, the song punctuates the brothers' removal of a threat and refusal to give up. However, "Rooster" has a deeper meeting. Guitarist Jerry Cantrell wrote the song for his father, a two-tour Vietnam War veteran, whose nickname was the "Rooster."[40] Rather than the immediate effects of war, the song was meant to address the long-term consequences of combat, specifically the baggage that soldiers are unable to leave behind on the field of battle.[41] Thus, "Rooster" foreshadows the cost of the Winchesters' endless war against supernatural evil.

many real-life combat veterans who struggle with returning to a mundane world devoid of the adrenaline rushes that combat provides, Sam and Dean need to hunt as much as the world needs them—the "narcotic effect" of war.[42]

### The Killer's Journey

Sam and Dean become killers as children. Trained by their father from a young age, they are taught to dehumanize their adversaries, including those unfortunate innocents possessed by demons.[43] Like combat soldiers conscripted into service, Sam and Dean convince themselves that their actions fulfill their ultimate calling: to live the lives of hunters and fight against the world's monsters.[44] Further, they begin to relish the thrill of the hunt and the kill, which becomes almost narcotic.[45]

Manifesting their own signs of *perpetrator-induced traumatic stress*,[46] Sam and Dean have difficulty maintaining relationships, are ever-vigilant and mistrusting, struggle with substance use, and engage in self-destructive behavior. As a result of the violence they inflict in their endless war, the brothers have summoned perhaps their most nefarious and persistent adversary: the demons of their actions that will continue to haunt their very souls. And, unlike the minions of Hell, the Winchesters' inner demons will remain after the fighting is over. No devil's trap or shot from the Colt can vanquish or control them.

*References*

Bertelsen, P. (1999). Free will in psychology—in search of a genuine compatibilism. *Journal of Theoretical & Philosophical Psychology, 19*(1), 41–77.

Blass, T. (2004). *The man who shocked the world: The life and legacy of Stanley Milgram.* New York, NY: Basic.

Boelen, P. A. (2015). Peritraumatic distress and dissociation in prolonged grief and posttraumatic stress following violent and unexpected deaths. *Journal of Trauma & Dissociation, 16*(5), 541–550.

Cantrell, J. (1999). *Music bank* [CD liner notes]. New York, NY: Columbia.

Ching, H., Daffern, M., & Thomas, S. (2012). Appetitive violence: A new phenomenon? *Psychiatry, Psychology & Law, 19*(5), 745–763.

DeSanti, B. (2015). The cannibal talking head: The portrayal of the windigo "monster" in popular culture and Ojibwe traditions. *Journal of Religion & Popular Culture, 27*(3), 186–201.

Downes, A. B. (2007). Restraint or propellant? Democracy and civilian fatalities in interstate wars. *Journal of Conflict Resolution, 51*(6), 872–904.

Forgas, J. P., & Fiedler, K. (1996). Us and them: Mood effects on intergroup discrimination. *Journal of Personality & Psychology, 70*(1), 28–40.

Grossman, D. (2009). *On killing: The psychological cost of learning to kill in war and society.* New York, NY: Back Bay.

Herman, J. L. (1992). Complex PTSD: A syndrome in survivors of prolonged and repeated trauma. *Journal of Traumatic Stress, 5*(3), 377–391.

Hedges, C. (2002). *War is a force that gives us meaning.* New York, NY: Anchor.

Irvine, A. (2007). *The Supernatural book of monsters, spirits, demons, and ghouls.* New York, NY: HarperCollins.

Junger, S. (2010). *War.* New York, NY: Twelve.

Kennedy, T. M., & Ceballo, R. (2016). Emotionally numb: Desensitization to community violence exposure among urban youth. *Developmental Psychology, 52*(4), 778–789.

King, C. (2016, February 18). *Why Supernatural season 11 is the best the show has been in years.* TV Overmind: http://www.tvovermind.com/supernatural/why-supernatural-season-11-is-the-best-the-show-has-been-in-years.

Kristensen, P., & Weisæth, L. (2012). Bereavement and mental health after sudden and
    violent losses: A review. *Psychiatry: Interpersonal & Biological Processes, 75*(1), 76–97.
Marlantes, K. (2011). *What it is like to go to war.* New York, NY: Atlantic Monthly
    Press.
Martens, A., Kosloff, S., & Jackson, L. E. (2010). Evidence that initial obedient killing
    fuels subsequent volitional killing beyond effects of practice. *Social Psychology &
    Personality Science, 1*(3), 268–273.
MacNair, R. M. (2002). Perpetration-induced traumatic stress in combat veterans.
    *Peace & Conflict: Journal of Peace Psychology, 8*(1), 63–72.
MacNair, R. M. (2015). Causing trauma as a form of trauma. *Peace & Conflict: Journal of
    Peace Psychology, 21*(3), 313–321.
McMahan, J. (2002). *The ethics of killing: Problems at the margins of life.* Oxford, UK:
    Oxford University Press.
Milgram, S. (1963). Behavioral study of obedience. *Journal of Abnormal & Social Psychol-
    ogy, 67*(4), 371–378.
Milgram, S. (1974). *Obedience to authority: An experimental view.* London, UK: Tavis-
    tock.
Mrug, S., Madan, A., Cook, E. W., & Wright, R. A. (2015). Emotional and physio-
    logical desensitization to real-life and movie violence. *Journal of Youth & Adolescence,
    44*(5), 1092–1108.
Nandi, C., Crombach, A., Bamboyne, J., Elbert, T., & Weierstall, R. (2015). Predic-
    tors of posttraumatic stress and appetitive aggression in active soldiers and former
    combatants. *European Journal of Psychotraumatology, 6,* ArtID 26553.
Protevi, J. (2008). Affect, agency, and responsibility: The act of killing in the age of
    cyborgs. *Phenomenology & the Cognitive Sciences, 7*(3), 405–413.
Quong, J. (2009). Killing in self-defense. *Ethics, 119*(3), 507–537.
Sasson-Levy, O. (2008). Individual bodies, collective state interests. *Men & Masculini-
    ties, 10*(3), 296–321.
Scharf, M., Mayseless, O., & Kivenson-Baron, I. (2012). Intergenerational concor-
    dance in adult attachment interviews with mothers, fathers, and adolescent sons and
    subsequent adjustment of sons to military service. *Attachment & Human Development,
    14*(4), 367–390.
Scull, N. C., Mbonyingabo, C. D., & Kotb, N. C. (2016). Transforming ordinary
    people into killers: A psychosocial examination of Hutu participation in the Tutsi
    genocide. *Peace & Conflict: Journal of Peace Psychology, 22*(4), 334–344.
Stec, F. J. (2016). Bringing attention to the human costs of war: Grievability, delibera-
    tion, and anti-war numbers. *Southern Communication Journal, 81*(5), 271–288.
Violanti, J. M., & Aron, F. (1994). Ranking police stressors. *Psychological Reports, 75,*
    824–826.

## Notes

1. Episode 5–9, "The Real Ghostbusters" (November 12, 2009).
2. Marlantes (2011).
3. King (2016).
4. Boelen (2015), Herman (1992), Kristensen & Weisæth (2012).
5. Bertelsen (1999).
6. Kennedy & Ceballo (2016), Mrug et al. (2015), Scull et al. (2016).
7. MacNair (2002).
8. Protevi (2008).

9. Downes (2007), MacNair (2015), Stec (2016).
10. Violanti & Aron (1994).
11. Grossman (2009).
12. Episode 1–20, "Dead Man's Blood" (April 20, 2006).
13. Milgram (1963).
14. Blass (2004).
15. Milgram (1974).
16. Grossman (2009).
17. Sasson-Levy (2008).
18. Scharf et al. (2012).
19. Martens et al. (2010).
20. Episode 5–9, "The Real Ghostbusters" (November 19, 2009).
21. As early as episode 1–1, "Pilot" (September 13, 2005), they acknowledge that ghosts are often suffering.
22. Marlantes (2011), p. 42.
23. Grossman (2009).
24. Forgas & Fiedler (1996).
25. Episode 1–15, "The Benders" (February 14, 2006).
26. Episode 10–18, "Book of the Damned" (April 15, 2015).
27. Episode 1–2, "Wendigo" (September 20, 2005).
28. DeSanti (2015), Irvine (2007).
29. Episode 4–4, "Metamorphosis" (October 9, 2008).
30. Episode 9–11, "First Born" (January 21, 2014).
31. Episode 9–23, "Do You Believe in Miracles?" (May 20, 2014).
32. Episode 1–6, "Skin" (October 18, 2005).
33. Marlantes (2011).
34. Grossman (2009).
35. Grossman (2009), Marlantes (2011).
36. Episode 12–6, "Celebrating the Life of Asa Fox" (November 17, 2016).
37. As early as episode 1–1, "Pilot" (September 13, 2005), when Dean asks Sam, "So what are you gonna do? Just live some normal, apple pie life? Is that it?"
38. Written by Jerry Cantrell (1993); episode 2–19, "Folsom Prison Blues" (April 26, 2007).
39. Episode 2–19, "Folsom Prison Blues" (April 26, 2007).
40. Cantrell (1999).
41. Cantrell (1999).
42. Hedges (2002).
43. Episodes 1–1, "Pilot" (September 13, 2005); 1–20, "Dead Man's Blood" (April 20, 2006); 3–8, "A Very Supernatural Christmas" (December 13, 2007).
44. Episodes 1–1, "Pilot" (September 13, 2005); 10–13, "Halt & Catch Fire" (February 10, 2015).
45. Ching et al. (2012), Nandi et al. (2015).
46. MacNair (2002).

## CHAPTER THIRTEEN

# Making a Deal with the Demon: Having Emotions Means Having Your Soul

### JANINA SCARLET
### AND JENNA BUSCH

*"That's what you get working with a demon. . . .
There's only one rule: Make a deal, keep it!"*
—Crowley[1]

*"Our contract with life is a contract that is brokered
with fragility, and with sadness, and with anxiety.
And if we're going to authentically and meaningfully
be in this world, we cannot focus on one dimension
of life and expect that focusing on that dimension
is going to then give us a well-rounded life."*
—clinical psychologist Susan David[2]

I f you had a chance to trade your soul with the demon on the crossroads in order to escape all your agonizing memories and avoid feeling physical and emotional pain, would you

187

take it? Many people naturally want to get rid of their painful emotions and experiences but, as with any demon-made deal, emotion avoidance comes at a high price.[3] Experiencing and exploring emotions can actually make people better adapted to withstand the demons of depression, the hexes of anxiety, and the monsters of past traumas.[4]

## Gambling with Your Soul: The Pros and Cons of Experiential Avoidance

People who, like the Winchester brothers, have experienced a lot of losses, trauma, and other painful events,[5] might struggle with intrusive thoughts and memories of these experiences.[6] Many might then want to try to avoid these painful experiences (*experiential avoidance*) as a way of immediately reducing their pain.[7] Some examples of experiential avoidance include drinking, evading reminders of painful events, and avoiding talking about these events.[8]

### Pros

Experiential avoidance may seem appealing, especially since it offers an immediate escape from painful sensations and memories.[9] For instance, Bobby Singer buries the memory of his father's violent behavior for most of his life in order to escape from his feelings about the violence he witnessed, endured, and returned while growing up. He also refuses to have children of his own, scared that he might harm them, and uses alcohol to manage his emotions.[10] This response to such behavior is common because denial and numbing pain may seem to be the easier path or safer than facing one's greatest fears.

# ROAD MUSIC

## Cons

On the other hand, experiential avoidance prolongs the recovery process.[16] Specifically, the more often people avoid painful experiences, the more likely they are to develop and/or struggle with depression and anxiety,[17] as well as posttraumatic stress disorder (PTSD).[18] Although Bobby is able to avoid the trauma of his childhood for most of his life, he also struggles in his marriage and ultimately has to confront his painful memories in order to move on to the next stage after his death.[19]

Avoidance of painful emotions, such as fear, anxiety, sadness, and grief, can also lead to emotional numbing, where the individual may be unable to experience emotions at all.[20] Such emotional numbing can lead to *anhedonia* (difficulty feeling any enjoyment), depression, anger, self-hatred, or hostility.[21] Indeed, when Sam loses his soul, he loses his ability to feel any

emotion at all, including guilt and joy.[22] Without the ability to
feel, it is hard or impossible to have empathy or compassion,
and to care, as indicated when soulless Sam admits to Dean that
he doesn't care about anyone.[23] Subsequently, these feelings and
behaviors can potentially affect the emotionally numbed individual's relationships with others.[24]

## Breaking Through the Mental Barrier:
## Name It and You Tame It

When Sam gets his soul back, he inevitably struggles with its
repercussions. Not having his soul for over a year after literally
surviving hellish torture arguably makes it so painful when he
finally gets his soul back.[25] When people finally allow themselves to face and process their painful emotions, they are more
likely to begin to recover.[26]

In the beginning, facing our past can be painful. In the
long run, though, it might help us recover and reduce painful
emotions.[27] Bobby visibly tries to avoid reliving the memory of
what his father did to him and his mother, but once he faces it,
he is able to move onto another stage in his death and become
a ghost so he can help Sam and Dean fight the Leviathans.[28]

When people allow themselves to feel painful emotions, they
might be able to name and process these emotions in a more
therapeutic way. For instance, people who experience a painful loss may feel an emotion of guilt in addition to sadness.
By acknowledging, naming, and recognizing these distinct
emotions, people might be able to better process their loss,
making it easier for them to recover.[29] For instance, during
his trial by the god Osiris, Dean has to confront his feelings of
guilt over the hunter Jo Harvelle's death. His own guilt over
being unable to save her seems to condemn him during the

trial. Recognizing and naming such emotions can help people accept and process their grief in healthy ways.[30] With Sam's help, Dean is then able to acknowledge that the emotion he is feeling is sadness, allowing him to move past his loss.[31]

### Getting Your Soul Back: Feel It and You Heal It

*"I deserve to be loved!"*
—Crowley[32]

> *"Why do we fear vulnerability? We are afraid that if someone finds out who we really are, they will reject us."*
> —compassion researcher Emma Seppälä[33]

One way to process and experience painful emotions is to practice *mindfulness* (present moment awareness of one's internal and external experiences).[34] Mindfulness may entail focusing on one's breath, physical sensations, or emotional experiences. Whereas most people spend much of their time focusing on the past or future problems, mindfulness requires us to pay attention to what is happening at the present time.[35] As Bobby Singer wisely advises the Winchesters, "How about we worry about today's problems?"[36]

Focusing on a current sensation, such as the breath, the feeling of our feet, the sensation of physical or emotional pain, or the sounds in our environment can help us better manage the symptoms of anxiety and depression,[37] as well as trauma and hallucinations.[38] Veterans with PTSD who practice mindfulness in terms of noticing their physical or emotional pain can demonstrate reductions in both PTSD and depression over time.[39] Sam uses this technique to help him after he cuts his left hand on broken glass. When he later experiences hallucinations

# EMOTION A DAY KEEPS
# THE REAPERS AWAY

The ability to connect with loved ones on a deep personal level can trigger "positive" emotions, such as love, gratitude, and happiness.[40] These emotions may even arise when people are supporting their loved one in a crisis.[41] For example, Dean connects on a deep level with Benny, a vampire, when they fight together in Purgatory. Even when the two arrive back in the land of the living, they express mutual gratitude and help each other[42] (increasing commitment through the *principle of reciprocity*, or repaying each other in kindness).[43] Dean even says that he feels more connected to Benny than to Sam because the two have experienced Purgatory together.[44] The ability to experience such positive emotions during a crisis can potentially increase a person's resilience to trauma, reduce depression,[45] and lengthen the lifespan.[46] Similarly, the practice of *self-compassion* (being kind toward oneself when struggling) can improve psychological and physical well-being.[47] A common self-compassion practice, for example, includes remembering a painful event, which occurred in one's childhood, and then offering compassion and soothing to oneself from a loving perspective.[48] This is what Bobby does when a reaper comes to take him into the afterlife. He has to connect with his worst memory of his abusive father and is able to offer compassionate words of comfort to his younger self for the abuse he has endured.[49]

of Lucifer, he uses a mindfulness exercise of squeezing and feeling the pain in his left hand, a concrete present–moment sensation that allows him to temporarily reduce his hallucinations.[50]

An important part of soothing painful emotions is the *willingness* to experience them. Most people naturally want to avoid unpleasant sensations. Paradoxically, trying to escape one's painful sensations can actually increase them. The willingness to experience these sensations can make them less overwhelming over time.[51] As Sam says to Dean before he gets his soul back, "Having a soul equals suffering." Dean explains that suffering can be helpful in that it can allow people to feel their emotions and recover faster.[52]

Although each Winchester often tries hunting solo, they usually find that they work better together. Facing painful emotions, as with facing terrifying demons or wicked hexes, can be easier with social support.[53] Veterans who have higher level of social support are less likely to experience post-deployment PTSD.[54] In order to cope with the pain of losing his brother, Dean turns to his girlfriend Lisa and her son Ben for comfort.[55] Such social support can help in reducing the symptoms of depression and loneliness,[56] anxiety,[57] grief, and trauma.[58]

## Emotion Is the Ultimate Anti-Demon Spell

Because the Winchesters face so much distress and trauma, and so many losses,[59] they need to adaptively process their emotions to ensure their mental health and overall survival.[60] As Death reminds Sam and Dean, the human soul is stronger than most people realize.[61] Through facing (rather than avoiding) their painful experiences, real people (not just the Winchesters) seem to function better and become more resilient.[62] Similarly, practices such as mindfulness, self-compassion, and the willingness to ask for others for help can be the ultimate keys to keeping the emotional monsters at bay.[63]

*References*

Allen, A. B., Goldwasser, E. R., & Leary, M. R. (2012). Self-compassion and well-being among older adults. *Self & Identity, 11*(4), 428–453.
Arch, J. J., Brown, K. W., Dean, D. J., Landy, L. N., Brown, K. D., & Laudenslager, M. L. (2014). Self-compassion training modulates alpha-amylase, heart rate variability, and subjective responses to social evaluative threat in women. *Psychoneuroendocrinology, 42*, 49–58.

Boeschen, L. E., Koss, M. P., Figueredo, A. J., & Coan, J. A. (2001). Experiential avoidance and post-traumatic stress disorder: A cognitive mediational model of rape recovery. *Journal of Aggression, Maltreatment & Trauma, 4*(2), 211–245.

Breheny, M., & Stephens, C. (2009). "I sort of pay back in my own little way": Managing independence and social connectedness through reciprocity. *Ageing & Society, 29*(8), 1295–1313.

Chapman, A. L., Gratz, K. L., & Brown, M. Z. (2006). Solving the puzzle of deliberate self-harm: The experiential avoidance model. *Behaviour Research & Therapy, 44*(3), 371–394.

Danner, D. D., Snowdon, D. A., & Friesen, W. V. (2001). Positive emotions in early life and longevity: Findings from the nun study. *Journal of personality and social psychology, 80*(5), 804–813.

David, S. (2016). *Emotional agility: Get unstuck, embrace change, and thrive in work and life.* New York, NY: Avery.

Dour, H. J., Wiley, J. F., Roy-Byrne, P., Stein, M. B., Sullivan, G., Sherbourne, C. D., Bystritsky, A., Rose, R. D., & Craske, M. G. (2014). Perceived social support mediates anxiety and depressive symptom changes following primary care intervention. *Depression & Anxiety, 31*(5), 436–442.

Escudero-Pérez, S., León-Palacios, M. G., Úbeda-Gómez, J., Barros-Albarrán, M. D., López-Jiménez, A. M., & Perona-Garcelán, S. (2016). Dissociation and mindfulness in patients with auditory verbal hallucinations. *Journal of Trauma & Dissociation, 17*(3), 294–306.

Feeny, N. C., Zoellner, L. A., Fitzgibbons, L. A., & Foa, E. B. (2000). Exploring the roles of emotional numbing, depression, and dissociation in PTSD. *Journal of Traumatic Stress, 13*(3), 489–498.

Forman, E. M., Herbert, J. D., Moitra, E., Yeomans, P. D., & Geller, P. A. (2007). A randomized controlled effectiveness trial of acceptance and commitment therapy and cognitive therapy for anxiety and depression. *Behavior Modification, 31*(6), 772–799.

Fredrickson, B. L., Tugade, M. M., Waugh, C. E., & Larkin, G. R. (2003). What good are positive emotions in crisis? A prospective study of resilience and emotions following the terrorist attacks on the United States on September 11th, 2001. *Journal of Personality & Social Psychology, 84*(2), 365–376.

Gallagher, M., Prinstein, M. J., Simon, V., & Spirito, A. (2014). Social anxiety symptoms and suicidal ideation in a clinical sample of early adolescents: Examining loneliness and social support as longitudinal mediators. *Journal of Abnormal Child Psychology, 42*(6), 871–883.

Guidances, C., & Watch, T. (2007). Social support and resilience to stress: from neurobiology to clinical practice. *Psychiatry, 4*(5), 35–40.

Han, S. C., Castro, F., Lee, L. O., Charney, M. E., Marx, B. P., Brailey, K., Proctor, S. P., & Vasterling, J. J. (2014). Military unit support, postdeployment social support, and PTSD symptoms among active duty and National Guard soldiers deployed to Iraq. *Journal of Anxiety Disorders, 28*(5), 446–453.

Hayes, S. C., Strosahl, K., Wilson, K. G., & Bissett, R. T. (2004). Measuring experiential avoidance: A preliminary test of a working model. *Psychological Record, 54*(4), 553–558.

Hofmann, S. G., Sawyer, A. T., Witt, A. A., & Oh, D. (2010). The effect of mindfulness-based therapy on anxiety and depression: A meta-analytic review. *Journal of Consulting and Clinical Psychology, 78*(2), 16–183.

Ironson, G., Wynings, C., Schneiderman, N., Baum, A., Rodriguez, M., Greenwood, D., Benight, C., Antoni, M., LaPerriere, A., Huang, H. S., & Klimas, N. (1997).

Posttraumatic stress symptoms, intrusive thoughts, loss, and immune function after Hurricane Andrew. *Psychosomatic Medicine, 59*(2), 128–141.

Kabat-Zinn, J. (2003). Mindfulness-based interventions in context: Past, present, and future. *Clinical Psychology: Science & Practice, 10*(2), 144–156.

Kashdan, T. B., Elhai, J. D., & Frueh, B. C. (2006). Anhedonia and emotional numbing in combat veterans with PTSD. *Behaviour Research & Therapy, 44*(3), 457–467.

Kearney, D. J., McDermott, K., Malte, C., Martinez, M., & Simpson, T. L. (2012). Association of participation in a mindfulness program with measures of PTSD, depression and quality of life in a veteran sample. *Journal of Clinical Psychology, 68*(1), 101–116.

Larsen, S. E., & Berenbaum, H. (2015). Are specific emotion regulation strategies differentially associated with posttraumatic growth versus stress? *Journal of Aggression, Maltreatment & Trauma, 24*(7), 794–808.

Levitt, J. T., Brown, T. A., Orsillo, S. M., & Barlow, D. H. (2004). The effects of acceptance versus suppression of emotion on subjective and psychophysiological response to carbon dioxide challenge in patients with panic disorder. *Behavior Therapy, 35*(4), 747–766.

Liu, L., Gou, Z., & Zuo, J. (2016). Social support mediates loneliness and depression in elderly people. *Journal of Health Psychology, (21)*5, 750–758.

McIlwaine, F., & O'Sullivan, K. (2015). "Riding the wave": Working systemically with traumatised families. *Australian & New Zealand Journal of Family Therapy, 36*(3), 310–324.

Neff, K. (2011). *Self-Compassion.* Chicago, IL: Hachette UK.

Neff, K. D., Kirkpatrick, K. L., & Rude, S. S. (2007). Self-compassion and adaptive psychological functioning. *Journal of Research in Personality, 41*(1), 139–154.

Parzefall, M. (2008). Psychological contracts and reciprocity: A study in Finnish context. *International Journal of Human Resource Management, 19*(9), 1703–1719.

Plumb, J. C., Orsillo, S. M., & Luterek, J. A. (2004). A preliminary test of the role of experiential avoidance in post-event functioning. *Journal of Behavior Therapy & Experimental Psychiatry, 35*(3), 245–257.

Ruscio, A. M., Weathers, F. W., King, L. A., & King, D. W. (2002). Male war-zone veterans' perceived relationships with their children: The importance of emotional numbing. *Journal of Traumatic Stress, 15*(5), 351–357.

Seppälä, E. (2014, October 29). *The best kept secret to intimacy: Vulnerability.* Huffington Post: http://www.huffingtonpost.com/emma-seppala-phd/the-best-kept-secret-to-i_b_5986870.html.

Simpson, T., Jakupcak, M., & Luterek, J. A. (2006). Fear and avoidance of internal experiences among patients with substance use disorders and PTSD: The centrality of anxiety sensitivity. *Journal of Traumatic Stress, 19*(4), 481–491.

Tull, M. T., & Gratz, K. L. (2008). Further examination of the relationship between anxiety sensitivity and depression: The mediating role of experiential avoidance and difficulties engaging in goal-directed behavior when distressed. *Journal of Anxiety Disorders, 22*(2), 199–210.

van Rooij, A. J., Kuss, D. J., Griffiths, M. D., Shorter, G. W., Schoenmakers, T. M., & Van De Mheen, D. (2014). The (co-)occurrence of problematic video gaming, substance use, and psychosocial problems in adolescents. *Journal of Behavioral Addictions, 3*(3), 157–165.

Wang, K., Weiss, N. H., Pachankis, J. E., & Link, B. G. (2016). Emotional clarity as a buffer in the association between perceived mental illness stigma and suicide risk. *Stigma & Health, 1*(4), 252–262.

Williams, D. P., Cash, C., Rankin, C., Bernardi, A., Koenig, J., & Thayer, J. F. (2015). Resting heart rate variability predicts self-reported difficulties in emotion regulation: A focus on different facets of emotion regulation. *Frontiers in Psychology, 6*, 261.

Xu, J., & Roberts, R. E. (2010). The power of positive emotions: It's a matter of life or death—Subjective well-being and longevity over 28 years in a general population. *Health Psychology, 29*(1), 9–19.

## Notes

1. Episodes 5–20, "The Devil You Know" (April 29, 2010); 7–8, "Time for a Wedding" (November 11, 2011).
2. David (2016).
3. Chapman et al. (2006).
4. Forman et al. (2007), Kearney et al. (2012).
5. Episode 2–1, "In My Time of Dying" (September 28, 2006).
6. e.g., Ironson et al. (1997).
7. Plumb et al. (2004).
8. Simpson et al. (2006).
9. Hayes et al. (2004).
10. Episode 7–10, "Death's Door" (December 2, 2011).
11. Written by B. Squier (1981); played in episode 9–14, "Captives" (February 25, 2014).
12. Gallagher et al. (2014), van Rooij et al. (2014).
13. Episode 9–16, "Thin Man" (March, 4, 2014).
14. Gallagher et al. (2014).
15. Episode 2–22, "Who We Are" (May 18, 2017).
16. Boeschen et al. (2001).
17. Tull & Gratz (2008).
18. Boeschen et al. (2001).
19. Episode 7–10, "Death's Door" (December 2, 2011).
20. Feeny et al. (2000).
21. Kashdan et al. (2006).
22. Episode 6–1, "Exile on Main Street" (September 24, 2010).
23. Episode 6–7, "Family Matters" (November 5, 2010).
24. Ruscio et al. (2002).
25. Episode 6–11, "Appointment in Samarra" (December 10, 2011).
26. Larsen & Berenbaum (2015).
27. McIlwaine & O'Sullivan (2015).
28. Episode 7–10, "Death's Door" (December 2, 2011).
29. Wang et al. (2016).
30. Wang et al. (2016).
31. Episode 7–4, "Defending Your Life" (October 14, 2011).
32. Episode 8–23, "Sacrifice" (May 15, 2013).
33. Seppälä (2014).
34. Hofmann et al. (2010).
35. Kabat-Zinn (2003).
36. Episode 7–3, "The Girl Next Door" (October 7, 2011).
37. Hofmann et al. (2010).
38. Escudero-Pérez et al. (2016).
39. Kearney et al. (2012).

40. Fredrickson et al. (2003).

41. Fredrickson et al. (2003).

42. e.g., Dean helps Benny in episode 8–5, "Blood Brother" (October 31, 2012); Benny helps Dean in 8–19, "Taxi Driver" (April 3, 2013).

43. Breheny et al. (2009), Parzefall (2008).

44. Episode 8–5, "Blood Brother" (October 31, 2012).

45. Fredrickson et al. (2003).

46. Danner et al. (2001), Xu & Roberts (2010).

47. Allen et al. (2012), Arch et al. (2014), Neff et al. (2007).

48. Neff (2011).

49. Episode 7–10, "Death's Door" (December 2, 2011).

50. Episodes 7–2, "Hello, Cruel World" (September 30, 2011); 7–3, "The Girl Next Door" (October 7, 2011).

51. Levitt et al. (2004).

52. Episode 6–9, "Clap Your Hands If You Believe" (November 11, 2010).

53. Guidances & Watch (2007), Han et al. (2014).

54. Han et al. (2014).

55. Episode 6–1, "Exile on Main Street" (September 24, 2010).

56. Liu et al. (2016).

57. Dour et al. (2014).

58. Han et al. (2014).

59. Episodes 1–1, "Pilot" (September 13, 2005); 2–1, "In My Time of Dying" (September 28, 2006).

60. Levitt et al. (2004).

61. Episode 6–11, "Appointment in Samarra" (December 10, 2010).

62. Episodes 7–2, "Hello, Cruel World" (September 30, 2011); 7–3, "The Girl Next Door" (October 7, 2011).

63. Allen et al. (2012), Arch et al. (2014), Kabat-Zinn (2003), Neff et al. (2007).

# Bargaining

*"Stage three: Bargaining."*
—Tessa, a Reaper[1]

*"I went to the crossroad, fell down on my knees. Asked the Lord above, 'Have mercy, now save poor Bob, please."*
—singer/songwriter Robert Leroy Johnson[2]

Regarding the so-called *bargaining stage*, psychiatrist Elisabeth Kübler-Ross mainly talked about terminally ill patients pleading for doctors to use science or God to use omnipotent power to extend their lives.[3] In her experience, the dying individual trying this would typically make some promise, the bargain, to do something for science (e.g., donate organs) or for God (e.g, perform charitable works), and these promises tend to reflect whatever he or she feels guilty about doing or not doing. A number of characters in *Supernatural* pray to God for deliverance for themselves or others.[4] Some of those at death's door plead for Reapers to let them live instead of moving on, but Reapers know the dangerous consequences of violating the natural order and they do not deal either.[5] Characters who turn elsewhere to make deals are the ones whose consequences create the kind of crises that drive plot.

The temptation to "deal with the devil" is not unique to fiction in which such deals can be literal. History is replete with examples of people making deals with dictators, drug lords, bandits, slave traders, robber barons, crooked businessfolk, and others whose actions hurt others.[6] How many people dealt with the Nazis to spare their lives, their communities, their art collections?[7] How many trade goods, even weapons, with despots in exchange for funds, information, technology, or items that benefit themselves no matter who their customers might turn around and destroy? Some characters who make deals with Crowley and other crossroad demons seek personal prosperity and achievements[8] while others seek revenge or retribution,[9] but some make their deals for selfless reasons, usually to extend their loved ones' lives.[10]

Kübler-Ross's patients' bargains included the promises, whether explicitly stated or implicitly understood, that each would ask for an extension only once and would not try to change the bargain after setting a self-imposed deadline when they would get what they wanted. "None of our patients have 'kept their promise,'" she reported. Each of those who survived to reach the first goal would purpose postponement of the death sentence once more. Setting a new goal after reaching one can be adaptive, of course. A few keep cheating death and proving their doctors wrong, and the hope of becoming one of those few keeps others going. Many characters who make crossroad deals go to great lengths to break those deals. Some succeed, such as Bobby Singer who blackmails Crowley into releasing after Crowley's "best efforts" fail to return Singer's soul to him.[11] Most fail. Notable among those is Dean Winchester himself, killed by hellhounds and sent to Hell where months pass like decades until the angel Castiel finally brings him back.[12]

John, Mary, Dean, and Sam Winchester each offer to give up their lives and sometimes their souls to save immediate family members. "Take me instead" is a common bargaining cry among those whose loved ones are at risk.[13] After death in the real world, the focus of bargaining changes, such as by praying for a respite from suffering more family tragedies once one tragedy has happened and entered the past, but some people try making deals of other kinds in order to reunite with departed loved ones. Séances for the dead are big business. Customers who grow disenchanted with such attempts to reach the dead may find peace in other ways, while some grow gloomier. When no one will bargain with Sam to retrieve Dean from Hell, his mood grows dark and his behavior takes a turn into an addictive, self-destructive spiral.[14]

## References

Benjamin, L. T., Jr., & Baker, D. B. (2004). *From Séance to science: A history of the profession of psychology in America.* Belmont, CA: Wadsworth.

Hoff, J. (2007). *A Faustian foreign policy from Woodrow Wilson to George W. Bush: Dreams of perfectibility.* Cambridge, UK: Cambridge University Press.

Kübler-Ross, E. (1969). *On death and dying: What the dying have to teach doctors, nurses, clergy, & their own families.* London, UK: Routledge.

Kübler-Ross, E., & Kessler, D. (2005/2014). *On grief and grieving: Finding the meaning of grief through the five stages of loss.* New York, NY: Scribner.

Lothane, Z. (2001). The deal with the devil to "save" psychoanalysis in Nazi Germany. *Psychoanalytic Review, 88*(2), 195–224.

Mellen, J. (2016). *Faustian bargains: Lyndon Johnson and Mac Wallace in the robber baron culture of Texas.* London, UK: Bloomsbury.

Petropoulos, J. (2000). *The Faustian bargain: The art world in Nazi Germany.* Oxford, UK: Oxford University Press.

## Notes

1. Episode 2–1, "In My Time of Dying" (September 28, 2006).
2. From "Cross Road Blues" a.k.a. "Crossroads" by Johnson, R. L. (1936 recording, 1937 release).
3. Kübler-Ross (1969); Kübler-Ross & Kessler (2005/2014).
4. e.g., Layla—episode 1–12, "Faith" (January 17, 2006); Dean—4–18, "The Monster at the End of This Book" (April 2, 2009), 5–14, "My Bloody Valentine" (February 11, 2010); Sam—11–2, "Form and Void" (October 14, 2015).
5. Episodes 2–1, "In My Time of Dying" (September 28, 2006); 6–11, "Appointment in Samarra" (December 20, 2010).
6. Hoff (2007); Mellen (2016).
7. e.g., Lothane (2001); Petropoulos (2000).
8. Episodes 2–8, "Crossroad Blues" (November 16, 2006);
9. Episode 3–15, "Time is on My Side" (May 8, 2008).
10. Episode 2–22, "All Hell Breaks Loose," part 2 (May 17, 2007).
11. Episode 6–4, "Weekend at Bobby's" (October 15, 2010).
12. Episode 3–16, "No Rest for the Wicked" (May 15, 2008); 4–1, "Lazarus Rising" (September 18, 2008).
13. Kübler-Ross (1969).
14. Season 4 (2008–2009).

# PART IV

# ABOVE AND BELOW

# CHAPTER FOURTEEN

# Personal Purgatories, Mental Illness, and a Manual of Lore

## TRAVIS LANGLEY

*"Now, you wanna stand there and therapize, or you wanna get me some coffee? Make it Irish."*
—Bobby Singer[1]

*"Not quite in hell, not quite on earth, even. Purgatory is now, somewhere in the middle of life's journey."*
—psychotherapist Dorothy Firman[2]

No matter how hellish a severe mental illness may feel, we try to maintain hope that it is purgatory, neither hell nor heaven but a state somewhere in between, and that instead of lingering in a dark place or descending somewhere darker, the individual who is suffering can one day rise into something better. To treat a mental illness, mental health professionals seek to identify the person's difficulty (to name it—*diagnosis*), and then estimate whether that person's future looks likely to

# ROAD MUSIC

darken, brighten, or remain much the same (*prognosis*). Over the course of several generations, the American Psychiatric Association (APA) developed its *Diagnostic and Statistical Manual of Mental Disorders* (DSM) to help with these categories, starting with diagnosis.[6] This text has become the psychiatric standard that still applies today in the real world and apparently the *Supernatural* world too: In one of Sam's hallucinations of Lucifer, he sees the Devil flipping through an edition of the manual.[7]

Early editions of the DSM were heavily influenced by the *psychoanalytic* approach, in other words, by the views of Sigmund Freud and his followers.[8] Freud classified mental illness as either *neurosis* (any of the nonpsychotic conditions that arise when a person does not adequately use defense mechanisms to manage unconscious conflicts) or *psychosis* (any condition disconnected from reality). His influential views on psychopathology entered a purgatory of their own, not fully accepted but not fully rejected either.

## Neurosis: Every Problem That's Not Psychosis?

Even though *neurotic* is not a modern diagnostic term, we still talk about what it means because the concept has infiltrated everyday language and become a stereotype, perhaps because of the common appearance of the "neurotic" character in entertainment. When Dean describes a TV character as "the sexy yet neurotic doctor over there" or Ketch calls Lady Toni Bevell "a neurotic, overreaching time bomb,"[9] viewers can easily understand that they're asserting that the women in question do not manage their worries well. Each may mean something more specific than that, but one key criticism of the word *neurotic* is the accusation that it is not specific.[10] In 1980, the APA dropped *neurosis* as a categorical term for mental disorders involving chronic distress because it lacked specificity and because not everyone agreed with the Freudian ideas regarding the term's origins.[11] Freud felt that every person is neurotic to one degree or another, having some area of life that he or she does not manage perfectly well even when those difficulties are not severe enough that we would think of them as mental illnesses. Out of all the Winchesters' many behaviors that might be considered neurotic, the characters discuss at least one by referring to a diagnostic term: Sam's phobia toward clowns.[12]

### Coulrophobia: Not Everybody Loves a Clown

Like some bit of ancient arcana, the origin of the term *coulrophobia* (clown phobia) may be lost to history. The term does not appear before the late twentieth century.[13] Its prefix *coulro-* means nothing in Greek or English,[14] and dictionaries disagree on how to pronounce it.[15] Is the first syllable pronounced "cool," "cole," "call," or "cowl"? The history of the phobia itself is difficult to pin down,[16] in part because many people think they have phobias when they do not. A person can fear something strongly without qualifying as having a mental illness, in this case a *phobic disorder.*

When Dean calls Sam's aversion "clown phobia,"[17] is he right? *Phobia* is a diagnostic term for an intense, unrealistic, maladaptive fear.[18] Rather than list thousands of stimulus-specific phobias such as *coulrophobia, aerophobia* (flying), and *claustrophobia* (enclosed spaces), the APA subsumes most under the diagnosis *specific phobia* (previously called *simple phobia*[19]), which would be the diagnosis for a person like Sam if he meets these criteria:

- The fear must be severe.
- Nearly every encounter with the feared stimulus produces fear or anxiety.
- The person either avoids the stimulus or endures it with intense distress.
- The fear is disproportionate to any real danger.
- The condition persists for at least six months.[20]

Intensity can be difficult to quantify when describing an emotional experience. Is the difficulty *maladaptive*? In other words, does it interfere with the person's ability to function, to adapt to life? Also, is the fear unrealistic? On their way to investigate a report of a deadly phantom clown, the brothers both argue that their respective fears are realistic:

**Sam:** "At least I'm not afraid of flying."
**Dean:** "Planes crash!"
**Sam:** "And apparently clowns kill."[21]

Not only is avoidant behavior a symptom of phobia, it also worsens anxiety in the long run when momentary relief rewards avoidance through *negative reinforcement* (reward by removing something).[22] The brothers show examples of both avoiding fears and facing them head on. Despite his aversion, Sam does not avoid clowns, as shown in an early episode when Sam is the one who decides he and Dean should investigate a possible killer clown.[23] In contrast, Dean goes to greater lengths to avoid flying, and on the rare occasions when he does fly, he has difficulty managing his discomfort.[24]

Treatment for aversion to clowns, as with any dreaded stimulus, will at some stage involve encountering the stimulus—facing the fear. Fighting a nightmare clown feels "therapeutic" to Sam,[25] and yet he later tenses up when a clown merely steps into an elevator with him.[26] The fact that the elevator clown then tries to kill him would not help prevent future fears. Although a gradual exposure technique such as *systematic desensitization* tends to be more effective,[27] some clinicians find value in abrupt, intense exposure to a feared stimulus (*flooding* or *implosive therapy*[28]). If not handled properly, such immersion risks creating yet another unpleasant experience that reinforces escape or avoidance.[29] A fight to the death in an elevator does not follow supervised therapeutic procedures.

## Psychosis: "Crazy Brains"

*Psychosis* remains a modern description for a range of symptoms and conditions in which the individual severely loses touch with reality, especially *hallucination* (a perception not based on real sensory experience) and *delusion* (a firm belief that severely distorts reality). Whereas Freud defined *neurosis* in terms of his assumptions about unconscious causes, he defined *psychosis* in terms of the manifest symptoms, and that suited the APA's eventual approach of categorizing mental disorders according to symptoms rather than causes.[30] Psychotic conditions arise from diverse origins, many of which are clearly biological in nature.

*Supernatural* touches on biological origins of mental illness when a wraith employed as a psychiatric nurse tells Sam that she likes "crazy brains. They get soaked in dopamine and adrenaline and just all sorts of hormones and chemicals that make them delicious—and the crazier they are, the better they taste."[31] Imbalances in *neurotransmitters* (chemicals that transmit signals in the nervous system) or *hormones* (regulatory chemicals produced by other cells and glands) are indeed associated with a variety of mental difficulties.[32] While we don't know how those chemicals taste to a wraith, we do know that pleasurable foods such as chocolate make the brain release dopamine,[33] a neurotransmitter important for emotion, movement, and many other functions.[34] People suffering schizophrenia often have too much dopamine. People also seek out caffeine, cocaine, and other substances that make the body quickly release *adrenaline* (a.k.a. *epinephrine*) and *noradrenaline* (*norepinephrine*), the body's natural stimulants. Elevated levels of both can be associated with *mania*, the extremely energized pole in bipolar disorder,[35] and severe mania can result in *manic psychosis* with symptoms such as delusions and hallucinations.[36]

However, could the opposite occur: a situation in which hallucinations cause an increase in dopamine levels? The wraith makes Dean start hallucinating. As soon as the creature dies, the hallucinations stops and Dean reports that he is no longer crazy, "not any more than usual."[37] Neurotransmitter levels should not return to normal so abruptly. Because the extra dopamine should not simply vanish, this would suggest that Dean's neurotransmitters were not the original cause of his hallucinations. What if, in *Supernatural*, instead of using dopamine to produce Dean's hallucinations, the wraith is using the hallucinations to start raising his dopamine levels? Our behavior can cause neurotransmitter release.[38] Mimicking happiness, sadness, and other mental states can make our brains begin to function as if those states were real, which can then make them real.[39] If hallucinations caused by means other than neurotransmitter elevation subsequently boost dopamine, that would explain why the wraith does not drain a brain right away. A number of disorders with known physiological signs such as abnormal neurotransmitter levels have a chicken-egg riddle about them regarding which came first, the obvious symptom or what seems to be the underlying cause.[40]

### How Well Can a Hallucination Diagnose?

After a hallucination of Lucifer (called "Hallucifer" by fans[41]) pesters Sam to keep him awake for five days straight, Sam lands in a psychiatric hospital in the throes of a "full-blown psychotic episode."[42] Even a person not already hallucinating will become psychotic if deprived of sleep long enough.[43]

At one point during his hospitalization, Sam hallucinates Lucifer flipping through the DSM-IV-TR and assessing himself: "Narcissistic personality disorder. Okay, now this one I could have." A person with *narcissistic personality disorder* is superegotistical, showing a pervasive pattern of selfish grandiosity and need for attention. A person can seem very egotistical without the trait defining who that individual is as a human being. The trait does, however, define the narcissist. "Sets unrealistic goals—check," Lucifer says, perhaps paraphrasing from the text because the DSM-IV-TR does not say that. Its diagnostic criteria instead include preoccupation with "fantasies of unlimited success, power, brilliance, beauty, or ideal love."[44] The hallucinated Devil continues, "But trouble keeping healthy relationships? Not so sure about that one. Thoughts?" Although this is not required in its diagnostic criteria, the manual does mention that narcissists' relationships "are typically impaired" [45] due to their self-absorption and insensitivity.

A hallucination will provide no information more accurate than anything its sufferer knows. So how could a hallucinatory tormentor read the DSM to Sam and get any of the book's information roughly correct even if it was paraphrased? Knowledge comes from somewhere. Without invoking psychic phenomena (admittedly a feature of *Supernatural* fiction[46]), information accurately conveyed by a hallucination or dream involves picking up something heard or seen around the psychotic or dreaming person, guessing correctly, or retrieving details already stored somewhere in that individual's brain.[47] Sam's disturbed brain might draw from personal experience such as his voluntary infiltration of a mental hospital when he is investigating the aforementioned wraith,[48] any psychology class he might have taken during college,[49] or simply the fact that he is a well-read person.

Why would a hallucination make the individual think about a specific personality disorder, though? Psychotic ramblings can be creative, illogical, beyond understanding, and simply without any fathomable connection to real life, especially if the individual experiences incoherence or the common schizophrenic symptom known as *loosening of associations*.[50] It might not be random, though. Hallucinatory content can make understandable connections that the conscious mind normally might miss or may draw from previous experience.[51] The meaning may be what the hallucination's obvious *manifest content* expresses: that narcissistic personality disorder fits Lucifer well. If there is a deeper meaning that Sam does not consciously recognize, such as projecting a narcissistic assessment of himself onto someone else, that would be what a Freudian could consider the hallucination's *latent content*.[52] A non-Freudian might consider it to be a simple *association* (connection between different situations or stimuli[53]) if Sam associates mental hospitals or his own hallucinations (because Sam is aware he's hallucinating even if he begins having trouble distinguishing which experiences are real) with that particular diagnosis—in this case, if he knows that a nonexistent doctor previously hallucinated by his brother accused Dean of being psychotic with narcissistic personality disorder.[54] Some professionals will consider all of these possibilities and more, but some fall into the trap of interpreting every client's experience in terms of a specific psychological paradigm.

Viewers familiar with the DSM, upon seeing Lucifer reading it to Sam in a rerun, could get the impression that the television program used an out-of-date edition of the manual. Not so! The American Psychiatric Association finally released the manual's fifth edition, called the DSM-5, in 2013.[55] The revised fourth edition (DSM-IV-TR[56]) seen on screen would not become out of date until after Sam's hallucination of Lucifer perusing it and would have been current during both of Sam's stays in mental hospitals.[57]

## Rising out of Purgatory

The DSM is a diagnostic tool, a starting point to help the clinician give a name to a person's difficulty out of the hundreds of mental disorders that the manual names. It provides a shared language so that different professionals can discuss these conditions and, it is hoped, generally understand what the others are talking about. It is a book of lore, not a spellbook filled with incantations and solutions. Mental illness rarely has an easy explanation. We can hope for every person to get better even though we know that not all will. We can hope that our methods of assessing their problems and trying to help them will also allow them to move away from the darkness and closer toward the light at the end of the tunnel.

## References

American Psychiatric Association (1952). *Diagnostic and statistical manual of mental disorders* (1st ed.) (DSM-I). Washington, DC: American Psychiatric Association.

American Psychiatric Association (1968). *Diagnostic and statistical manual of mental disorders* (2nd ed.) (DSM-II). Washington, DC: American Psychiatric Association.

American Psychiatric Association (1980). *Diagnostic and statistical manual of mental disorders* (3rd ed.) (DSM-III). Washington, DC: American Psychiatric Association.

American Psychiatric Association (1987). *Diagnostic and statistical manual of mental disorders* (3rd ed., rev.) (DSM-III-R). Washington, DC: American Psychiatric Association.

American Psychiatric Association (2000). *Diagnostic and statistical manual of mental disorders* (4th ed., text revision) (DSM-IV-TR). Washington, DC: American Psychiatric Association.

American Psychiatric Association (2013). *Diagnostic and statistical manual of mental disorders* (5th ed.) (DSM-5). Washington, DC: American Psychiatric Association.

Aschebrock, Y., Gavey, N., McCreanor, T., & Tippett, L. (2003). Is the content of delusions and hallucinations important? *Australasian Psychiatry, 11*(3), 306–311.

Auchincloss, E. L., & Samberg, E. (Eds.) (2012). *Psychoanalytic terms and concepts.* New Haven, CT: Yale University Press.

Bartels-Velthuis, A. A., van de Willige, G., Jenner, J. A., Wiersma, D., & van Os, J. (2012). Auditory hallucinations in childhood: Associations with adversity and delusional ideation. *Psychological Medicine, 42*(3), 583–593.

Beentjes, T. A., Goossens, P. J., & Poslawsky, I. E. (2012). Caregiver burden in bipolar hypomania and mania: A systematic review. *Perspectives in Psychiatric Care, 48*(1), 187–197.

Bleuler, E. (1911/1950). *Dementia praecox or the group of schizophrenias* (H. Zinkin, Trans.). New York, NY: International Universities Press.

Brébion, G., Ohlsen, R. I., Bressan, R. A., & David, A. S. (2012). Source memory errors in schizophrenia, hallucinations, and negative symptoms: A synthesis of research findings. *Psychological Medicine, 42*(12), 2543–2554.

Carlson, N. R. (2008). *Foundations of physiological psychology* (7th ed.). Boston, MA: Pearson.

Chawla, N., & Ostafin, B. (2007). Experiential avoidance as a functional dimensional approach to psychopathology: An empirical review. *Journal of Clinical Psychology, 63*(9), 871–890.

Culbertson, F. (1995, July 17). *The phobia list.* The Phobia List: http://phobialist.com.

D'Onofrio, M. A., & D'Onofrio, E. (1998). *Psychiatric words and phrases* (2nd ed.). Modesto, CA: Health Professions Institute.

Ekman, P., & Davidson, R. J. (1993). Voluntarily smiling changes regional brain activity. *Psychological Science, 4*(5), 342–345.

Firman, D. (2010, August 3). *Twixt heaven and hell.* Psychology Today: https://www.psychologytoday.com/blog/living-life-purpose/201008/twixt-heaven-and-hell.

Freud, S. (1900/2010). *The interpretation of dreams* (J. Strachey, Trans.). New York, NY: Sterling.

Gilleland, M. (2010, June 18). *Coulrophobia?* Laudator Temporis Acti: https://laudator-temporisacti.blogspot.ca/2010/06/coulrophobia.html.

Hayes, S. C., Wilson, K. G., Gifford, E. V., Follette, V. M., & Strosahl, K. (1996). Experiential avoidance and behavioral disorders: A functional dimensional approach to diagnosis and treatment. *Journal of Consulting & Clinical Psychology, 64*(6), 1152–1168.

Iversen, L., Iversen, S., Dunnett, S., & Bjorklund, A. (2009). *Dopamine handbook.* Oxford, UK: Oxford University Press.

Joyce, P. R., Fergusson, D. M., Woollard, G., Abbott, R. M., Horwood, L. J., & Upton, J. (1995). Urinary catecholamines and plasma hormones predict mood state in rapid cycling bipolar affective disorder. *Journal of Affective Disorders, 33*(4), 233–243.

Kalanthroff, E., Abramovitch, A., Steinman, S. A., Abramowitz, J. S., & Simpson, H. B. (2016). The chicken or the egg: What drives OCD? *Journal of Obsessive-Compulsive & Related Disorders, 11*(1), 9–12.

Kramer, P. D. (2008, November 18). *Chicken and egg: Does depression cause brain change, or does brain change cause depression?* Psychology Today: https://www.psychologyto-day.com/blog/in-practice/200811/chicken-and-egg.

Kühn, S. Müller, B. C. N., van der Leij, A., Dijksterhuis, A., Brass, M., & van Baaren, R. B. (2011). Neural correlates of emotional synchrony. *Social Cognitive & Affective Neuroscience, 6*(3), 368–374.

Langley, T. (2017, February 24). *The lost origin of coulrophobia, the abnormal fear of clowns,* Psychology Today: https://www.psychologytoday.com/blog/beyond-heroes-and-villains/201702/the-lost-origin-of-coulrophobia-the-abnormal-fear-clowns.

Malinowski, J. E., & Horton, C. L. (2014). Memory sources of dreams: The incorporation or autobiographical rather than episodic experiences. *Journal of Sleep Research, 23*(4), 441–447.

Merikangas, K. R., & Pato, M. (2009). Recent developments in the epidemiology of bipolar disorder in adults and children: Magnitude, correlates, and future directions. *Clinical Psychology: Science & Practice, 16*(2), 122–133.

Merriam-Webster (n.d.). *Coulrophobia.* Merriam-Webster Medical Dictionary: https://www.merriam-webster.com/medical/coulrophobia.

Nehlig, A. (2013). The neuroprotective effects of cocoa flavanol and its influence on cognitive performance. *British Journal of Clinical Psychopharmacology, 75*(3), 716–727.

Oxford Living Dictionaries (n.d.). *Coulrophobia.* Oxford Living Dictionaries: https://en.oxforddictionaries.com/definition/coulrophobia.

Patten, S. B. (2006). A major depression prognosis calculator based on episode duration. *Clinical Practice & Epidemiology in Mental Health, 2*, Article D: 13.

Petrovsky, N. Ettinger, U., Hill, A., Frenzel, L., Meyhöfer, I. Wagner, M., Backhaus, J., & Kumari, V. (2014). Sleep deprivation disrupts inhibition and induces psychosis-like symptoms in healthy humans. *Journal of Neuroscience, 34*(7), 9134–9140.

Radford, B. (2016). *Bad clowns.* Albuquerque, NM: University of New Mexico Press.

Rhodes, J. E., & Jakes, S. (2004). The contribution of metaphor and metonymy to delusions. *Psychology & Psychotherapy: Theory, Research & Practice, 77*(1), 1–17.

Solesvik, M., Joa, I., Larsen, T. K., Langeveld, J., Johannessen, J. O., Bjørnestad, J., Anda, L. G., Gisselgård, J., Velden Hegelstad, W. T., & Brønnick, K (2016). Visual hallucinations in first-episode psychosis: Association with childhood trauma. *PLoS ONE, 11*(5), Article D e0153458.

Stampfl, T. G., & Lewis, D. J. (1967). Essentials of implosive therapy: A learning-theory-based psychodynamic behavioral therapy. *Journal of Abnormal Psychology, 72*(6), 496–503.

Steiner, J., Bernstein, H., Schiltz, K., Müller, U. J., Westphal, S., Drexhage, H. A., & Bogerts, B. (2014). Immune system and glucose metabolism interaction in schizophrenia: A chicken-egg dilemma. *Progress in Neuro-Psychopharmacology & Biological Psychiatry, 48*(3), 287–294.

Sundel, M., & Stone-Sundel, S. (2005). *Behavior change in the human services.* Thousand Oaks, CA: SAGE.

Supernatural Wiki (n.d.). *Hallucifer.* Supernatural Wiki: http://www.supernaturalwiki.com/index.php?title=Hallucifer.

Swann, A. C., Katz, M. M., Bowden, C. L., Berman, N. G., & Stokes, P. E. (1999). Psychomotor performance and monoamine function in bipolar and unipolar affective disorders. *Biological Psychiatry, 45*(8), 979–988.

Swensen, C. H., Jr., & Pascal, G. R. (1954). Duration of illness as a prognostic indicator in mental illness. *Journal of Consulting & Clinical Psychology, 18*(5), 363–365.

Thorndike, E. L. (1931). *Human learning.* New York, NY: Appleton.

Weinstein, A., Livny, A., & Weizman, A. (2017). New developments in brain research of internet and gaming disorder. *Neuroscience & Biobehavioral Reviews, 75*, 314–330.

Wittlink, M. N., Oslin, D., Knott, K. A., Coyne, J. C., Gallo, J. J., & Zubritsky, C. (2005). Personal characteristics and depression-related attitudes of older adults and participation in stages of implementation of a multi-site effectiveness trial (PRISE-E). *International Journal of Geriatric Psychiatry, 20*(1), 927–937.

Wolpe, J. (1969). *The practice of behavior therapy.* New York, NY: Pergamon.

## Notes

1. Episode 6–17, "My Heart Will Go On" (April 15, 2011).
2. Firman (2010).
3. Written by T. Scholz (1977); featured in episode 1–7, "Hook Man" (October 25, 2005).
4. Patten (2006); Swensen & Pascal (1954); Wittlink et al. (2005).
5. American Psychiatric Association (2013).
6. American Psychiatric Association (1952; 1968; 1980; 2000; 2013).
7. American Psychiatric Association (2000).
8. American Psychiatric Association (1952; 1968).
9. Respectively, episodes 5–8, "Changing Channels" (November 5, 2009); 12–14, "The Raid" (March 2, 2017).
10. Auchincloss & Samberg (2012).
11. American Psychiatric Association (1980).
12. Episode 7–14, "Plucky Pennywhistle's Magical Menagerie" (February 10, 2012).
13. Possibly no earlier than Culbertson (1995) online and D'Onofrio & D'Onofrio (1998) in print.
14. Gilleland (2010); Langley (2017).
15. Compare Merriam-Webster (n.d.) and Oxford Living Dictionary (n.d.).
16. Radford (2016).
17. Episode 7–14, "Plucky Pennywhistle's Magical Menagerie" (February 10, 2012).
18. American Psychiatric Association (2013).
19. American Psychiatric Association (1987).
20. American Psychiatric Association (2013).
21. Episode 2–2, "Everybody Loves a Clown" (October 5, 2006).
22. Chawla & Ostafin (2007); Hayes et al. (1996).
23. Episode 2–2, "Everybody Loves a Clown" (October 5, 2006).

24. Episode 1–4, "Phantom Traveler" (October 4, 2005).
25. Episode 7–14, "Plucky Pennywhistle's Magical Menagerie" (February 10, 2012).
26. Episode 11–7, "Plush" (November 18, 2015). He tenses before he spies the clown's bloody scalpel.
27. Wolpe (1969).
28. Stampfl & Lewis (1967).
29. Sundel & Stone-Sundel (2005).
30. American Psychiatric Association (1980).
31. Episode 5–11, "Sam, Interrupted" (January 23, 2010).
32. Carlson (2008).
33. Nehlig (2013).
34. Iversen et al. (2009).
35. Joyce et al. (1995); Swann et al. (1999).
36. Beentjes et al. (2012).
37. Episode 5–11, "Sam, Interrupted" (January 23, 2010).
38. Weinstein et al. (2017).
39. Ekman & Davidson (1993); Kühn et al. (2011).
40. Kalanthroff et al. (2016); Kramer (2008); Steiner et al. (2014).
41. Supernatural Wiki (n.d.).
42. Episode 7–17, "The Born-Again Identity" (March 23, 2012).
43. Petrovsky et al. (2014).
44. American Psychiatric Association (2000), p. 717.
45. American Psychiatric Association (2000), p. 716.
46. As shown by psychics (among others) such as Missouri Moseley in episode 1-9, "Home" (November 15 2005).
47. Aschebrock et al. (2003); Brébion et al. (2012); Malinowski & Horton (2014).
48. Episode 5-11, "Sam, Interrupted" (January 23, 2010).
49. Before leaving Stanford University in episode 1-1, "Pilot" (September 13, 2005).
50. Bleuler (1911/1950).
51. Bartels-Velthuis et al. (2012); Solesvik et al. (2016).
52. Freud (1900/2010); Rhodes & Jakes (2004).
53. Thorndike (1931).
54. Episode 5–11, "Sam, Interrupted" (January 23, 2010).
55. American Psychiatric Association (2013).
56. American Psychiatric Association (2000).
57. Episodes 1–9, "Home" (November 15 2005); 5-11, "Sam, Interrupted" (January 23, 2010).

## CHAPTER FIFTEEN

# Going Through Hell: How Torture Affects the Tormentor and the Tormented

### JUSTINE MASTIN
### AND COLT J. BLUNT

*"You know something, Alastair? I could still dream. Even in Hell. And over and over and over, you know what I dreamt? I dreamt of this moment. And believe me, I got a few ideas. Let's get started."*
—Dean Winchester[1]

> *"The healthy man does not torture others—generally it is the tortured who turn into torturers."*
> —psychiatrist Carl Jung[2]

Whether it's caused by sitting through a boring lecture or being stuck in traffic, most people have expressed feeling tortured. Similarly, when looking at the face of a friend as we tell a long story or a child as we tell him or her it's time to leave the playground, we've experienced the feeling that we might be torturing someone else. True torture, however, is quite different, and many fewer people have experienced this. Dean Winchester has experienced being both the tortured and the torturer. Torture is an evil action, but are those who torture as reprehensible as their actions? In some cases, the answer is resoundingly yes, but in some complicated situations, roles can be more permeable, with individuals sometimes fitting into more than one category or in some cases changing roles completely. Through his own trials and tribulations at the hands of Hell's minions, Dean begins as a tortured soul and comes full circle to become the torturer. Even though torturers in real life do not go through literal Hell, not all feel that they have another choice.[3] Both roles—that of the tortured and that of the torturer—have their own psychological challenges.

## Why Torture?

In the simplest sense, *torture* is the infliction of physical or psychological harm in order to achieve an objective. The end goal could be *coercion*—such as to extract information, assist in confession, or compel an action—or it could be simply to inflict suffering on the victim. The goal of torture runs the gamut in *Supernatural*. Crossroads demon turned King of the Crossroads turned King of Hell, Crowley often sends his minions to extract information from those who have stirred his ire. Stepping up when he considers it necessary, Crowley tortures Samandriel not once[4] but twice.[5] The protagonists themselves are not above using torture to learn the information they need. An example would be the Winchester brothers' torture of the demon Redd to learn the whereabouts of another demon, whom they also plan on torturing, in their attempts to locate Crowley.[6] Though it might be easy to dismiss real-world

# ROAD MUSIC

### "Cheek to Cheek" by Irving Berlin[7]

Humans find both pleasure and release in skin-to-skin contact.[8] When we touch, the hormone oxytocin, colloquially referred to as the "cuddle hormone," is released, encouraging both physical and emotional bonding.[9] Irving Berlin's "Cheek to Cheek" is evocative of the pleasure stimulated by physical touch, but when this song is sung by Alastair before his torture, the effect is eerie rather than erotic.

research as not applying to demons, modern findings indicate that, contrary to popular belief, torture is unlikely to result in the discovery of useful or accurate information; rather, subjects of torture are motivated through coercion or the desire to avoid pain to say whatever they believe will result in the end of suffering and may even make efforts to mislead their torturer.[10]

Though Crowley's vision for Hell is one of bureaucratic torture and ennui, viewers are initially introduced to a more traditional version of Hell in which its denizens are subject to eternal torture at the hands of Hell's minions.[11] The average torture in Hell doesn't serve a purpose beyond making eternity as awful as possible for those unfortunate enough to end up there at the end of their days. This ultimately results in some of those tortured souls becoming demons themselves. It is this fate that Dean Winchester is bound to, having sold his soul to a crossroads demon in exchange for the resurrection of his brother, Sam.[12]

## On Being Tortured: Immediate and Long-Term Effects

By all accounts, Dean is a tortured character because of all he's been through in life—abusive and absent father, never-ending parade of demons to fight, the deaths of almost everyone he loves—but at the end of season 3, he is literally dragged into Hell. Hellhounds rip his body to shreds, and his soul is strapped to the rack to be tortured for all eternity. He screams from Hell for Sam to help him, but Sam cannot hear his cries.[13] Dean spends the next four months in Hell being tortured daily. Although this would be horrific enough, time in Hell moves differently, so that the four months that pass on Earth are equivalent to 40 years in Hell for Dean.[14]

The purpose for Dean's time on the rack is twofold. Ostensibly, he has earned an eternity of torture by merit of the contract he agreed to and his residence in Hell. However, it is revealed that Alastair, Hell's most adept torturer, inflicted his craft upon Dean in order to open the first of the 66 Seals with the ultimate goal of bringing about the biblical Apocalypse. Ultimately, Alastair's goal is to use torture to coerce Dean to engage in actions contrary to his nature: Alastair needs Dean, the proverbial righteous man, to shed blood in Hell.[15] But first Alastair needs to break him.

Torture is intended to be horrific. Unlike many peripherally related procedures, such as investigative interviewing and noncapital punishment, torture by its very nature is meant to have a lasting effect, whether physical, psychological, or both. The physical effects of torture are readily apparent and have an obvious cause-and-effect relationship: Placing a hot iron against someone's abdomen can be expected to cause a burn, and subjection to the rack can result in damage to joints, bones, and nerves. Beyond this, torture leads to an elevated physiological state, including rapid heart rate and elevated blood pressure;[16] the experience of such physiological symptoms is interpreted by the body and manifested psychologically in the forms of extreme stress and anxiety. Nineteenth-century theorists William James and Carl Lang were the first to describe this phenomenon, in which the brain monitors physiological data, interprets it, and translates it into an emotional state; this has been collectively referred to as the *James-Lange theory*, which has been modified and expanded upon to reflect advances in our understanding of both the mind and the body.[17] Like the emotional state we experience when confronted with any adverse stimuli, whether an angry dog or an ominous landscape on a moonless night, this explains the immediate distress resulting from torture. Dean's torture (the hooks, the stretching, the tearing) leads to clear physical distress, creating an emotional state reflective of terror. This increases Dean's susceptibility to Alastair's influence, making him increasingly more amenable to fulfilling Hell's purpose for him. However, torture has significant effects beyond the immediate, many of which have the potential to be psychologically scarring and lifelong.

Following his ordeal in Hell, Dean awakes in his coffin, alone and terrified.[18] As ever, Dean is a survivor, and once he makes his way out of his own grave, his first order of business is attending to his base needs: water, food, an inventory of his body (a handprint burn on his shoulder but no sign of hellhound evisceration), and a pornographic magazine.

After reuniting with his brother, Sam, and surrogate father, Bobby, Dean denies having any memory of his time in the pit. But, viewers know that he remembers at least something as they begin to see the damage that his time in Hell has done to him. Dean has flashbacks each time he closes his eyes to sleep. It's typical of Dean to keep secrets, especially when revealing them might cause others pain, but he eventually opens up to Sam. He reveals that he does in fact remember his time in Hell but won't allow Sam to give him support.[19]

The long-term physical effects of torture are fairly easy to predict. Torturers aren't known for providing the best medical care to their victims. As such, broken bones may not be

properly set, cuts may not be stitched, and needed medi-
cines and treatments may not be provided; without necessary treatment, serious injuries to the organs or head could
result in system failures, epilepsy, cognitive decline, or even
death.[20] However, Dean escapes his torture in Hell relatively
unscathed, at least physically: no scars from hooks, no burns
from the fires of the pit, just a handprint on his shoulder to
remind him of his ordeal.

The long-term psychological effects of torture are a bit
trickier. Injuries that maim, amputate appendages, or result in
life-limiting damage carry particular baggage. Severe injuries
can impact quality of life and destroy the victim's ability to
function independently; beyond this, significant injuries and
scarring inflicted during torture can result in anxious and
depressive symptoms, including social anxiety and withdrawal,
feelings of hopelessness, suicidal ideation and attempts, and a
lack of motivation to engage in the daily functions of life.[21]
Even remnants of torture and its escape that do not cause physical pain or limit life (such as Dean's handprint scar, a remnant
of Castiel's role in his escape) can serve as reminders of the
torture, dredging up bad memories whenever the victim sees
them in the mirror or an observer asks about them. Indeed,
research suggests that a large proportion of torture survivors
experience significant long-term psychological consequences.[22]

Perhaps the most salient outcome of traumatic experiences
is *posttraumatic stress disorder* (PTSD), which involves the re-ex-
periencing of traumatic events, avoidance of similar stimuli,
psychological distress when the victim is involved in analogous
situations, hypervigilance, changes in behavior, a feeling of
detachment from reality, and dissociation. However, PTSD, as
it is most commonly characterized, focuses on individuals who
have been subjected to circumscribed trauma, such as those
involved in major accidents, natural disasters, and other inci-

dents with the potential for loss of life. As a result, clinicians and researchers have described a distinct subcategory of PTSD called *complex PTSD*, which is particular to victims of prolonged trauma, such as torture. Complex PTSD is typically considered more difficult to treat; these individuals can display significant personality changes and are at an increased risk of harm, both self-inflicted and at the hands of others.[23] One of the most overt clues to Dean's inner struggle is his abuse of alcohol. Over the course of the fourth season and the seasons that follow, Dean's drinking, along with his apparent tolerance to alcohol, increases steadily. Although Dean never truly loses his playfulness, viewers begin to see a more serious Dean who is clearly struggling with his own demons. However, his self-destructive behavior may serve more as a maladaptive coping strategy for his time as a torturer than as a means of dealing with his own torture.

## Becoming the Torturer

Dean later reveals to Sam that he not only remembers the torture but became a torturer himself. Dean experiences feelings of shame that he does not know how to process.[24] He later acknowledges that he actually began to derive pleasure from torturing others:

> I enjoyed it, Sam. They took me off the rack, and I tortured souls, and I liked it. All those years, all that pain. Finally getting to deal some out yourself. I didn't care who they put in front of me. Because that pain I felt, it just slipped away. No matter how many people I save, I can't change that. I can't fill this hole. Not ever.[25]

Dean Winchester is a bit of an anomaly when it comes to torturers, and this is fitting in light of Alastair's intention for him in opening the first of the 66 Seals. As the prophetical righteous man, Dean is not expected to be the prototypical torturer, yet similarly to those identified by Huggins, he enjoys torturing others, has a history that is notable for aggression, and abuses substances (though this is likely more of a coping strategy than a premorbid factor). However, Dean takes responsibility for his actions, blaming himself and thinking himself weak for not resisting Alastair's offer. He does not forget his actions, and those memories tear at him. Combined with the effects from his time being tortured on the rack, Dean is a broken man who believes he is beyond saving.

## The Path to Salvation Is Long and Winding

Dean discovers that he was "raised from perdition" by an angel of the Lord, Castiel. Dean cannot believe that he is worthy of saving, especially not by God, and does not understand how the Lord could possibly have work for him to do.[26] His self-loathing is so deep that even with all the people he has saved over the years, he believes himself to be undeserving of this act. When Castiel gripped Dean tight, he left a literal mark, one physical scar from Dean's time in Hell—an instant and constant reminder of what was done to him, what he did, and what God deemed his worth to be.

Alastair eventually appears on Earth, and Dean is asked to torture him for information.[27] Dean has a strong and immediate reaction to this request but realizes quickly that refusing isn't an option. Before confronting his former torturer, Dean shares a moment of compassion with his rescuer, Castiel: "For what it's worth, I would give anything not to have you do this."

# HELL AND OTHER PEOPLE

**Travis Langley**

The expression "Hell is other people" comes from the existentialist play *No Exit*, about three characters damned to annoy each other for eternity.[28] Most humans, though, find prolonged solitude to be so unnerving that many prisons will send inmates to solitary confinement as punishment.[29] Dean does not yet grasp this when a distraught vampire says, "I've lost everyone I ever loved. I'm staring down eternity alone. Can you think of a worse hell?" and Dean replies, "Well, there's Hell."[30]

As psychiatrist Carl Jung originally conceived the terms, an *introvert* is energized by privacy and feels drained by others whereas an *extravert* is the opposite.[31] While recognizing that we each have a blend of these qualities, Jung noted that many people tend to need people less (studious Sam more than Dean[32]) while others need people more (Dean). Dean, who spends four months (which passes like forty years[33]) in Hell, later finds two months confined to a small cell so unbearable that he would rather die than remain utterly alone.[34] Nearly a decade after suggesting to a vampire that Hell would be worse than aloneness, Dean tells his mother, "Being locked in that cell with nothing. . . . I've been to Hell. This was worse."[35] For the extravert who needs people to feel alive, the real hell is having no other people.

*"People have different fears, and Hell's such a personal torment."*
— *Supernatural* art director John Marcynuk[36]

Dean does go on to interrogate Alastair, the source of so much of his pain. During this encounter, Alastair adds insult to injury by informing Dean that his father was one of Alastair's previous victims and withstood 100 years of torture without succumbing to Alastair's offer to get off the rack: "Pulled out all the stops, but John, he was, well, made of something unique.

The stuff of heroes." Dean begins to torture him. Alastair continues to torment Dean, explaining he has ". . . carved [him] into a new animal" and there is ". . . no going back."[37]

Before escaping his bonds, Alastair explains to Dean that his breaking was necessary to open the first seal, which required the righteous man to shed blood in Hell, further compounding Dean's shame. This is confirmed by Castiel, who offers Dean his first glimmer of hope: "It's not blame that falls on you, Dean, it's fate. The righteous man who begins it is the only one who can finish it."

*References*

Bradley, L., & Tawfiq, N. (2006). The physical and psychological effects of torture in Kurds seeking asylum in the United Kingdom. *Torture, 16*(1), 41–47.

chris684 (2015, March 15). *Supernatural—discussion—the flattening of Sam Winchester.* Spoiler TV: http://www.spoilertv.com/2015/03/supernatural-discussion-flattening-of.html.

Dalgleish, T. (2004). The emotional brain. *Nature Reviews Neuroscience, 5*(7), 583–589.

Dixit, V., & Kumar, A. (2015). Attachment: The roots of love. *International Journal of Education & Psychological Research, 4*(4), 40–45.

Franklin, J. (2009). Evidence gained from torture: Wishful thinking, checkability, and extreme circumstances. *Cardozo Journal of International and Comparative Law, 17*(2), 281–290.

Glancy, G. D., & Murray, E. L. (2006). The psychiatric aspects of solitary confinement. *Victims & Offenders, 1*(4), 361–368.

Herman, J. L. (1992). Complex PTSD: A syndrome in survivors of prolonged and repeated trauma. *Journal of Traumatic Stress, 5*(3), 377–391.

Jung, C. G. (1921). *Psycholgische Typen [Psychological types].* Zurich, Switzerland: Rascher Verlag.

Jung, C. G. (1939). *The symbolic life* (transcript). In C. G. Jung (Author) (1977), *The symbolic life: Miscellaneous writings.* Princeton, NJ: Princeton University Press.

Knight, N. (2009). *Supernatural; The official companion season 3.* London, UK: Titan.

Morris, R. G. (2015). Exploring the effect of exposure to short-term solitary confinement among violent prison inmates. *Journal of Quantitative Criminology, 32,* 1–22.

Morrison, I. (2016). Keep calm and cuddle on: Social touch as a stress buffer. *Adaptive Human Behavior & Physiology, 2*(4), 344–362.

Occam's Chainsaw (2016, January 25). *Sam Winchester: INFJ.* The Book Addict's Guide to MBTI: https://mbtifiction.com/2016/01/25/sam-winchester-double-check/.

O'Mara, S. (2011). On the imposition of torture, an extreme stressor state, to extract information from memory. *Zeitschrift für Psychologie, 219*(3), 159–166.

Quiroga, J. & Jaranson, M. (2005). Politically-motivated torture and its survivors: A desk study review of the literature. *Torture, 16*(2-3), 1–111.

Rasmussen, A., Rosenfeld, B., Reeves, K., & Keller, A. S. (2007). The effects of torture-related injuries on long-term psychological distress in a Punjabi Sikh temple. *Journal of Abnormal Psychology, 116*(4), 734–740.

Sartre, J. (1944/1989). *No exit and three other plays*. London, UK: Vintage.

## Notes

1. Episode 4–16, "On the Head of a Pin" (March 19, 2009).
2. Jung (1939/1977), p. 587.
3. Hoffman et al. (2015); Lankford (2009); Wolfendale (2006).
4. Episode 8–7, "A Little Slice of Kevin" (November 14, 2012).
5. Episode 8–10, "Torn and Frayed" (January 16, 2013).
6. Episode 6–20, "The Man Who Would Be King" (May 6, 2011).
7. Written by Irving Berlin (1935); played in episode 4–16, "On the Head of a Pin" (March 19, 2009).
8. Morrison (2016).
9. Dixit & Kumar (2015).
10. Franklin (2009).
11. Episode 3–16, "No Rest for the Wicked" (May 15, 2008).
12. Episode 2–22 "All Hell Breaks Loose: Part Two" (May 17, 2007).
13. Episode 3–16, "No Rest for the Wicked" (May 15, 2008).
14. Episode 4–10, "Heaven and Hell" (November 20, 2008).
15. Episode 4–16, "On the Head of a Pin" (March 19, 2009).
16. O'Mara (2011).
17. Dalgleish (2004).
18. Episode 4–1, "Lazarus Rising" (September 18, 2008).
19. Episode 4–8, "Wishful Thinking" (November 6, 2008).
20. Rasmussen et al. (2007).
21. Quiroga & Jaranson (2005).
22. Bradley & Tawfiq (2006).
23. Herman (1992).
24. Episode 4–10, "Heaven and Hell" (November 20, 2008).
25. Episode 4–11, "Family Remains" (January 15, 2009).
26. Episode 4–1, "Lazarus Rising" (September 18, 2008).
27. Episode 4–16, "On the Head of a Pin" (March 19, 2009).
28. Sartre (1944/1989).
29. Glancy & Murray (2006); Morris (2015).
30. Episode 3–7, "Fresh Blood" (November 15, 2007).
31. Jung (1921).
32. chris684 (2015); Occam's Chainsaw (2016).
33. Episode 4–10, "Heaven and Hell" (November 20, 2008).
34. Episode 12-9, "First Blood" (January 26, 2017).
35. Episode 12-9, "First Blood" (January 26, 2017).
36. Quoted by Knight (2009), p. 100.
37. Episode 4–16, "On the Head of a Pin" (March 19, 2009).

## CHAPTER SIXTEEN

# From Heaven to Hell: An Examination of Leadership Style

### JENNIFER BONDS-RAACKE
### AND JOHN RAACKE

*"I think I need to confer with our fearless leader for a minute. Why not go get washed up for the orgy?"*
—angel Castiel calling mortal Dean his leader[1]

*"Charisma is a fire, a fire that ignites followers' energy and commitment, producing results above and beyond the call of duty."*
—management professors Katherine Klein and Robert House[2]

We are drawn to those who lead due to psychological needs for affiliation with those who are endowed with power or perceived power.[3] Therefore, pointing to a leader seems easy. However, ask someone to define the qualities and characteristics that are associated with leaders or leadership styles and the task becomes much more complex and the definitions become far less agreed upon.

*Supernatural* presents many leaders or characters possessing (no pun intended) leadership qualities—both heroes and villains among them, including God and Lucifer, angels and demons, and even monsters and mortals.[4] Prominent among those mortals, the Winchester brothers can represent the leadership in the light. (After all, Chuck Himself expresses His faith in them.[5]) Who else should represent leadership in the dark but the demon who works his way up to King of Hell?

## Leadership Elements

What is leadership? Psychologists and others who study leadership have debated and investigated this for the better part of the last century, yet after all this time there is no agreed-upon definition. In fact, leadership research has evolved from looking at individual characteristics or differences to evaluating more complex models of leadership and its development.[6] Nevertheless, three defining elements emerge across the literature: group phenomenon, goal-directed and action-oriented, and hierarchy within a group.[7] Using these elements, we can define leadership as a social contract between the followers in a group and an individual to make decisions and pursue actions that are beneficial and in the best interest of the group.[8]

### Group Phenomenon

Leadership does not take place without followers.[9] Specifically, the people who follow are not solely the beneficiaries of influence from a leader; rather, they are active in the emergence of leadership development (*group phenomenon*).[10] The Winchesters' followers include Castiel, Bobby, Sheriff Jody Mills, Kevin Tran, and a host of others who believe in protecting and saving the world. Crowley's followers include the demons of Hell, hellhounds, and other monster groups.

### Goal-Directed, Action-Oriented

Leadership is *goal-directed and action-oriented*. In other words, leaders must have a vision in which followers are inspired to perform at high levels to achieve a goal.[11] The Winchesters' goal is to protect people from monsters and often to prevent the end of world as we know it, which they accomplish. Crowley's goal is to rise from his simple beginnings to create a powerful dominion in which he maintains his role as Hell's leader. To achieve this goal, he will take any and all actions necessary, including eliminating subordinates and rivals, double-crossing potential partners, and preserving alliances with those (i.e., the Winchesters) who do not want to see him removed and replaced as King.

### Hierarchy within a Group

The group must have a structure, whether formal or informal, for leaders to rise in position within its hierarchy. Among hunters, the Winchesters have become revered over the years. Even their followers tend to recognize their leadership roles when a course of action must be chosen. Similarly, Crowley's dominion is hierarchical, with certain demons having different responsibilities and serving in different roles (e.g., crossroad demons). We can define both our heroes and our villain as leaders in their respective organizations (hunters and Hell).

## Leadership Style

Defining *what* a leader is differs from defining *how* a leader leads. Leaders can demonstrate many different types of leadership styles: *autocratic* leadership,[12] in which a leader seeks very little input from others and makes all decisions solely on the basis of his or her own ideas and judgement (e.g., the angel Castiel when he conquers Heaven[13]); *democratic* leadership,[14] in which leaders encourage participation from followers in the decision-making process before ultimately making the decision on the basis of input from the group (e.g., the angel Hannah when she emerges as leader in Heaven[15]); *transactional leadership,*[16] in which leaders focus on results through reward and punishment and the way individuals fit within an organizational structure (e.g., the fallen angel Lucifer when he isn't throwing a tantrum[17]); and *dissonant leadership,*[18] in which leaders maintain a social and emotional distance in an attempt to remain logical and objective in dealing with followers (e.g., their version of God[19]), to name a few. The leadership characteristics shown by the Winchesters and Crowley, however, best fit another type: the charismatic leadership style.

### Charismatic Leadership

Charismatic leaders possess extreme self-confidence in their abilities, unconventional behavior that instills confidence, strong belief in their personal righteousness, and excellent rhetorical and articulation skills.[20] Yet the aspect that allows charismatic leaders to inspire followers most is the existence of a crisis in which followers are ready to be saved or merely are looking for a change in direction.[21] It is this combination that leads to charismatic leadership development in the boys and Crowley.

Sam and Dean begin as ordinary hunters from an ordinary hunter family[22] with very little cachet in the *Supernatural* universe. Over time, the interactions and crises created by demons and monsters as well as the response of their small number of followers ignite the development of charismatic leadership in the Winchesters: Stopping Azazel from opening Hell,[23] stopping Lilith from releasing Lucifer,[24] and returning

Lucifer to the Cage[25] create early situations in which an ever growing cadre of followers are inspired to join Sam and Dean in their fight against threats to human life. Simply, it is the intersection of leadership of brothers, followers, and crisis that creates or encourages the Winchesters' charismatic leadership style.

Lucifer's return to the Cage results in a "win" for Crowley by leading to his new title of King of Hell. Quickly, we see Crowley become an expert in using his influence and success to further his leadership development. Situations such as attempting to capture all the Alphas so that Crowley may learn the location of Purgatory,[26] ridding the world of Dick Roman and the Leviathans,[27] and stopping the Winchesters from sealing all demons in Hell forever[28] demonstrate Crowley's charismatic leadership development. It is in these situations that Crowley's charismatic leadership qualities lead to a response from his followers to sacrifice and eliminate threats to demonkind survival.

### Motivation and Power: Same Style, Different Outcomes

There is vast overlap in the charismatic leadership style of the Winchesters and that of Crowley. However, subtle differences produce varying outcomes when facing oppositional forces. These differences manifest themselves in two personal attributes: motivation to lead and sources of power.

People are motivated to meet perceived needs for power, dominance, achievement, affiliation, or responsibility.[29] The motivation to become a leader is different for the Winchesters and Crowley. Crowley is motivated by the need for power and dominance. After his rise to power, he utilizes every trick, deal, double-cross, and move to maintain his power and dominance. Crowley is not above forming alliances with enemies in order to maintain his power and protect his privileged position.[30] Often, Crowley teams up with the Winchesters to maintain his position and power. This is evident when he helps Dean locate the First Blade in order to restore himself to his place as King of Hell and to kill Abaddon[31] or when he helps the Winchesters stop Amara from ending all of existence.[32] Crowley further uses his leadership power to act within his own interest[33] when a demonic Dean embarrasses him and Crowley turns Dean over to Sam so that Dean can be restored to a human state.[34] In each instance, Crowley is motivated by personal gain to maintain his control of power and dominance over Hell.

Conversely, the Winchesters are initially motivated by a need for responsibility. Sam and Dean want to protect others from the horrors of their childhood. As time goes on, they feel a responsibility to protect all of humankind. Their motivation to lead is augmented by the need for affiliation. As a result of their need for affiliation, they make multiple attempts to rescue each other from death in addition to their friends and followers; this can be seen in the cases of Castiel and Bobby Singer. Thus, their growth into a leadership role is born from positive forms of motivation, whereas Crowley's leadership arguably is born from negative motivation.

There is also great difference in the Winchesters' and Crowley's sources of power. An individual's power in leadership can take any of five forms: *legitimate power* (based on a position in an organization), *reward power* (based on access to rewards), *coercive power* (based on punishment), *expert power* (based on expertise), and *referent power* (based on respect).[35] Followers respond differently to these sources of power,[36] with some showing resistance to coercive or reward power and others showing commitment to expert or referent power.

The Winchesters are most closely aligned with referent power and expert power. In the beginning, they lead individuals against Azazel and Lilith through their relationships with their friends, such as Bobby Singer, Sheriff Jody, Ellen, Ash, and even the demon Ruby. The Winchesters also rely heavily on the journal of John Winchester and the knowledge that Bobby is able to provide. As time progresses, people who are initially followers because of referent power begin to recognize the expert power the Winchesters hold. New hunters such as Garth, Mary Winchester, Castiel, and Kevin Tran begin to turn to the Winchesters because of their knowledge of the supernatural, leading to a high level of commitment from their followers.

The source of Crowley's power, in contrast, moves from legitimate power to coercive and reward power. Early on, his followers view him as the legitimate King of Hell because of his title. These followers—demons—react in compliance with his position within the hierarchy of Hell. As time progresses, Crowley begins to utilize coercive and reward power to maintain his leadership position. Demons who do not agree with his leadership are dealt with quickly and severely, typically by being killed or punished. The use of coercive and reward power leads Crowley's followers to be more resistant to his leadership, as demonstrated by the number of demons who are willing to follow anyone else who may try to assume a leadership role in Hell.[37] This includes demons who side with Abaddon to overthrow Crowley and/or Lucifer since his return.

The commonality of these two personal attributes—motivation and power—results in very different outcomes for the charismatic leadership styles of the Winchesters and Crowley. In one instance, the motivating factors of need of responsibility and affiliation with referent as well as expert power yield followers who are loyal, supportive, and devoted and have respect for their leaders—Sam and Dean. In contrast, the motivating factors of power and dominance with legitimate, coercive, and reward power sources eventually lead to followers

# MARK SHEPPARD ON THE REAL CROWLEY[38]

**Janina Scarlet**

> **Janina Scarlet:** "Which version of Crowley do you think is the real character—the more villainous one or the more helpful one?"
>
> **Mark Sheppard:** "There's no versions of Crowley. They're all the same Crowley. You have no idea. Seriously, you never quite know whether he's telling the truth or not. I love playing Crowley. It's fun."

who are disloyal, undermining, and unenthusiastic and who fail to comply with their leader's demands—Crowley.

## Better to Reign...

Both heroes and villains can develop into charismatic leaders. Despite the fact that there are plenty of similarities in their leadership styles, there are also some obvious differences that shape the direction of the characters as time continues. Although Sam and Dean arguably develop and continue to develop a strong leadership style, Crowley loses his position as a charismatic leader because of his motivation and sources of power. Once the primary antagonist to Sam and Dean Winchester, Crowley nicknames the brothers Moose (Sam) and Not Moose (Dean), as exhibited on his cell phone when the rivals communicate.[39] In fact, although Crowley maintains his role as King of Hell, he begins to develop many of the same characteristics of someone who would be a follower of the Winchesters, while the Winchesters enable this behavior. The result is a form of leadership bromance. Leadership roles and styles are not set in stone and are fluid concepts in which individuals may find themselves a leader, a follower, or both depending on the situation.

> *"You and Sam don't understand.*
> *I'm not your bloody sidekick!"*
> —Crowley[40]

> *"Some people bring out the worst in you, others bring out*
> *the best, and then there are those remarkably rare, addictive*
> *ones who just bring out the most. Of everything. They make*
> *you feel so alive that you'd follow them straight into hell."*
> —author Karen Marie Moning[41]

## References

Avolio B. J. (2007). Promoting more integrative strategies for leadership theory-building. *American Psychologist, 62*(1), 25–33.

Bass, B. M., & Avolio, B. J. (1994). *Improving organizational effectiveness through transformational leadership.* London, UK: Sage.

Bhatti, N., Maitlo, G., Shaikh, N., Hasmi, M., & Shaikh, F. (2012). The impact of autocratic and democratic leadership style on job satisfaction. *International Business Research, 5*(2), 192–201.

Chan, K. Y., & Drasgow, F. (2001). Toward a theory of individual differences and leadership: Understanding the motivation to lead. *Journal of Applied Psychology, 86*(3), 481–498.

French, J. R. P., Jr., & Raven, B. (1959). The bases of social power. In D. Cartwright (Ed.), *Studies in social power* (pp.150–167). Ann Arbor, MI: University of Michigan Press.

Goleman, D., Boyatzis, R., & McKee, A. (2002). *The new leaders: Transforming the art of leadership into the science of results.* London, UK: Time Warner.

House, R. J. (1977). A 1976 theory of charismatic leadership. In J. G. Hunt & L. L. Larson (Eds.), *Leadership: The cutting edge.* Carbondale, IL: Southern Illinois University Press.

Kipnis, D. (1972). Does power corrupt? *Journal of Personality & Social Psychology, 24*(1), 33–41.

Kirkpatrick, S. A., & Locke, E. A. (1996). Direct and indirect effects of three core charismatic leadership components on performance and attitudes. *Journal of Applied Psychology 81*(1), 36–51.

Klein, K. J., & House, R. (1995). On fire: Charismatic leadership and levels of analysis. *Leadership Quarterly, 6*(2), 183–198.

Lapierre, L. M., Bremner, N., & McMullan, A. D. (2012). Strength in numbers: How employees' acts of followership can influence their manager's charismatic leadership behavior. *Zeitschrift für Psychologie, 220*(4), 251–261.

Maner, J. J., & Mead, N. L. (2010). The essential tension between leadership and power: When leaders sacrifice group goals for the sake of self-interest. *Journal of Personality & Social Psychology 99*(3), 482–497.

Moning, K. M. (2011). *Shadowfever.* New York, NY: Random House.

Nahavandi, A. (2012). *The art and science of leadership* (6th ed.). Upper Saddle River, NJ: Prentice Hall.

Pastor, J. C., Mayo, M., & Shamir, B. (2007). Adding fuel to fire: The impact of followers' arousal on ratings of charisma. *Journal of Applied Psychology 92*(6), 1584–1596.

Shamir, B., & Howell, J. M. (1999). Organizational and contextual influences on the emergence and effectiveness of charismatic leadership. *Leadership Quarterly, 10*(2), 257–283.

Smith, P.K., & Trope, Y. (2006). You focus on the forest when you are in charge of the trees: Power priming and abstract information processing. *Journal of Personality & Social Psychology, 90*(3), 578–596.

TVForTheRestOfUs (2015, July 13). *Interview with Supernatural's Mark Sheppard— Comic Con 2015.* YouTube: https://www.youtube.com/watch?v=rjCtUvd28pM.

Vugt, M. V. (2006). Evolutionary origins of leadership and followership. *Personality & Social Psychology Review 10*(2), 354–371.

Vugt, M. V., Jepson, S. F., Hart, C. M., & De Cremer, D. (2004). Autocratic leadership in social dilemmas: A threat to group stability. *Journal of Experimental Social Psychology, 40*(1), 1–13.

Yorges, S. L., Weiss, H. M., & Strickland, O. J. (1999). The effect of leader outcomes on influence, attributions, and perceptions of charisma. *Journal of Applied Psychology, 84* (3), 428–436.

Yukl, G. A. (2006). *Leadership in organizations.* Upper Saddle River, NJ: Prentice Hall.

## Notes

1. Episode 5–4, "The End" (October 1, 2009).
2. Klein & House (1995), p. 183.
3. Kipnis (1972).
4. Examples: God according to Castiel in episode 4–1, "Lazarus Rising" (September 18, 2008); Lucifer—5–1, "Sympathy for the Devil" (September 10, 2009); Amara, the Darkness—11–1, "Out of the Darkness, into the Fire" (October 7, 2015); Death—

5–21, "Two Minutes to Midnight" (May 6, 2010); Hannah, angel—10–17, "Inside Man" (April 1, 2015); Crowley, demon—flashback, episode 12–12, "Stuck in the Middle (with You)" (February 16, 2017); alpha vampire, monster—6–4, "Live Free or Twihard" (October 22, 2010); Garth, "the new Bobby," mortal—8–6, "Southern Comfort" (November 7, 2012).

5. Episode 11–23, "Alpha and Omega" (May 25, 2016).
6. Yukl (2006).
7. Nahavandi (2012).
8. Maner & Mead (2010).
9. Nahavandi (2012).
10. Lapierre et al. (2012).
11. Kirkpatrick & Locke (1996).
12. Vugt et al. (2004).
13. Episode 6–22, "The Man Who Knew Too Much" (May 20, 2011).
14. Bhatti et al. (2012).
15. Episode 10–18, "Book of the Damned" (April 15, 2015).
16. Bass & Avolio (1994).
17. Episode 5–19, "Hammer of the Gods" (April 22, 2010).
18. Goleman et al. (2002).
19. Who explains His reasons for staying distant in episode 11–21, "All in the Family" (May 11, 2016).
20. Yorges et al. (1999).
21. House (1977); Pastor et al. (2007); Shamir & Howell (1999).
22. Episode 1–1, "Pilot" (September 13, 2005).
23. Episodes 2–21, "All Hell Breaks Loose, Part 1" (May 10, 2007); 2–22, "All Hell Breaks Loose, Part 2" (May 17, 2007).
24. Episode 4–22, "Lucifer Rising" (May 14, 2009).
25. Episode 5–22, "Swan Song" (May 13, 2010).
26. Episode 6–7, "Family Matters" (November 5, 2010).
27. Episode 7–23, "Survival of the Fittest" (May 18, 2012).
28. Episode 8–23, "Sacrifice" (May 15, 2013).
29. Chan & Drasgow (2001).
30. Vugt (2006).
31. Episode 9–11, "First Born" (January 21, 2014).
32. Episode 11–23, "Alpha and Omega" (May 25, 2016).
33. Smith & Trope (2006).
34. Episode 10–3, "Soul Survivor" (October 21, 2014).
35. French and Raven (1959).
36. Nahavandi (2012), p. 253.
37. Episode 12–15, "Somewhere between Heaven and Hell" (March 9, 2017).
38. TVForTheRestOfUs (2015).
39. Episode 9–16, "Blade Runners" (March 18, 2014).
40. Episode 11–2, "Form and Void" (October 14, 2015).
41. Moning (2010).

## CHAPTER SEVENTEEN

# The Hero's Road Trip

## LARISA A. GARSKI
## AND JUSTINE MASTIN

*"Well, as fate would have it, I adopted two boys and they grew up great. They grew up heroes. So you can go to Hell!"*
—Bobby Singer[1]

*"Once having traversed the threshold, the hero moves in a dream landscape of curiously fluid, ambiguous forms, where he must survive a succession of trials. . . . "*
—mythologist Joseph Campbell[2]

The *monomyth*—the "one myth" popularly known as the Hero's Journey—is the global representation of the hero and the process by which she or he becomes heroic. Literally or figuratively, the hero crosses the divide separating the ordinary world from the supernatural realm, faces a series of tests, receives aid from mystical guides or helpers, and eventually emerges triumphant with an extraordinary gift that he or she is

243

charged with bringing back to the ordinary world to help save or improve it.[3] Sam and Dean Winchester cross this divide with surprising regularity, and the audience stays with them because the monomyth innately speaks to us. Sam and Dean's hunters' narrative is a call to adventure that resonates beyond fandom and into the therapy room where clients work with their own helpers—psychotherapists—to cross the threshold dividing the conscious and unconscious minds to achieve increased self-understanding and deeper integration.

## The Hero's Journey

Joseph Campbell, a twentieth-century mythologist and writer, built his model of the Hero's Journey on a foundation laid down by psychiatrist Carl Jung, the founding father of *analytical psychology*. Jung postulated the existence of a *collective unconscious*, an instinctive part of the unconscious mind inherited by all people separate from—but linked to—each individual's *personal unconscious*.[4] He envisioned this collective unconscious as a repository of shared motifs and narratives common to all humans across time and space.[5] From the *Mahabharata*[6] to *Star Wars* to *Supernatural*, these stories resonate because they have the same narrative of symbols or unconscious themes, *archetypes*. For Jung, the two worlds of the monomyth, the ordinary and the supernatural, represent the conscious self and the unconscious self. Only by crossing the threshold from the conscious mind to the unconscious mind can a person draw "a hatful of water from a stream" and carry this bit of deeper unconscious understanding (elixir) back into conscious life, where it can be fully integrated into the personality.[7] In myth this final act of integration is symbolized by the hero restoring himself or others with a supernatural elixir. Dean's rescue from Hell by

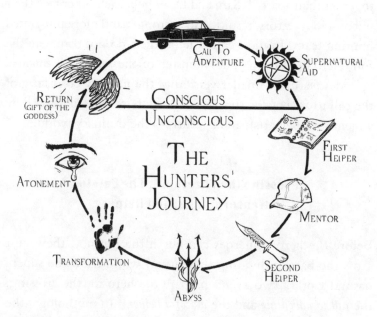

Although not all heroes follow this format exactly, their journey tends to follow this paradigm.[8] In *Super-natural*, Sam and Dean are united on a cyclical Hunters' Journey, repeatedly going through these stages.[9]

Castiel exemplifies this final act. In his case, knowledge of the underworld is his supernatural elixir, and he carries it with him both literally via a celestial handprint and figuratively as hunting wisdom that he later uses to prevent the Apocalypse.

Together, Sam and Dean Winchester cross the threshold between the ordinary (conscious) and supernatural (unconscious) worlds numerous times to vanquish demons, save innocents, and battle their shadow selves. Although the hero never walks entirely alone on the Hero's Journey, *Supernatural* shows us that heroes can achieve even greater heights by working (in this case hunting) together. Sam and Dean's insistence that they cannot live without the other isn't just a case of brotherly love. As Dean explains, "The universe is trying to tell us something we both should already know. We're stronger together than apart."[10] Sam and Dean help each other face their unconscious terrors, resulting in a stronger and more integrated hunting team. In most cases the brothers do not complete the full Hero's Journey. The monster-of-the-week *Supernatural* episodes feature a smaller version of the journey consisting of the call to adventure, supernatural aid, tests and trials aided by a mentor or helper(s), and a return to the ordinary world.

## Crossing the Threshold: The Call to Adventure, Tests, and Helpers

Before the hero or heroes can begin the journey, they must cross the barrier dividing the natural world from the super-natural world. Two events prepare the hero for the crossing: the *call to adventure* and the *aid of a helper*.[11] In mythology, the call to adventure is often represented as a literal herald or either from a magical being or from nobility,[12] such as when the angel Castiel tells Dean that he has a mission from God.[13]

In Jungian psychology, the call to adventure symbolizes a crisis or transition that pushes the individual toward greater self-understanding.[14] The catalyst may be interior, as in the case of biological puberty, or exterior, such as the sudden death of a loved one. The death of Mary Winchester is a major turning point for her husband, John, and their sons, Sam and Dean.[15] If she had lived, the Winchester brothers might never have become hunters.[16] Such a turning point is an opportunity for the conscious mind to encounter the unconscious. *Supernatural* opens with Sam's fraught response to the call.[17] Though he fights his destiny (resisting the call), Sam eventually commits to life on the hunter's road, as exemplified by the moment at the end of the pilot when he throws his shotgun in the trunk of the Impala and states that "we got work to do."[18]

Before crossing the threshold, the hero encounters a helper who offers guidance, a tool, or a potion that catalyzes the hero's commitment to the path. Dean is both the harbinger of Sam's call to adventure and Sam's first helper as he prepares to join him on a joint Hero's Journey. He provides Sam with advice, comfort, and support: "Nothing bad will happen to you as long as you've got me."[19] Once they cross the threshold, the real work begins as they face the tests or trials of the supernatural realm. Whether defeating a malevolent djinn[20] or battling a house of vampires,[21] the hero continues to receive aid via helpers. As Campbell notes, not all helpers are unambiguously good or bad.[22] Many are ferocious in their aid. Thus, the demon called Ruby is an example of an *awful helper*, inspiring both disgust and wonder.

### Flight to the Return: Integrating the Unconscious Elixir into the Conscious Self

Once the heroes have vanquished the demon, freed the angel, or escaped from the underworld, they must cross over the threshold that divides the supernatural (unconscious) world from the daily (conscious) world and bring some "boon" or gift they have gained, such as new skill, secret knowledge, supernatural power, mighty weapon, or magical elixir.[23] The Colt, a gun that can kill almost anything thanks to its magic, is the classic example of such a boon. The heroes return to the natural realm with this gift and use it to enhance themselves, their community, or the world. This circuit symbolizes the psychotherapeutic process of integration in which a part of the unconscious self is added to the conscious self.

Unlike the hero who makes the journey once and then returns home, Sam and Dean are defined by their commit-

## ROAD MUSIC

### "Ramble On" by Led Zeppelin[24]

The monomyth can be found in stories across time and space; humans are hardwired to understand the framework of story.[25] Dean Winchester says that one of his favorite songs is "Ramble On," which draws on imagery from another famous Hero's Journey, *The Lord of the Rings*, as it describes a cyclical journey without end.[26]

ment to a Hero's Journey without end. In mythological terms, this means that each cycle of the journey brings them closer to a transcendent state. Not all heroes are destined for this final transformation, but despite Dean's insistence that he is just a "dropout with 6 bucks to his name" and that Sam is "an ex-blood junkie," Sam and Dean are not your average heroes.[27] Even *Supernatural's* symbolic God, better known as Chuck, is confident in their abilities, saying to Dean, "Earth will be fine. It's got you. And Sam"[28]

### Archetypes on the Road

Within the monomyth, we find a cast of recurring characters and motifs known as *archetypes*.[29] Jung conceptualized each archetype as a highly developed aspect of the collective unconscious, often depicted in the monomyth as a character or narrative theme.[30] In *Supernatural*, we find symbols for many of these archetypes: the shadow self, the anima and animus, and death and resurrection. *Supernatural's* writers make clever use of these archetypes, enabling them to create complex narrative arcs that cycle back to the start of the monomyth.

## My Anima Is Your Impala

An inventive representation of an archetype is the way *Supernatural* test drives the anima. Anima and animus are gendered terms: Men have access to the collective unconscious via their female anima, whereas women access the collective unconscious via their male animus.[31] Arguably one of the more divisive of the Jungian archetypes,[32] the anima is the figurative bridge connecting a man's unconscious to the collective unconscious.[33] For men, the anima is supposedly the access point and the means for travel into the mythic world. How do Sam and Dean travel into the supernatural world? They do this via their female-gendered Impala, Baby.

John Winchester, father to these heroes, keeps the Impala safe. But Sam and Dean claim the Impala and make her their own. Their connection to the Impala is made poignantly clear via a series of flashbacks: the boys scrambling over backseats, squabbling over junk food, and playing warrior games with army men.[34] The scenes shift backward and forward through time to show the ways the Impala has functioned as both the bridge and the vehicle for every hunting journey.

The supernatural world of the hunters is the world of the collective unconscious brought to life, and the Impala is Sam and Dean's personal vehicle to this mythic realm, their home without a roof and four walls.[35] In Jungian psychology as in mythology, the client or patient's journey often begins with the anima or the animus. The male patient uses his anima to gain deeper understanding of the collective unconscious, readying him for the later encounter with the shadow self. Sam and Dean begin almost every adventure in their Impala; she takes them across the threshold into the supernatural realm where they face each trial. Often, she is the conduit for the brothers to face their shadow selves.

## Shadow

The shadow self represents the hidden aspect of the self. Although it can be evil, it is not always so and thus defies the strict duality common in many variations of the monomyth. The shadow generally contains the wilder impulses of the unconscious from which the conscious self runs.[36] One goal of Jungian psychoanalysis is to bring these two selves into greater knowing via an encounter or series of encounters between the self and the shadow self.[37] *Supernatural* uses symbols of this archetype both to develop Sam and Dean's individual journeys and to integrate their journeys together as co-heroes of one epic narrative. When they enter the abyss, each brother must face the shadow within himself. Sam faces the demonic heritage he has inherited as a baby poisoned by demon's blood: "There's something in me that scares the hell out of me, Dean."[38] Dean faces the broken hero inside of him, eventually becoming a demonic torturer before ascending to earth via a celestial transformation.[39]

## Death and Resurrection

The death and resurrection of the hero "encompasses the oldest [archetypes] known to researchers."[40] Sam and Dean encounter both death and resurrection numerous times on their drives down the hunting road. It is through death in the abyss and a resurrected emergence that a hero is reborn into a transformed hero. When Sam returns after a prolonged stint in Hell, his hunting skills surpass those of every hunter around him, including his grandfather.[41] He may not be the nicest Sammy on the block, but heroic transformation does not always result in a kinder, gentler hero, though it does have that effect on Dean.[42] In psychotherapy, themes of death and resurrection are often symbolic of the relinquishing of old habits or ways of being. Now the client or patient can access new awareness or learn new skill sets. In mythology, death and resurrection are mortal means to a cosmic end: transcendence. But what does transcendence mean?

For heroes of the monomyth, transcendence is the end result of numerous rebirths; the hunters Sam and Dean have died and been resurrected so many times that they have lost count.[43] After completing numerous cycles of the Hero's Journey, the hero transcends, moving beyond the daily dualities of good and evil, death and life, male and female to become divine or godlike. In psychotherapy, the transcendent state symbolizes total integration or complete intermingling of the conscious mind and the unconscious mind.[44] Not all heroes are capable of transcendence. Most return to their communities after a single Hero's Journey and "live happily ever after" in the natural world. But Sam and Dean are heroes by birthright and choice. Because they are committed to the hunting life, their cyclical Hunters' Journey is moving toward ever greater illumination and a point at which they will transcend all archetypal dualities[45] to become "that divine being," the fully integrated self.[46]

## The Future Is Divine

The monomyth teaches that the transcendent state can be achieved in one of two ways: by a battle or series of battles[47] with the archetypal "Universal Father," at which point the hero integrates the father in a process Campbell terms "at-one-ment with the father," or via divine communion with a god or goddess.[48] The *divine marriage* describes the union—sexual or marital—between the hero and the god or goddess, symbolizing the hero's worth and ability to attain enlightenment.[49] Sam's journey takes him on the mythic path of "the Atonement with the father."[50] With a history of entrenched paternal conflict, Sam battles first with his biological father and then with a series of father figures, gaining a deeper understanding of himself and his motivations. Ever since divine intervention at the hands of Castiel, Dean's path has arced toward "the Meeting with the Goddess"[51] or celestial being. He has slept with a fallen angel[52] and been chosen as a human vessel for the archangel Michael. Perhaps most important, he has been the object of Castiel's interest since the angel first gripped him tight. The two "share a more profound bond."[53] Does divine marriage await one of our hunters? It is difficult to know. Regardless of how the show ends, it is clear that the hunters are destined to transcend. As *Supernatural's* most transcendent character, Chuck, aka God, explains, "No doubt—endings are hard. But then again, nothing ever really ends, does it?"[54]

*References*

Campbell, J. (1949/2008). *The hero with a thousand faces* (3rd ed.). Novato, CA: New World Library.
Campbell, J., & Moyers, B. (1988). *The power of myth*. New York, NY: Anchor.
Jung, C.G. (1963). *Memories, dreams and reflections* (C. Winston & R. Winston, Trans.). New York, NY: Random House.
Jung. C. G. (1966). *Two essays on analytical psychology* (*Complete Works*, Vol. 7). Princeton, NJ: Princeton University Press.
Jung. C. G. (1969). *The archetypes and the collective unconscious* (*Complete Works*, Vol. 9). Princeton, NJ: Princeton University Press.
Jung, C. G. (2009). *The red book*. New York, NY: Norton.
Lewis, D. (1995). *The complete guide to the music of Led Zeppelin*. London, UK: Omnibus.

*Notes*

1. Episode 7–10, "Death's Door" (December 2, 2011).
2. Campbell (1949/2008), p. 81.
3. Campbell (1949/2008).
4. Jung (1969).
5. Jung (1969).
6. One of two major Hindu epics that form the foundation of ancient Indian narrative tradition (Campbell, 1949/2008).
7. Jung (1963).
8. Campbell (1949/2008); Campbell and Moyers (1988).
9. Special thanks to A. Catherine Duthie, who helped design and create this *Supernatural* Hunter's Journey graphic.
10. Episode 10–19, "The Werther Project" (April 22, 2015).

11. Campbell & Moyers (1988).
12. Campbell (1949/2008); Campbell and Moyers (1988).
13. Episode 4–1, "Lazarus Rising" (September 18, 2008).
14. Jung (1963).
15. Episode 1–1, "Pilot" (September 13, 2005).
16. Episode 1–20, "Dead Man's Blood" (April 20, 2006).
17. Episode 1–1, "Pilot" (September 13, 2005). In the pilot, Sam has abandoned the hunter's life for college.
18. Episode 1–1, "Pilot" (September 13, 2005).
19. Episode 1–14, "Nightmare" (February 7, 2006).
20. Episode 2–20, "What Is and What Should Never Be" (May 3, 2007).
21. Episode 1–20, "Dead Man's Blood" (April 20, 2006).
22. Campbell (1949/2008).
23. Campbell and Moyers (1988).
24. Written by Led Zeppelin; mentioned in episode 4–18, "The Monster at the End of This Book" (April 2, 2009).
25. Brown (2017).
26. Lewis (1995).
27. Episode 5–13, "The Song Remains the Same" (February 4, 2010).
28. Episode 11–23, "Alpha and Omega" (May 25, 2016).
29. Jung (1969).
30. Jung (1963; 1969).
31. Jung (1963).
32. By modern psychotherapy's standards, we would argue that the anima/animus notion is both myopically Western and overly heteronormative.
33. Jung (1963).
34. Episode 5–22, "Swan Song" (May 13, 2010).
35. Episode 5–22, "Swan Song" (May 13, 2010).
36. Jung (1966).
37. Jung (2009).
38. Episode 5–2, "Good God Y'all" (September 17, 2009)
39. Episode 4–10, "Heaven and Hell" (November 20, 2008)
40. Campbell (1949/2008).
41. Episode 6–1, "Exile on Main Street" (September 25, 2010).
42. Episode 6–6, "You Can't Handle the Truth" (October 29, 2010).
43. Episode 5–16, "Dark Side of the Moon" (April 2, 2010).
44. In psychotherapy such complete integration is understood as the unattainable goal to which the client and the psychotherapist aspire.
45. Life and death, good and evil, male and female.
46. Campbell (1949/2008).
47. These battles represent the process of healing with the father.
48. Campbell (1949/2008).
49. Campbell (1949/2008).
50. Campbell (1949/2008).
51. Campbell (1949/2008), p.91
52. Episode 4–10, "Heaven and Hell" (November 20, 2008).
53. Episode 6–3, "The Third Man" (October 8, 2010).
54. Episode 5–22, "Swan Song" (May 13, 2010).

# Depression

*"I'm tired, Sam. I'm tired of this job, this life, this*
*weight on my shoulders, man. I'm tired of it."*
—Dean Winchester[1]

> *"When the terminally ill patient can no longer deny his*
> *illness, when he is forced to undergo more . . . he cannot*
> *smile it off anymore. His numbness or stoicism, his anger*
> *and rage will soon be replaced with a great sense of loss."*
> —psychiatrist Elisabeth Kübler-Ross[2]

A person's mood can be depressed without qualifying as a mental disorder. A person can feel empty, miserable, and unmotivated without the severity, duration, or variety of behavioral, cognitive, and other maladaptive symptoms associated with a condition such as *major depression* (also known as *clinical depression* or *major depressive disorder*).[3] When terminally ill patients seemed to be in the depression period, psychiatrist Elisabeth Kübler-Ross viewed this not as a mental illness but instead as a normal response to their situations: "We withdraw from life, left in a fog of intense sadness, wondering, perhaps, if there is any point in going on alone. Why go on at all?"[4] Both Winchester brothers die (a lot), but because it is Dean who more often has reason to anticipate his death,[5] he experiences more *anticipatory grief* (which Kübler-Ross also called *preparatory grief*[6]) for the upcoming loss of his life. From the perspective of the terminal individual, losing life means losing everything and everyone he or she values. Repeatedly doomed Dean Winchester keeps reaching the point at which he says he's tired of it all and for a time stops fighting his fate.[7] "I'm tired of burying friends, Sam," he says on one of these many occasions. "I'm just—I'm just getting tired." [8]

In the *Diagnostic and Statistical Manual of Mental Disorders* (known as the DSM or DSM-5 for its fifth edition), the American Psychiatric Association cautions professionals against labeling bereavement depression without more carefully considering the client's life,[9] and this note of caution might logically apply to those facing their own deaths. Knowing they're dying does not normally make people happy, and so unhappiness about it is normal. At some point, giving up may be a normal thing to do. When none of them see any way to stop the Darkness from ending the universe, hopelessness crushes both Castiel and Chuck Himself, and each resigns himself to a gloomy end. "Now's kinda all we got," says Chuck.[10]

When a grieving person also has a depressive disorder, the symptoms, impairment, and *prognosis* (estimated outcome) all tend to be worse. Bereavement-related depression occurs more often in people who are already prone to depressive symptoms.[11] Dean Winchester qualifies on that count,[12] and Bobby Singer even more so. The death of Bobby's wife pushes him into a number of depressive symptoms, notably his heavy drinking, and when Dean returns from his summer in Hell, he learns that misery over Dean's death has worsened Bobby's alcohol abuse. "Like I said," Bobby acknowledges when Dean picks up one of the many empty liquor bottles scattered around Singer's home, "last few months ain't been that easy."[13]

Feeling unhappy about dying may be normal enough, yet a dying person can reach the point of feeling better. For some, there can be inner peace.

## References

American Psychiatric Association (2013). *Diagnostic and statistical manual of mental disorders* (5th ed.) (DSM-5). Washington, DC: American Psychiatric Association.

Kübler-Ross, E. (1969). *On death and dying: What the dying have to teach doctors, nurses, clergy, and their own families.* London, UK: Routledge.

Kübler-Ross, E., & Kessler, D. (2005/2014). *On grief and grieving: Finding the meaning of grief through the five stages of loss.* New York, NY: Scribner.

Morales, D. (n.d.). *Psychology of supernatural: The mark of Cain and depression.* Psycholo-geek: http://www.psycholo-geek.com/2015/06/the-psychology-of-supernatural-mark-of.html.

Wakefield, J. C., & Schmitz, M. F. (2013). Normal vs. disordered bereavement-related depression: Are the differences real or tautological? *Acta Psychiatrica Scandinavica, 127*(2), 159–168.

## Notes

1. Episode 2–9, "Croatoan" (December 7, 2006).
2. Kübler-Ross (1969), p. 97.
3. Wakefield & Schmitz (2013).
4. Kübler-Ross & Kessler (2005/2014), p. 20.
5. Episodes 1–12, "Faith" (January 17, 2006); 2–22, "All Hell Breaks Loose," part 2 (May 17, 2007).
6. Kübler-Ross (1969).
7. Episodes 2–9, "Croatoan" (December 7, 2006); 3-1, "The Magnificent Seven" (October 4, 2007); 4–16, "On the Head of a Pin" (March 19, 2009); 4–20, "The Rapture" (April 30, 2009); "Shut Up, Dr. Phil" (October 21, 2011).
8. Episode 4–16, "On the Head of a Pin."
9. American Psychiatric Association (2013).
10. Episode 11–23, "Alpha and Omega" (May 25, 2016), whereas Crowley continues to think ahead and waits until a Winchester rallies the troops. "Bingo."
11. American Psychiatric Association (2013).
12. Morales (n.d.).
13. Episode 4–01, "Lazarus Rising" (September 18, 2008).

# PART V

# FACT AND FANTASY

## CHAPTER EIGHTEEN

# Cognitive Biases: Sometimes Seeing Isn't Believing

### ERIN CURRIE

*"Give me one good reason why I should believe you."*
—Sam Winchester[1]

*"When men wish to construct or support a theory,
how they torture facts into their service."*
—author Charles Mackay[2]

How is it that one person can fail to see and appropriately act on something that seems to be clear and obvious to another person? A common mission throughout the field of psychology is to help people accurately understand their world and make effective decisions on the basis of that understanding. Through research, a multitude of biases have been identified that affect what information is taken in, how information is processed, and the resulting decisions and behaviors.[3] Sam and Dean Winchester interact with a lot of people who, in the face of strong evidence of the supernatural, refuse to believe their supernatural explanations. This is especially problematic when they need help from those people to defeat the monsters.

Dean and Sam have their work cut out for them when they need the help of the local citizens and law enforcement in their hunting grounds.

## Cognitive Bias

The human brain has a lot to manage. There is the continuous stream of sensory data from the environment as well as the internal bodily processes, thoughts, and feelings to be assessed. Then all of it has to be integrated into a comprehendible, useful whole. To manage everything, the brain has shortcuts that allow it to process the onslaught of information more efficiently. Without these mechanisms, each bit of information would have to be measured for its merit against all the other immediate information and our preexisting body of knowledge.[4] The delay in reaction time this would cause would make it almost impossible to function in the everyday world and possibly affect basic survival.[5] For example, when a noose-bearing ghost appears, a detailed analysis of internal and external information, weighing all possible conclusions, may not be an effective survival strategy.[6] Running first and asking questions later is more likely to keep the average person alive.

Cognitive shortcuts (*heuristics*) may be useful for survival, but they aren't accurate enough when a nuanced and detailed analysis is needed.[7] The term *cognitive bias* is used when the otherwise useful cognitive mechanisms create errors in perception, attention, information processing, or decision making.[8] If a cognitive bias in attention causes a hunter to overlook a key piece of supernatural information, that hunter could find himself or herself bringing a gun to a wendigo fight.[9]

As if simple bias alone isn't enough to contend with, the body of research on cognitive biases shows that biases can range from being completely outside of conscious awareness to being fully conscious and intentional. Usually there is some amount of both.[10] With the exception of the occasional demonic possession, the local sheriff isn't deliberately making poor decisions and endangering the community. Unfortunately, sheriffs are up against both supernatural and cognitive forces that they do not understand.[11]

## Perception and Attention

The brain uses heuristic shortcuts to filter out what is unimportant and focus on what is most important. This can help people ignore the little background noises of life and focus on the task at hand.[12] Without this cognitive feature, a person would be constantly inundated with sensory information. With it, a person may ignore the old house noises that are actually deadly poltergeist noises.[13]

*Confirmation bias* is the tendency for the brain to notice and process information that is consistent with a person's beliefs about the world. When people search their environment for information to understand an event, they are more likely to pay attention to information that is consistent with what they know and have experienced.[14] Before Sam and Dean came to town and even afterward, most civilians and law enforcement officers did not believe monsters are real. Therefore, if the police officers see a mauled dead body, they are going to look for what they've dealt with before, such as wolves.[15]

Although the confirmation bias can be caused by the conscious desire to be proved right, there is an underlying unconscious cognitive shortcut. People typically look for the presence of features over the absence of features even when beliefs are not involved.[16] The unfortunate consequence of this shortcut is that people are more likely to miss important information that comes from absence, such as the repeated lack of a heart in bodies or the lack of wolves in the area of the attack.[17]

As the amount of information increases or when there are multiple possible conclusions that could be drawn, people are more likely to overlook information that does not fit neatly into their established knowledge frameworks.[18] Thus, even when Sam and Dean point out that the victim of a werewolf was attacked in their office and there was no other evidence of an animal presence, animal attack still is listed as the official cause of death.[19] The research shows that once people reach a viable conclusion that fits the information well enough, they are unlikely to fully consider alternative explanations presented to them later.[20] The evidence that the detective sees is close enough to a wolf attack to prevent him from seeking or considering other explanations.[21]

There is also the *Pollyanna effect*, which is the tendency to give preference to information that is pleasant over information that is unpleasant.[22] Sam and Dean hunt a vengeful ghost that is killing local men and leaving no bodies. Despite knowing the related lore, local officers hold to their theory that it is a serial kidnapper or killer.[23] Kidnapping isn't pleasant generally, but in this case if it's a kidnapper, there is a chance to save the victims. Even if it's a serial killer, most of the law enforcement professionals Sam and Dean work with are better equipped to deal with a flesh-and-blood killer than with a ghost.

The human brain is hardwired to seek patterns, whether seeing a face in the craters of the moon or looking for otherworldly portents to figure out the location of the yellow-eyed demon.[24] The man in the moon is an example of an *illusory correlation*, in which a person perceives a relationship between things that happen together even though they aren't actually related.[25] When citizens cannot avoid the unexplainable, they often use recent mundane happenings to create an explanation. Drug use may be the most common mundane scapegoat, blamed for everything from unusual witness testimonies to supernatural possession. In Gunnison, Colorado, marijuana tourism resulting from recent legalization is used to explain the odd behavior of hikers and mass disappearances of locals. Instead, it's a 27-year supernatural breeding cycle.[26]

## Information Processing

People tend to default to automatic information processing until their attention is unavoidably directed to information that indicates that their reasoning is false. They may even start to question their larger ability to understand their world.[27] This is similar to Sam, Dean, and Bobby Singer going back and digging through more archaic lore to determine which monster they are facing when the facts no longer support their initial assumptions. Occasionally, they even question their sense of expertise.[28]

The *availability heuristic* is an information-processing shortcut that uses the sense of ease of information recall to determine whether a fact is true. The easier a piece of information is to remember, the truer it feels. High frequency of use of a piece of information is one way to make information come to mind more quickly and easily.[29] Thus, at the beginning of the Apocalypse when a scientist is asked why the light output of the sun has decreased by 6 percent, he says that the sun's fluctuation is natural even though the length of time and the degree of fluctuation are unusual. The scientist is able to call to mind far more times that he has observed the sun's energy fluctuating than times when the world ending.[30]

## Decision Making

It has been noted that people tend to be overconfident in their understanding of the world and the judgments they make about it. This is true for supernatural experts as well as civilians.[31] Hunter Rufus Turner interprets evidence related to repeated deaths in the same house as signs of a ghost, ignoring the incongruent but pivotal information that the creature put its victims into a coma. When salting and burning the bones of the past residents doesn't work, Bobby recalls hunting a similar, though unidentified, monster in the past and how he defeated it. They never figured out that it was a soul eater.[32]

The *fundamental attribution error* is an illusory correlation that causes a lot of interpersonal and social issues. It is the tendency to neglect situational factors that influence another person's behavior. Instead, the person's short-term behavior is connected to his or her long-term character.[33] This is a bias that many of the hunters show, even Dean.[34] The underlying need that this error satisfies is simplicity of structure.[35] One is able to create an understanding of a situation and a corresponding set of rules quickly when one considers only the immediate behavior of another person. That person now can be categorized as good or bad, human or monster, and so on, and the corresponding set of rules for engagement can be applied quickly. Is it a monster? Yes. The monster rule is you kill it, call it a day, and have a beer.[36]

## Overcoming Bias and Saving the Day

*"Look, we're not asking you to believe that this is true. Just act like you do. People do it all the time."*
—Dean Winchester[37]

*"Rational beliefs bring us closer to getting*
*good results in the real world."*
—psychologist Albert Ellis[38]

What is a hunter to do when he or she needs the help of the
locals to kill the monster or at least prevent more deaths?
Cognitive bias researchers have found some methods for getting
around and even dismantling biases.[39] Some of these methods
the hunters already use; others they should consider adding to
their repertoires.

One method of dismantling bias is to point out to a person
how his or her perception and understanding of the situation
are flawed. People who are made to attend to information that
disconfirms their preferences are able to remember confirming
and disconfirming information equally well.[40] This is Sam's
preferred method early in his adult hunting career. Even though
he runs into a lot of resistance from Dean and the people he is
trying to save, Sam isn't entirely wrong in his plan.[41] Research
shows that people can reduce the impact of biased information
processing and decision making when they are aware of their
faulty thinking.[42] The *identified victim effect* is another option
for beating bias. This is the phenomenon in which people are
more likely to intervene when they are aware of the needs of a
single identifiable person than when they are informed that a
group of people needs help.[43] This is the reason Sam and Dean
have better luck persuading people to believe them and help
them when they can point to a specific person who will be
hurt if they don't cooperate. It is easier to empathize with one
sympathy-arousing victim and his or her distress. The more
distress a person feels about another's suffering, the more likely
that person is to get involved. This is especially true when the
person identifies with the victim, such as a member of his or
her family or the community to the point where Sam and Dean
literally go to Hell and back for each other.[44]

*Cognitive busyness*, which is the state of trying to do too many mental tasks at once, can override efforts to overcome bias and must be guarded against.[45] Sam's time as a pseudo-demon forces Dean to question his Fae monster bias, but that didn't stop him from killing Sam's kitsune friend. Dean's distraction with Sam's Lucifer hallucinations may have prevented him from challenging his biases even after Sam explained the circumstances of her killings and her resolution never to kill another human.[46]

Cognitive biases aren't always a barrier to Sam and Dean while they are hunting. There is one type of shortcut that they use to their benefit on a regular basis: *authority bias*. A classic study in psychology shows that people follow the orders of those with the appearance of authority even past the point where they violate their own values of not causing harm. The people in the study obeyed authority even when there was no chance of punishment.[47] Sam and Dean take advantage of the appearance of authority when they need to get people to cooperate by regularly impersonating law enforcement and even child psychologists. They occasionally resort to threatening people with legal consequences while impersonating law enforcement, but most often the identification with authority is enough to get them what they need.[48]

What conclusion can be drawn from the research on cognitive shortcuts and the biases they cause? The same conclusion that should be drawn from the hunting experiences of the Winchester boys: Don't be too hasty. These biases can help people manage everyday life and survive immediate disaster. However, whenever possible, we should try to understand these biases and the problems they are capable of causing. This is necessary if we want to have a real understanding of our world and make the best decisions. Whether we are trying to slay the right monster or doing something more mundane such as deciding whether to go into the family business, it helps to see the situation clearly.[49]

# ROAD MUSIC

## Just World Fallacy

The belief that people get what they deserve is called the *just world fallacy*. The theory underlying this bias is that people want a predictable and stable existence. One way to achieve that is to believe that doing good things will cause good things to happen to you and doing bad things will cause bad things to happen.[53] Sam and Dean rely on this logic to justify killing monsters that hurt humans.[54]

The fallacy of this logic comes when one is faced with a victim of unfortunate circumstance in which a good person experiences harm. People who strongly believe in a just world experience *cognitive dissonance*, which is the distress experienced when one is confronted with two conflicting facts.[55] They must choose between their belief in a just world and the goodness of the victim. For those who choose the latter, the more serious the harm and the more innocent the victim, the more negative the attitudes that need to be generated toward the victim to justify the harm.[56] By just world logic, repeatedly

# HUNTERS, INTERRUPTED:
# CONFIRMATION BIAS

**Travis Langley**

In order to investigate mysterious deaths at a mental hospital, Sam and Dean Winchester get themselves committed simply by telling the insane-sounding truth about their lives.[58] Doctors and other staff members they encounter make the same kind of mistake made by real people in a famous investigation of mental hospitals. Psychologist David Rosenhan and his colleagues once infiltrated twelve different facilities, getting themselves committed in order to investigate admission and treatment procedures.[59] Akin to how fictional staff members fail to discern the Winchesters' true purpose, none of the real staffers identified Rosenhan's *pseudopatients* as pretenders.

After getting themselves admitted by reporting a single auditory hallucination (a voice saying, "empty," "hollow," and "thud"[60]), the Rosenhan researchers stopped feigning the symptom. Staff members committed *confirmation bias*, interpreting any behavior as if it confirmed their existing beliefs (the admitting diagnoses).[61] For example, a nurse referred to one researcher's note-taking as pathological "writing behavior." Thirty-five out of 118 fellow patients, however, eyed such behavior more critically and expressed suspicions that the pseudopatients were mentally healthy and possibly journalists investigating the hospital. The respective hospitals only released each researcher when he finally called himself insane, when he affirmed the staff's beliefs. The Winchesters, of course, skip normal release procedures and break out of the place after they kill a monster.

saving the world should get Sam and Dean a wonderful life, but this is clearly not the case. Sam and Dean justify their suffering by turning this bias on themselves, focusing more on their misdeeds than on the people they save.[57]

## References

Darley, J. M., & Latané, B. (1968). Bystander intervention in emergencies: Diffusion of responsibility. *Journal of Personality & Social Psychology, 8*(4, pt. 1), 377–383.

Devine, P. G., Plant, E. A., Amodio, D. M., Harmon-Jones, E., & Vance, S. L. (2002). The regulation of explicit and implicit race bias: The role of motivation to respond without prejudice. *Journal of Personality & Social Psychology, 82*(5), 835–848.

Dolinski, D., & Grzyb, T. (2016). One serious shock versus gradated series of shocks: Does "multiple feet-in-the-door" explain obedience in Milgram studies? *Basic & Applied Social Psychology, 38*(5), 276-283.

Epstein, R. (2001, January). *The prince of reason.* Psychology Today: https://www.psychologytoday.com/articles/200101/the-prince-reason.

Fazio, L. K., Brashier, N. M., Payne, B. K., & Marsh, E. J. (2015). Knowledge does not protect against illusory truth. *Journal of Experimental Psychology: General, 144*(5), 993–1002.

Festinger, L. (1957). *A theory of cognitive dissonance.* Stanford, CA: Stanford University Press.

Frost, P., Casey, B., Griffin, K., Raymundo, L., Farrell, C., & Carrigan, R. (2015). The influence of confirmation bias on memory and source monitoring. *Journal of General Psychology, 142*(4), 238–252.

Griffin, D. W., & Tversky, A. (1992). The weighing of evidence and the determinants of confidence. *Cognitive Psychology, 24*(3), 411–435.

Jang, S. M. (2014). Challenges to selective exposure: Selective seeking and avoidance in a multitasking media environment. *Mass Communication & Society, 17*(5), 665–688.

Klauer, K. C., Musch, J., & Naumer, B., (2000). On belief bias in syllogistic reasoning. *Psychological Review, 107*(4), 852–884.

Kogut, T., & Ritov, I. (2005). The "identified victim" effect: An identified group, or just a single individual? *Journal of Behavioral Decision Making, 18*, 157–167.

Lerner, M. J. & Miller, D.T. (1978). Just world research and the attribution process: Looking back and looking ahead. *Psychological Bulletin, 85*(5), 1030–1058.

Mack, A. (2003). Inattentional blindness: Looking without seeing. *Current Directions in Psychological Science, 12*(5), 180–184.

Mackay, C. (1852/1932). *Extraordinary popular delusions and the madness of crowds* (2nd ed.). Boston, MA: Page.

Matlin, M. W., & Stang, D. J. (1978). *The Pollyanna principle: Selectivity in language memory and thought.* Cambridge, MA: Shenkman.

Milgram, S. (1963). Behavioral study of obedience. *Journal of Abnormal & Social Psychology, 67*(4), 371–378.

Nickerson, R. S. (1998). Confirmation bias: A ubiquitous phenomenon in many guises. *Review of General Psychology, 2*(2), 175–220.

Pezdek, K., Whetstone, T., Reynolds, K., Askari, N., & Dougherty, T. (1989). Memory for real-world scenes: The role of consistency with schema expectation. *Journal of Experimental Psychology: Learning, Memory, & Cognition, 15*, 587–595.

Rajsic, J., Wilson, D. E., & Pratt, J. (2015). Confirmation bias in visual search. *Journal of Experimental Psychology: Human Perception & Performance, 41*(5), 1353–1364.

Rosenhan, D. L. (1973). On being sane in insane places. *Science, 179*, 250–258.

Ross, L. (1977). The intuitive psychologist and his shortcomings: Distortions in the attribution process. In L. Berkowitz (Ed.). *Advances in Experimental Social Psychology* (Vol. 10). New York, NY: Academic Press.

Scherer, L. D., de Vries, M., Zikmund-Fisher, B. J., Witteman, H. O., & Fagerlin, A. (2015). Trust in deliberation: The consequences of deliberative decision strategies for medical decisions. *Health Psychology, 34*(11), 1090–1099.

Schwarz, N., Bless, H., Strack, F., Klumpp, G., Rittenauer-Schatka, H., & Simons, A. (1991). Ease of retrieval as information: Another look at the availability heuristic. *Journal of Personality & Social Psychology, 61*(2), 195–202.

Stalder, D. R. (2009). Competing roles for the subfactors of need for closure in committing the fundamental attribution error. *Personality & Individual Differences, 47,* 701–705.

Turk, D. C. & Salovey, P. (1985). Cognitive structures, cognitive processes, and cognitive-behavior modification: II. Judgments and inferences of the clinician. *Cognitive Therapy & Research, 9*(1), 19–33.

Van den Bos, K. & Maas, M. (2009). On the psychology of the belief in a just world: Exploring experiential and rationalistic paths to victim blaming. *Personality & Social Psychology Bulletin, 35*(12), 1567–1578.

Van den Bos, K., Peters, S. L., Bobocel, D. R., & Ybema, J. F. (2006). On preferences and doing the right thing: Satisfaction with advantageous inequity when cognitive processing is limited. *Journal of Experimental Social Psychology, 42,* 273–289.

## Notes

1. Episode 2-3, "Bloodlust" (October 12, 2006).
2. Mackay (1852/1932).
3. Jang (2014); Nickerson (1998); Scherer et al. (2015).
4. Winter & Uleman (1984).
5. Freidrich (1993).
6. Episode 1–17, "Hell House" (March 30, 2016).
7. Scherer et al. (2015).
8. Nickerson (1998).
9. Episode 1–2, "Wendigo" (September 20, 2005).
10. Nickerson (1998).
11. Episodes 3–12, "Jus in Bello" (February 21 2008); 8–11, "LARP and the Real Girl" (January 23, 2013); 11–19, "The Chitters" (April 27, 2016).
12. Mack (2003).
13. Episode 1–9, "Home" (November 15, 2005).
14. Frost et al. (2015).
15. Episode 6–8, "All Dogs Go to Heaven" (November 12, 2010).
16. Klauer et al. (2000); Rajsic et al. (2015).
17. Episode 2–17, "Heart" (March 22, 2007).
18. Nickerson (1998).
19. Episode 2–17, "Heart" (March 22, 2007).
20. Fazio et al. (2015).
21. Griffin & Tversky (1992).
22. Matlin & Stang (1978).
23. Episode 1–1, "Pilot" (September 13, 2005).
24. Turk & Salovey (1985); episode 2–2, "Everybody Loves a Clown" (October 5, 2006).
25. Fazio et al. (2015).
26. Episodes 8–11, "LARP and the Real Girl" (January 23, 2013); 11–19, "The Chitters" (April 27, 2016).

27. Fazio et al. (2015).
28. Episode 6–4, "Weekend at Bobby's" (October 15, 2010); 11–16, "Safe House" (March 23, 2016).
29. Shwarz et al. (1991).
30. Episode 11–23, "Alpha and Omega" (May 25, 2016).
31. Scherer et al. (2015).
32. Episode 11–16, "Safe House" (March 23, 2016).
.33. Ross (1977).
34. Episode 2–3, "Bloodlust" (October 12, 2006).
35. Stadler (2009).
36. Episodes 2–3, "Bloodlust" (October 12, 2006); 7-3, "The Girl Next Door" (October 7, 2011).
37. Episode 11–21, "All in the Family" (May 11, 2016).
38. Epstein (2001).
39. Devine et al. (2002).
40. Pezdek et al. (1989).
41. Episode 1–8, "Bugs" (November 8, 2005).
42. Devine et al. (2002); Pezdek et al. (1989).
43. Kogut & Ritov (2005); episode 1–3, "Dead in the Water" (September 27, 2005).
44. Kogut & Ritov (2005); episodes 3–5, "Bedtime Stories" (November 1, 2007); 4–1, "Lazarus Rising" (September 18, 2008); 5–22, "Swan Song" (May 13, 2010).
45. Van den Bos et al. (2006).
46. Episode 7–3, "The Girl Next Door" (October 7, 2011).
47. Dolinski & Grzyb (2016); Milgram (1963).
48. Episodes 5–15, "Dead Men Don't Wear Plaid" (March 25, 2010); 11–8, "Just My Imagination" (December 2, 2015); 7–13, "The Slice Girls" (February 3, 2012).
49. Nickerson (1998); episode 1–2, "Wendigo" (September 20, 2005); 7–3, "The Girl Next Door" (October 7, 2011).
50. Townshend (1971); episode 5–8, "Changing Channels" (November 5, 2009).
51. Pezdek et al. (1989).
52. Episodes 1–1, "Pilot" (September 13, 2005); 5–15, "Dead Men Don't Wear Plaid" (March 25, 2010); 6–4, "Weekend at Bobby's" (October 15, 2010).
53. Lerner & Miller (1978).
54. Episode 2–3, "Bloodlust" (October 12, 2006).
55. Festinger (1957).
56. Van den Bos & Maas (2009).
57. Episodes 4–22, "Lucifer Rising" (May 14, 2009); 7–4, "Defending Your Life" (October 14, 2011).
58. Episode 5–1, "Sam, Interrupted" (January 23, 2010).
59. Rosenhan (1973).
60. Though Rosenhan sometimes referred to one word as "dull" rather than "hollow," he reported it as "hollow" in the original 1973 report.
61. Darley & Latané, B. (1968).

## CHAPTER NINETEEN

# Wild Folklore: Driving Through Normal with "Two Boys, an Old Drunk, and a Fallen Angel"

### J. SCOTT JORDAN

*"I remember the most remarkable event—remarkable because
it never came to pass. It was averted by two boys, an old
drunk, and a fallen angel. The grand story, and we
ripped up the ending and the rules and destiny,
leaving nothing but freedom and choice."*
—Castiel[1]

*"At its core, the idea of purpose is the idea that what
we do matters to people other than ourselves."*
—psychologist Angela Duckworth[2]

**"S**he's from Hell. I'm from Normal, Illinois—1958."[3] This
is not the type of phrase a person often hears in daily
life, but imagine you overheard someone say it at a party. How
would you respond? You'd probably look around the room,

# ROAD MUSIC

### "Born to Be Wild" by Steppenwolf[4]

As Sam and Dean drive their Chevy Impala through small-town USA, they are constantly surprised by the behavior of demons and angels—and even themselves. As a result, they become increasingly *metacognitive;* that is, they begin to have thoughts about their own thoughts, including the unconscious assumptions they make about the worthiness of demons, angels, and themselves. Regardless of any resulting guilt or remorse, however, their compulsion to confront the world *as it is* and protect others from the things they don't want to know pushes the brothers back into their car and out onto the open road.

trying to find some grumpy old guy in the act of introducing a woman he wasn't particularly fond of. If you actually saw such a couple, you'd think to yourself, "Okay. Everything's cool. Everything's normal. But man, who invited them?" The point is that the way we experience the world depends on what we think is normal. When Sam and Dean Winchester hear their grandfather, Henry Winchester, say these very words, it is obvious to them he is talking about an actual demon from Hell. However, since Henry looked to be the same age as the brothers, they had a hard time believing he was their grandfather. In short, for Sam and Dean, demons are normal but time-traveling grandparents are not.

These types of plays on the idea of what is normal occur throughout *Supernatural* and serve to remind us that like Henry Winchester, we are from Normal. Not in the geographic sense but in the developmental sense that we grew up in a place that became *our* Normal, a place where our family and friends held beliefs that we either agreed with or rebelled against. Does God exist? Should I go to college? Should I get married? Or in the case of Sam and Dean, should we kill monsters? Should we impersonate FBI agents? Should we become the vessels of Lucifer and Michael? Although the questions faced by Sam and Dean are obviously different from those faced by most people, they are asked for the same reasons, specifically, to figure out what is normal for oneself.

## Navigating Between Different Normals

Most psychologists agree that what is normal depends on the individual and the group.[5] Although each individual has his or her own usual (i.e., normal) pattern of behaviors and beliefs, groups and societies also have normal patterns of behaviors and beliefs that they expect individuals to follow. Psychologists often refer to these group expectations as *norms*.[6]

Sam and Dean, for example, regularly hunt and kill demons. Those behaviors and the belief that they should engage in them are normal for their lives but not for society at large. The brothers' awareness that their lifestyle violates societal norms often puts them in a state of *cognitive dissonance*,[7] the experience of having thoughts, behaviors, and/or beliefs that contradict one another. Such dissonance often leads the brothers to disparage their hunter lifestyle, as Dean does when discussing the fact that they are hunting a ghost: "What the hell? I mean, normal people, they see a monster and they run, but not us. No, no, no we search out things that want to kill us. . . . You know who does that? Crazy people. We are insane."[8]

Sam and Dean experience such norm-driven bouts of uncertainty because they live *inside* both sets of norms. Research in social psychology indicates that if members of normal society were to witness the brothers engaging in hunter behaviors that violated societal norms, the brothers would be treated as

What looks normal in Supernatural often is not. Cathedral featured in episode 2–13, "Houses of the Holy" (February 1, 2007).[9]

members of a morally or mentally inferior out-group.[10] Social psychologists refer to this tendency to hold derogatory views about members of out-groups as *stigma*.[11]

Since the brothers know they belong to a stigmatized group, they have to engage in "normal" hunter behaviors such as killing vampires, conjuring demons, and preventing multiple apocalypses by blending in with normal society and making sure they do not get caught violating majority, in-group expectations. Researchers refer to this ability to navigate different systems of norms in daily life as *code switching*.[12] Sam and Dean repeatedly engage in code switching when they impersonate FBI agents by dressing like them, standing like them, and talking like them— at least in a way that is consistent with television-driven stereotypes. Research in developmental psychology indicates that members of minority groups report engaging in code-switching types of behaviors when they have to participate in contexts that are dominated by majority norms and expectations.[13]

## Aren't All Main Streets Really the Same?

In addition to addressing the tensions between individual and group norms, Sam and Dean's extended road trip through the various Main Streets of American normativity draws our attention to ways in which different normative systems are actually similar. Specifically, believing in demons is normal for Sam and Dean because they have encountered them many, many times during their lives. As a matter of fact, Sam and Dean are fully aware that their unique life history is responsible for their norms being so different from everyone else's. While once again doubting their hunter norms and the fact that they hate vampires so much, Dean says, "What if we killed things that didn't deserve killing? I mean, the way Dad raised us. . . ."[14] Here Dean is experiencing cognitive dissonance because he knows his loathing of vampires is due to the way he was raised and knows that his upbringing was not normal.

Although it might seem obvious that Sam and Dean's bizarre system of norms developed from their equally bizarre pasts, their self-awareness on this issue invites us to ask to what extent our own normal norms are the result of our own past experiences. That is, might it be the case that all systems of normality are similar in that they emerge developmentally, like Sam and Dean's, out of a person's unique past? As an example from the field of psychology, contemporary norms regarding sexuality and identity are radically different from what they were half a century ago. As recently as 1972, the American Psychiatric Association considered homosexuality a treatable *mental disorder.* On the basis of a combination of scientific research[15] and social activism, homosexuality was declassified as a mental disorder in 1973 and classified instead as a normal variant of human sexuality. Because of this change in professional and societal norms, today's youths tend not to consider an attraction to members of the same sex *abnormal.*[16] As a matter of fact, many reject labels such as "gay" and "lesbian" because their own norms do not see their sexual preference as playing an extremely important role in their personal identity.[17]

If it is true that norms come and go, historically for societies and developmentally for individuals, it also seems true that nothing is ever normal because it is *supposed* to be. Rather, things are normal simply because they have happened *over and over again* and/or because people have told us *over and over again* that certain behaviors and beliefs are normal. Of course, such a past-driven take on norms is at odds with the way people experience them, for people tend to experience their norms *intuitively,*[18] which means they experience them automatically, without conscious effort. As a result, norms feel as if they are norms because they are *supposed to be.*

As an example of the intuitive *feel* of norms, Castiel says the following while praying to God: "I'm asking you, Father, one last time: Am I doing the right thing? Am I on the right path? You have to tell me. You have to give me a sign."[19] Clearly, Castiel at this point intuitively believes that God is in charge of the universe and has a plan for all of us, and he believes this because he has been told it is true his entire existence. But in light of his recent experience with freedom and choice, that is, helping the Winchesters save the world from the Apocalypse, he experiences the ideas of freedom and choice *in relation to* his normative, and thus intuitive, belief that God has a plan. Interestingly, recent findings in cognitive neuroscience clarify why norms emerge from past experiences yet simultaneously feel as if they don't.

## Why Norms Feel Like Intuitions:
## The Brain Is a Hope-Filled Cage

Have you ever been talking to a friend while walking down a set of stairs and suddenly realized you were falling? Research indicates that you experienced surprise because your brain was *unconsciously* anticipating when your foot would reach the next step and for some reason or another the brain's expectations were wrong.[20] Maybe you thought you had reached the last step but there was still one left. Whatever the reason, the example reveals that the brain is continuously creating anticipations, unconsciously, about what our bodies are going to do next. Although we do not experience our brains creating these unconscious expectations, when they are violated, we experience *surprise.*

Surprise plays a major role in *Supernatural* as characters continually experience events that violate their norms. In almost every episode, particularly in the first few minutes, a "normal" character is surprised because he or she sees a creature or event he or has never seen before. For Sam and Dean, who have experienced such events most of their lives, it is rather normal to see people surprised by supernatural phenomena. This familiarity with surprise allows Sam and Dean to help people who feel they may be going crazy. When Sam tries to coax a young girl to talk to him about her recent supernatural experiences, he tells her about his similar experiences as a way to help her feel more normal about hers: "I've been right where you're standing right now. Hearing things, even seeing things that can't be explained."[21]

What the girl's surprise and Dean's lack of surprise have in common is that both are based on *past experiences.* The girl has never heard dead people talking to her on the phone. As a result, she is surprised when it happens. Sam, in contrast, has experienced many people being surprised by supernatural experiences and as a result is not surprised by her surprise. The point here is that the unconscious expectations our brains continuously generate are based on our past experiences. This means that our past is continuously and unconsciously fed forward into the present as anticipation about the future, as if our brains were telling us stories all the time about what will happen next that are based on what has happened before. An example of such unconscious storytelling is when Castiel tries to persuade Dean that he is an angel, that he saved Dean from Hell, and that good things actually do happen in this world, and Dean responds, "Not in my experience."[22] Here we have two examples of how past experiences underlie norms and expectations. Dean has never experienced an angel, and so he refuses to believe they exist, and because he has not lived a pleasant life, he refuses to believe someone or something would ever rescue him from Hell.

Although it may seem strange that our brains continuously generate predictions about the future that are based on the past, it turns out that such predictions are necessary for *normal* perception.[23] For example, most people find it very difficult to tickle their own arms. This difficulty is due to the fact that when you start to stroke your arm with your finger, the brain *anticipates* the stroking sensation on the arm and reduces your sensitivity to the stroking sensation.[24] Reducing your sensitivity to sensations that you yourself produce is important for normal perception because it allows the brain to distinguish experiences caused by you from experiences caused by the environment. For example, if we see a ghost in the hallway in the middle of the night, the first thing we do after we stop screaming is rub our eyes and look again. Why do we rub our eyes? Because if we still see a ghost, we believe the experience is being caused by something in the environment, in this case an actual ghost. But if we don't see the ghost again, we believe the ghost experience was somehow caused by our own brain and swear never to drink again.

The point is that the brain's ability to generate anticipations about what we should experience next allows us to make the fundamental psychological distinction between *self* and *not-self*[25] as well as the distinction between what is real and what is not. Sam attempts to make this distinction by knocking on the wall of the crappy motel room in which they have suddenly appeared. Sam's fist makes a knocking sound and does not go through the wall, both of which Sam anticipated would happen if the wall were real. Given the positive results of the test, Sam says, "Solid. It's real. Nice."[26]

The idea that we need to distinguish self-produced experiences from environment-produced experiences is also supported by the finding that schizophrenics actually can tickle themselves.[27] This is possible because their brains do not generate anticipations the same way nonschizophrenic brains do. This difference in the way the brain uses anticipation also explains why schizophrenics experience hallucinations and delusions. They truly are hearing voices or truly believe that others are out to get them. The problem is that their brains are not able to detect that the voices and beliefs are being created by themselves. As a result, they experience the voices and beliefs as if they were coming from the environment.[28] This difficulty in tracking the cause of one's experiences is expressed by a vampire named Lucy when Sam and Dean try to persuade her that she has killed many people and is actually a vampire. Lucy says, "No. No, it wasn't real! It was the drug!"[29] Because Lucy has no previous experiences killing people, it is not an expectation she unconsciously generates about herself. And since she has no expectations of killing to compare to her actual experiences of killing, she experiences the killing as a hallucination—something that happened in her mind, not in the environment.

## The Curse of Anticipation: Escape the Cage by Telling a New Story

Although we may think that schizophrenics are somewhat trapped in their own minds, it seems that nonschizophrenics are trapped as well. We all continuously tell ourselves unconscious stories about the future that are based on the past, and we experience the present through these unconscious expectations. In daily life we refer to these stories as prejudices, stereotypes, and hasty decisions, and when we generate them, we don't experience them as being about ourselves. Rather, we experience our biases and stereotypes *intuitively*. Thus, we experience the person or event that activated our unconscious biases in terms of how it violated or did not violate our norms. Thus, we seem cursed—caged in our own expectations.

How do we escape the cage? How do we live our lives so that we are not forever slaves to our biases? *Supernatural* provides an answer: Set out on a road less traveled. In addition to all the surprises the characters experience throughout the series, the show reveals its commitment to surprise by putting the characters in settings that violate the norms of television tropes in general. When visiting an alternative reality as actors who simply play Sam and Dean on a TV show called *Supernatural*, the brothers discover that actor Jensen Ackles (who plays Dean) used to have a role in a soap opera, and we actually see a clip from the show. This is *metafiction*: fiction that makes reference to its status as fiction to surprise the reader or viewer and invite the audience members to ask questions about the nature of stories and the contexts they reference.[30]

By engaging in metafiction, *Supernatural* allows us to be *meta-cognitive* about our status as observers. That is, the story invites us to consciously examine the unconscious expectations we are continuously generating as we watch the show. Research indicates that metacognition can be used by schizophrenics to resist the negative stereotypes they believe others have of them.[31] Perhaps metacognition can help everyone escape the cage of expectations. When we make expectations conscious, we escape from the cage ever so briefly and are able to imagine alternative stories we might learn to tell ourselves. To make these alternatives a reality however, we have to do the hard work of living them day in and day out until eventually they become our new unconscious stories about ourselves. In short, we have to live a new story until it can become our new cage—our new normal.

## Wild Folklore: No Matter How Many Times You Die, Keep Moving

By engaging in metafiction, *Supernatural* continuously breaks free of its own cage and creates a new type of folklore for contemporary America. It is not a folklore about good and evil, right and wrong, or in-groups and out-groups but a *wild* folklore—a folklore that recognizes the past-driven nature of all normative systems and admonishes us to be ever vigilant of the cages we necessarily create for ourselves. Bobby explains the essence of such wild folklore rather well as Dean finds himself lamenting the normal life with Lisa and Ben he chose to leave behind. Bobby says, "Come on, now. You tried to hang it up and be a person with Lisa and Ben. And now here you are with a mean old coot and a van full of guns. That ain't person behavior, son. You're a hunter, meaning you're whatever the job you're doing today."[32]

Coming from a broken down old metacognitive drunk, that's pretty sound advice, particularly for someone trying to understand his own cage as they drive from Normal to Normal, helping others deal with the traumas they find in theirs. Of course, helping others is what brings purpose to Sam and Dean's wild ride. And for those they have helped, the brothers' continuing willingness to choose the road less traveled has made all the difference.

## References

Barreto, M., & Ellemers, N. (2010). Current issues in the study of social stigma: Some controversies and unresolved issues. *Journal of Social Issues, 66*(3), 431–445.

Blakemore, S. J., Wolpert, D., & Frith, C. (2000). Why can't you tickle yourself? *Neuroreport, 11*(11), R11–R16.

Brauer, M. (2001). Intergroup perception in the social context: The effects of social status and group membership on perceived out-group homogeneity and ethnocentrism. *Journal of Experimental Social Psychology, 37*(1), 15–31.

Coates, T. N. (2015). *Between the world and me.* New York, NY: Spiegel & Grow.

Cohler, B. J., & Hammack, P. L. (2007). The psychological world of the gay teenager: Social change, narrative, and "normality." *Journal of Youth & Adolescence, 36*(1), 47–59.

Duckworth, A. (2016). *Grit: The power of passion and perseverance.* New York, NY: Simon & Schuster.

Festinger, L. (1957). *A theory of cognitive dissonance.* Evanston, IL: Row, Peterson.

Fine, M., & Weis, L. (2010). Crime stories: A critical look through race, ethnicity, and gender. *International Journal of Qualitative Studies in Education, 11(3),* 435–459.

Fiske, S. T. (2002). What we know now about bias and intergroup conflict, the problem of the century. *Current Directions in Psychological Science, 11*(4), 123–128.

Frith, C. D., Blakemore, S. J., & Wolpert, D. M. (2000). Abnormalities in the awareness and control of action. *Philosophical Transactions of the Royal Society B, 355*(1404), 1771–1788.

Garcia, A. N. (2011). Breaking the mirror: Metafictional strategies in "Supernatural." In S. Abbott & D. Lavery (Eds), *TV goes to hell: An unofficial road map of Supernatural* (pp. 146–160). Toronto, Ontario, Canada: ECS.

Gerrig, R. J., & Zimbardo, P. G. (2002). *Psychology and life* (16th ed.). Boston, MA: Allyn & Bacon.

Haidt, J., & Joseph, C. (2004). Intuitive ethics: How innately prepared intuitions generate culturally variable virtues. *Daedalus, 133*(4), 55–66.

Jordan, J. S. (2003). Emergence of self and other in perception and action: An event-control approach. *Consciousness & Cognition, 12*(4), 633–646.

Jordan, J. S., & Hershberger, W. A. (1994). Timing the shift in retinal local signs that accompanies a saccadic eye movement. *Perception & Psychophysics, 55 (6),* 657–666.

Kinsey, A. C., Pomeroy, W. B., & Martin, C. E. (1948). *Sexual behavior in the human male.* Philadelphia, PA: Saunders.

Rabin, S. J., Hasson-Ohayon, I., Avidan, M., Rozencwaig, S., Shalev, H., & Kravetz, S. (2014). Metacognition in schizophrenia and schizotypy: Relation to symptoms of schizophrenia, traits of schizotypy and social quality of life. *Israel Journal of Psychiatry & Related Sciences, 51*(1), 44–53.

Savin-Williams, R. C. (2001). A critique of research on sexual-minority youths. *Journal of Adolescence, 24*(1), 5–13.

Schultz, P. W., Nolan, J. M:, Cialdini, R. B., Goldstein, N. J., & Griskevicius, V. (2007). The constructive, destructive, and reconstructive power of social norms. *Psychological Science, 18*(5), 429–434.

Strauss, L. C., & Cross W. E., Jr. (2005). Transacting black identity: A two-week daily-diary study. In G. Downey, J., Eccles, & C. M. Chatman (Eds.): *Navigating the future: Social identity, coping, and life tasks* (pp. 67–95).

## Notes

1. Episode 6–20, "The Man Who Would Be King" (May 6, 2011).
2. Duckworth (2016), p. 145.
3. Episode 8–12, "As Time Goes By" (January 30, 2013).
4. Written by Mars Bonfire; played in episode 7–23, "Survival of the Fittest" (May 18, 2012).
5. Gerrig & Zimbardo (2002).
6. Schultz et al. (2007).
7. Festinger (1957).
8. Episode 4–6, "Yellow Fever" (October 23, 2008).
9. Wheeler & Swords (2006).
10. Fiske (2002).
11. Barreto & Ellemers (2010).
12. Strauss & Cross (2005).
13. Strauss & Cross (2005).
14. Episode 2–3, "Bloodlust" (October 12, 2006).
15. Kinsey et al. (1948).
16. Cohler & Hammack (2007).
17. Savin-Williams (2001).
18. Haidt & Joseph (2004).
19. Episode 6–20, "The Man Who Would Be King" (May 6, 2011).
20. Jordan (2003).
21. Episode 3–14, "Long-Distance Call" (May 1, 2008).
22. Episode 4–1, "Lazarus Rising" (September 18, 2008).
23. Jordan & Hershberger (1994).
24. Blakemore et al. (2000).
25. Jordan (2003).
26. Episode 6–15, "The French Mistake" (February 25, 2011).
27. Frith et al. (2000).
28. Blakemore et al. (2000).
29. Episode 3–7, "Fresh Blood" (November 15, 2007)
30. Garcia (2011).
31. Rabin, et al.
32. Episode 7–9, "How to Win Friends and Influence Monsters" (November 18, 2011).

# CHAPTER TWENTY

# Natural Supernaturalism:
# Why Believe in Magic and Monsters?

ERIC D. WESSELMANN
AND JAMES S. NAIRNE

*"Of all the things we've hunted, how many of them
exist just because people believed in them?"*
—Sam Winchester[1]

*". . . supernatural beliefs are inevitable. At least knowing
where they come from and why we have them
makes it easier to understand belief in the
supernatural as part of being human."*
—experimental psychologist Bruce M. Hood[2]

Superstition, magic, and the spirit world: Why do people believe in the *supernatural* when these concepts are unsubstantiated by and sometimes even contradict direct scientific evidence?[3] Sam and Dean repeatedly have to give "the talk" to explain the supernatural to those who did not previously believe,[4] but sometimes they encounter individuals who already believe.

# ROAD MUSIC

### "(Don't Fear) the Reaper" by Blue Oyster Cult[5]

Contemplating our mortality and what (if anything) lies beyond death can provoke intense existential anxiety.[6] The Winchesters face reminders of mortality such as lethal threats, corpses, murders, and otherworldly beings (e.g., ghosts, reapers, angels, and demons[7]). Research indicates that religious or spiritual beliefs, especially belief in an afterlife and therefore some kind of continued existence, can help reduce death-related anxiety.[8] The Winchester brothers are not particularly religious, but at various points they visit Hell, Purgatory, and Heaven,[9] thus confirming that an afterlife exists and probably emboldening them to face death willingly to achieve their goals.[10]

Why does anyone who has not encountered the uncanny already believe? Early developmental psychologists assumed that supernatural beliefs were common in childhood but faded as mentally healthy individuals grew older.[11] However, much evidence shows that magical and rational thinking co-exist in both children and adults around the world.[12] These beliefs may offer assurance that beyond the world's chaos there exists order and beyond this mortal coil there exists something after death.

## Hunting for Agency and Meaning

Our survival depends on social relationships, and humans evolved to process and remember information relevant to one another.[13] Humans (newborns through adults) attend selectively to information about *animacy*—objects moving with a presumed purpose—probably because this information is associated with various survival-relevant agents (e.g., predators, wild game, friends or foes).[14] When the Ghostfacers investigate a haunted house, Ed Zeddmore misperceives a branch hitting the window as paranormal activity.[15] Humans are overly sensitive to animacy cues, especially when objects move in ambiguous ways.[16] This hyperactivity may help explain people's tendencies to attribute "bumps in the night" to supernatural agents,[17] as when Zeddmore recalls hearing a vase fall over and interprets it as evidence of ghosts.[18]

Humans also have a natural tendency to look for *meaningful* patterns in our environment in order to make causal predictions about both natural events (e.g., weather) and other people's actions (e.g., their reliability).[19] One of the first tactics the Winchesters or Bobby will use when investigating supernatural occurrences is to look for patterns such as shared characteristics among victims[20] or a pattern in a victim's bloodstains that forms a demonic sigil.[21] Psychologists argue that this orientation toward meaningful patterns may explain why individuals sometimes make spurious connections between coincidental events and ascribe supernatural explanations to those presumed connections.[22] The more religious Winchester, Sam, seems motivated to find meaning in the events he connects, especially when they involve his traumatic family history or his emerging psychic powers.[23] Even Dean entertains the possibility that the accidental (and eerily coincidental) death of a murderer he is chasing could have been an act of divine justice.[24]

## Supernaturally Memorable

Traditionally, people expect supernatural beings to perform actions outside anything natural: ghosts to walk through walls or teleport,[25] demons to cast spells and possess others,[26] and vampires to drink blood.[27] Typically, these properties violate our existing beliefs about the world (e.g., nothing can walk through walls) or represent unusual transfers of abilities from one thing to another (e.g., a haunted object). The Winchesters often avoid discussing the supernatural with nonhunters, especially the people they care about, because they know that most people would not believe them or would be distressed by the knowledge.[28]

Enduring supernatural concepts must have properties that are *minimally counterintuitive*: They generally conform to schemas that we have about everyday categories but possess only a few characteristics that violate those schemas. If a supernatural concept is too strange or counterintuitive, it limits our ability to make inferences and will not be remembered well.[29] Vampires are a good example because they generally fit a natural category—humans—but with minimally counterintuitive properties (they are dead and drink blood). Vampire-type creatures in various cultures,[30] as well as the ones faced by the Winchesters,[31] generally have these characteristics. However, if vampires also had six legs, disappeared on Tuesdays, and relied on photosynthesis, they would be tough to categorize and probably would not be remembered well. Most supernatural creatures that the Winchesters hunt are minimally counterintuitive.[32]

### Supernatural Control and Connection

The Winchesters often find themselves investigating cases in which people invoke supernatural agents to achieve desired outcomes, whether it is prosperity, protection, or retribution.[33] Individuals have a psychological need for control over their environments[34] even if the perceived control is illusory.[35] Superstitious behaviors (e.g., carrying luck charms) are good examples of ways in which individuals may satisfy this perceived need.[36] When Bela Talbot fights the Winchesters over a rabbit's foot, presumably it is because her employer wants the foot for its "lucky" properties.[37] Superstitious behavior may be especially attractive during times of stress or conflict.[38] When Sam and Dean are fighting demons, they draw sigils (such as their antipossession tattoos or the devil's traps) as protection against the demons' powers.[39]

There are several examples from *Supernatural* that involve characters using rituals from established religions (e.g., Christianity, Hoodoo, Zoroastrianism).[40] An important focus of many primitive and modern religious rituals is to exercise control over the environment either directly through one's actions or indirectly by influencing supernatural entities to intervene on one's behalf.[41] These practices follow the laws of *sympathetic magic*: contagion and similarity. Those laws hold that objects possess definitive magical properties—"essences."[42] It is through those essences that objects can influence one another, such as by acting on an object that physically resembles (and thus shares an essence with) another object (*similarity*) or by transferring an essence via direct contact (*contagion*).[43] Effigies or dolls used in magical practices exemplify the power of similarity: Acting on the doll is tantamount to acting on the person it represents. Sam and Dean investigate mysterious murders and find both Hoodoo markings and dolls suspiciously resembling the victims; they suspect that Hoodoo was used to murder the victims (although in this case they are incorrect).[44] In another example, Sam and Dean discuss how mandrake root, a plant used in folk remedies because of its humanlike shape, is an ingredient for making artificial humans called homunculi.[45]

Many tools and methods that the Winchesters use to combat supernatural entities evoke the psychological power of contagion. Paradoxically, there are several phenomena they investigate that also involve contagion. Because essences can be positive or negative, people's evaluations of the affected object differ depending on the perceived essence.[46] An object with a perceived *positive* essence will be valued for its potential to transmit that beneficial essence. John Winchester puts a rosary in a water tank and chants a Latin blessing in order to consecrate the water so that it will burn demonically possessed individuals.[47] Sam and Dean use salt, considered a purifying agent in the folklore of many cultures,[48] to deter against both ghosts and demons.[49]

Many hauntings the Winchesters investigate involve the law of contagion: Their family home where their mother was murdered became inhabited by a poltergeist, and they have encountered objects possessed by malevolent spirits (e.g., mirror, painting, truck).[50] Individuals will devalue and avoid an object with a perceived *negative* essence for fear of contamination. This avoidance tendency probably evolved as a way to deal with the constant threat of disease or infection.[51] Although adaptive, the law of contagion also promotes supernatural thinking. Individuals could fear physical contamination, as when they avoid touching something owned long ago by a sick individual, or they could fear moral contamination by touching an object previously owned by an immoral person (e.g., Hitler's sweater).[52] In either case, contamination is impossible, yet people still avoid those objects.

## Hunting for Immortality

Both Sam and Dean have difficulty accepting that their parents are dead and become upset when they think about the prospect that they are truly "gone."[53] Why do the Winchester brothers, and indeed most people, have difficulty contemplating someone's mortality and the possibility of nonexistence? People, typically within the first year of life, develop the concept of *object permanence*: They recognize that objects still exist when they are no longer physically present.[54] Object permanence applies to the concept of "people" as well; children recognize that others both exist physically and continue to have thoughts and feelings when not directly visible.[55] Concepts of spirits or ghosts are compatible with these natural tendencies.

Adults are used to assuming people exist even though they are not physically present, which helps sustain belief in an

# STIGMA MAGIC

## John B. Pryor and Eric D. Wesselmann

*Stigmas* (negative characteristics that socially devalue their bearer)[56] often subsume the bearer's identity, completely defining that person's essence in the eyes of others.[57] Groups often view stigmatized persons as strange, frightening, and unpredictable[58]—potential threats to be removed from society.[59] When vampire hunter Gordon refuses to believe Lenore that her vampire group has sworn off human blood, he tries to destroy them simply for *being* vampires.[60] Similarly, individuals who endorse essentialist beliefs (everyone and everything have unique, fixed, and unobservable essences that define them) are likely to endorse stereotypes about stigmatized groups.[61]

Once objects, persons, or things become associated with a stigma, they are contaminated in the eyes of perceivers.[62] Both John and Dean become suspicious of Sam because he was given demon blood as a child by Azazel.[63] Even the prophet Chuck suggests that others would judge Sam negatively for his continued consumption of demon blood even if it is for the greater good of preventing Armageddon.[64]

Beliefs about essentialism and contamination seem to be linked to intuitive cognitive processes. Intuitive processes exist largely because they are heuristics, helping individuals make split-second decisions that could affect their survival. Dean typically relies on intuition,[65] and several characters argue that this makes him a natural and successful hunter.[66] Intuitive negative reactions to stigmatized individuals, like other supernatural thinking processes,[67] can be overridden by analytical or deliberative thinking.[68] Deliberative thinking requires motivation, ability, and time. Sam, the more analytical of the two brothers,[69] overcomes his initial misgivings about the reformed vampires relatively quickly. Dean, however, takes considerably more convincing before he begins to trust those vampires.[70]

afterlife.[71] When a person dies, he or she is no longer physically present, but it is virtually impossible to turn off our beliefs in his or her permanence. We continue to make inferences about deceased people as if they were still alive, such as "he would have liked the service" or "she's probably rolling over in her grave." After John Winchester's death, Sam ruminates on what their father would want even though he has spent most of his life resisting his father's wishes.[72]

### We Are Being Watched

Many supernatural creatures, such as the angels Castiel and Zachariah and the demon Lilith, possess surprisingly personal knowledge about the Winchesters or other characters such as the prophet Chuck.[73] Cross-culturally, many supernatural entities have a property that makes them especially attractive and compelling to human cognitive architecture: *strategic knowledge*. Cultures often teach that gods, spirits, angels, and demons know things about us because they are specifically watching us to make sure we are obeying cultural standards of morality. Thus, we cooperate and obey society's rules to gain favor and avoid being punished either in this life or in the afterlife.[74] Psychological experiments demonstrate that individuals are more likely to behave morally when they are reminded of supernatural agent concepts, whether these are traditional gods, ghosts, or other invisible entities.[75] The preacher who heals Dean makes it clear that he believes God rewards the just and punishes the unjust and that his faith-healing ability is simply an instrument of that divine will.[76]

## We Are Born to Believe

Why do people believe in phenomena that lack empirical backing or are even refuted by science? The diverse characters in *Supernatural*, both hunters and mortal bystanders, reflect the everyday psychological intricacies of supernatural thinking. Hunters have direct experience with supernatural phenomena, but some believers, such as the Ghostfacers, do not (at least initially).[77] Many psychologists argue that supernatural beliefs are related to natural intuitive thought processes that have helped humans survive throughout history. In short, people have minds that are born ready to believe. Indeed, even as people grow and develop the cognitive skills for analytical reasoning, supernatural beliefs persist. Analytic skills afford people the ability to override intuitive processes but do not supplant them. Both analytic and intuitive processes co-exist in individuals, and both can influence thoughts, feelings, and actions even in individuals who resist relying on intuition.[78] Even Sam and Dean, prototypical analytic and intuitive thinkers, respectively, sometimes rely on their less-preferred cognitive process.[79]

We are not advocating that people should *necessarily* reject supernatural beliefs. Supernatural beliefs, even if they are inaccurate or unsubstantiated, do not automatically cause harm.[80] Indeed, many researchers argue that certain types of these beliefs can be beneficial.[81] Even so, there are situations in which supernatural beliefs can have negative implications for believers, such as when people avoid evidence-based medical interventions in favor of supernatural-based methods[82] or assume that victims of misfortunes are being punished by a deity.[83] As the terminally ill Layla Miller tells Dean, though, true faith may require no evidence: "I guess if you're gonna have faith, you can't just have it when the miracles happen. You have to have it when they don't."[84]

> "I have to admit that I'm skeptical. I've become more
> skeptical of the supernatural since doing this show. . . . But
> I hope it's out there; I want to have an experience. I want to
> believe in this stuff. . . ."
> —*Supernatural* creator Eric Kripke[85]

## References

Abell, F., Happe, F., & Frith, U. (2000). Do triangles play tricks? Attribution of mental states to animated shapes in normal and abnormal development. *Cognitive Development, 15*(1), 1–16.

Asser, S. M., & Swan, R. (1998). Child fatalities from religion-motivated medical neglect. *Pediatrics, 101*(4), 625–629.

Atran, S., & Norenzayan, A. (2004). Religion's evolutionary landscape: Counterintuition, commitment, compassion, communion. *Behavioral & Brain Sciences, 27*(6), 713–730.

Barrett, J. L. (2000). Exploring the natural foundations of religion. *Trends in Cognitive Sciences, 4*(1), 29–34.

Bastian, B., & Haslam, N. (2006). Psychological essentialism and stereotype endorsement. *Journal of Experimental Social Psychology, 42*(2), 228–235.

Bering, J. M. (2006). The folk psychology of souls. *Behavioral & Brain Sciences, 29*(5), 453–498.

Bering, J. M., & Johnson, D. (2005). "O lord . . . you perceive my thoughts from afar": Recursiveness and the evolution of supernatural agency. *Journal of Cognition & Culture, 5*(1), 118–142.

Bering, J. M., McLeod, K., & Shackelford, T. K. (2005). Reasoning about dead agents reveals possible adaptive trends. *Human Nature, 16*(4), 360–381.

Bleak, J. L., & Frederick, C. M. (1998). Superstitious behavior in sport: Levels of effectiveness and determinants of use in three collegiate sports. *Journal of Sport Behavior, 21*(1), 1–15.

Bos, A. E. R., Pryor, J. B., Reeder, G .D., & Stutterheim, S. (2013) Stigma: Advances in theory and research. *Basic & Applied Social Psychology, 36*(1), 1–9.

Bouvet, R., & Bonnefon, J. F. (2015). Non-reflective thinkers are predisposed to attribute supernatural causation to uncanny experiences. *Personality & Social Psychology Bulletin, 41*(7), 955–961.

Boyer, P. (2001). *Religion explained: The evolutionary origins of religious thought.* New York, NY: Basic.

Boyer, P., & Ramble, C. (2001). Cognitive templates for religious concepts: Cross-cultural evidence for recall of counter-intuitive representations. *Cognitive Science 25*(4), 535–564.

Bretherton, I., McNew, S., & Beeghly-Smith, M. (1981). Early person knowledge as expressed in gestural and verbal communication: When do infants acquire a "theory of mind"? In M. E. Lamb & L. R. Sherrod (Eds.), *Infant social cognition: Empirical and theoretical considerations* (pp. 333–373). Hillsdale, NJ: Erlbaum.

Brown, N. R. (2011). *The mythology of Supernatural.* New York, NY: Berkley Boulevard.

Burger, J. M. (1992). *Desire for control: Personality, social and clinical perspectives.* New York: Plenum.

Chevalier, J., & Gheerbrant, A. (1996). *A dictionary of symbols.* London, UK: Penguin.

Cohen, A. B., Pierce, J. D., Chambers, J., Meade, R., Gorvine, B. J., & Koenig, H. G. (2005). Intrinsic and extrinsic religiosity, belief in the afterlife, death anxiety, and life satisfaction in young Catholics and Protestants. *Journal of Research in Personality, 39*(3), 307–324.

Corrigan, P. (2004). How stigma interferes with mental health care. *American Psychologist, 59*(7), 614–625.

Cosmides, L., & Tooby, J. (1992). Cognitive adaptations for social exchange. In J. Barkow, L. Cosmides, & J. Tooby (Eds.), *The adapted mind* (pp. 163–228). New York, NY: Oxford University Press.

Dag, I. (1999). The relationships among paranormal beliefs, locus of control and psychopathology in a Turkish college sample. *Personality & Individual Differences, 26*(4), 723–737.

Damisch, L., Stoberock, B., & Mussweiler, T. (2010). Keep your fingers crossed! How superstition improves performance. *Psychological Science, 21*(7), 1014–1020.

Davies, M. F., & Kirkby, H. E. (1985). Multidimensionality of the relationship between perceived control and belief in the paranormal: Spheres of control and types of paranormal phenomena. *Personality & Individual Differences, 6*(5), 661–663.

Dechesne, M., Pyszczynski, T., Arndt, J., Ransom, S., Sheldon, K. M., Van Knippenberg, A., & Janssen, J. (2003). Literal and symbolic immortality: The effect of evidence of literal immortality on self-esteem striving in response to mortality salience. *Journal of Personality and Social Psychology, 84*(4), 722–737.

Epley, N., Waytz, A., & Cacioppo, J. T. (2007). On seeing human: A three-factor theory of anthropomorphism. *Psychological Review, 114*(4), 864–886.

Florian, V., & Mikulincer, M. (1998). Symbolic immortality and the management of the terror of death: The moderating role of attachment style. *Journal of Personality & Social Psychology, 74*(3), 725–734.

Frable, D. E. (1993). Dimensions of marginality: Distinctions among those who are different. *Personality & Social Psychology Bulletin, 19*(4), 370–380.

Frazer, J. G. (1890/1959). *The new golden bough: A study in magic and religion* (abridged ed.). New York, NY: Macmillan.

Froese, P., & Bader, C. (2010). *America's four Gods: What we say about God—and what that says about us.* New York, NY: Oxford University Press.

Gao, J., Fan, J., Wu, B. W., Chau, M., Fung, P. C., Chang, C., Zhang, Z., Hung, & Sik, H. H. (2016). Repetitive religious chanting modulates the late-stage brain response to fear-and stress-provoking pictures. *Frontiers in Psychology, 7*, 2055.

Gelman, S. A. (2004). Psychological essentialism in children. *Trends in Cognitive Sciences, 8*(9), 404–409.

Gervais, W. M., & Norenzayan, A. (2012a). Analytic thinking promotes religious disbelief. *Science, 336*(6080), 493–496.

Gervais, W. M., & Norenzayan, A. (2012b). Like a camera in the sky? Thinking about God increases public self-awareness and socially desirable responding. *Journal of Experimental Social Psychology, 48*(1), 298–302.

Gray, K., & Wegner, D. M. (2010). Blaming God for our pain: Human suffering and the divine mind. *Personality & Social Psychology Review, 14*(1), 7–16.

Greenberg, J., Koole, S. L., & Pyszczynski, T. A. (Eds.). (2004). *Handbook of experimental existential psychology.* New York, NY: Guilford Press.

Greenberg, J., Pyszczynski, T., & Solomon, S. (1986). The causes and consequences of the need for self-esteem: A terror management theory. In R. Baumeister (Ed.), *Public self and private self* (pp. 189–212). New York, NY: Springer-Verlag.

Guiley, R. M. (2005). *The encyclopedia of vampires, werewolves, and other monsters.* New York, NY: Checkmark.

Heider, F., & Simmel, M. (1944). An experimental study of apparent behavior. *American Journal of Psychology, 57*(2), 243–259.

Hood, B. M. (2009). *Supersense: Why we believe in the unbelievable.* San Francisco, CA: HarperOne.

Irvine, A. (2007). *The Supernatural book of monsters, spirits, demons, and ghouls.* New York, NY: HarperCollins.

Irvine, A. (2011). *Supernatural: John Winchester's journal.* New York, NY: HarperCollins.

Johnson, D., & Bering, J. (2006). Hand of God, mind of man: Punishment and cognition in the evolution of cooperation. *Evolutionary Psychology, 4*(1), 219–233.

Jonas, E., & Fischer, P. (2006). Terror management and religion: Evidence that intrinsic religiousness mitigates worldview defense following mortality salience. *Journal of Personality & Social Psychology, 91*(3), 553–567.

Keinan, G. (1994). Effects of stress and tolerance of ambiguity on magical thinking. *Journal of Personality & Social Psychology, 67*(1), 48–55.

Keinan, G. (2002). The effects of stress and desire for control on superstitious behavior. *Personality & Social Psychology Bulletin, 28*(1), 102–108.

Kerr, N. L., & Levine, J. M. (2008). The detection of social exclusion: Evolution and beyond. *Group Dynamics: Theory, Research, & Practice, 12*(1), 39–52.

Knight, N. (2014). *The essential Supernatural: On the road with Sam and Dean Winchester.* San Rafael, CA: Insight Editions.

Kurzban, R., & Leary, M. R. (2001). Evolutionary origins of stigmatization: The functions of social exclusion. *Psychological Bulletin, 127*(2), 187–208.

Lieberman, M. D. (2013). *Social: Why our brains are wired to connect.* New York, NY: Crown.

Lifshin, U., Greenberg, J., Weise, D., & Soenke, M. (2016). It's the end of the world and I feel fine: Soul belief and perceptions of end-of-the-world scenarios. *Personality & Social Psychology Bulletin, 42*(1), 104–117.

Lindeman, M., & Aarnio, K. (2007). Superstitious, magical, and paranormal beliefs: An integrative model. *Journal of Research in Personality, 41*(4), 731–744.

Lobato, E., Mendoza, J., Sims, V., & Chin, M. (2014). Examining the relationship between conspiracy theories, paranormal beliefs, and pseudoscience acceptance among a university population. *Applied Cognitive Psychology, 28*(5), 617–625.

Lobmeyer, D. L., & Wasserman, E. A. (1986). Preliminaries to free throw shooting: Superstitious behavior. *Journal of Sport Behavior, 9*(2), 70–78.

Lundberg, B., Hansson, L., Wentz, E., & Björkman, T. (2007). Sociodemographic and clinical factors related to devaluation/discrimination and rejection experiences among users of mental health services. *Social Psychiatry & Psychiatric Epidemiology, 42*(4), 295–300.

Lundh, L. G., & Radon, V. (1998). Death anxiety as a function of belief in an afterlife: A comparison between a questionnaire measure and a Stroop measure of death anxiety. *Personality & Individual Differences, 25*(3), 487–494.

Markson, L., & Spelke, E. S. (2006). Infants' rapid learning about self-propelled objects. *Infancy, 9*(1), 45–71.

Mauss, M. (1902/1972). *A general theory of magic.* New York, NY: Norton.

Melton, J. G. (1994). *The vampire book: The encyclopedia of the undead.* Detroit, MI: Visible Ink.

Norenzayan, A., Atran, S., Faulkner, J., & Schaller, M. (2006). Memory and mystery: The cultural selection of minimally counterintuitive narratives. *Cognitive Science, 30*(3), 531–553.

Osarchuk, M., & Tatz, S. J. (1973). Effect of induced fear of death on belief in afterlife. *Journal of Personality & Social Psychology, 27*(2), 256–260.

Over, H., & Carpenter, M. (2009). Priming third-party ostracism increases affiliative imitation in children. *Developmental Science, 12*(3), F1–F8.

Padgett, V. R., & Jorgenson, D. O. (1982). Superstition and economic threat: Germany, 1918–1940. *Personality & Social Psychology Bulletin, 8*(4), 736–741.

Pargament, K. I., Ano, G. G., & Wachholtz, A. B. (2005). The religious dimension of coping: Advances in theory, research, and practice. In R. F. Paloutzian & C. L. Park (Eds.), *Handbook of the psychology of religion and spirituality* (pp. 479–495). New York, NY: Guilford.

Pargament, K. I., & Hahn, J. (1986). God and the just world: Causal and coping attributions to God in health situations. *Journal for the Scientific Study of Religion, 23,* 193–207.

Pennycook, G., Cheyne, J. A., Seli, P., Koehler, D. J., & Fugelsang, J. A. (2012). Analytic cognitive style predicts religious and paranormal belief. *Cognition, 123*(3), 335–346.

Pepitone, A., & Saffiotti, L. (1997). The selectivity of nonmaterial beliefs in interpreting life events. *European Journal of Social Psychology, 27*(1), 23–35.

Peterson, C., & Seligman, M. E. (1984). Causal explanations as a risk factor for depression: Theory and evidence. *Psychological Review, 91*(3), 347–374.

Piaget, J. (1928). *The child's conception of the world.* London, UK: Routledge & Kegan Paul.

Piazza, J., Bering, J. M., & Ingram, G. (2011). "Princess Alice is watching you": Children's belief in an invisible person inhibits cheating. *Journal of Experimental Child Psychology, 109*(3), 311–320.

Pickett, C. L., & Gardner, W. L. (2005). The Social Monitoring System: Enhanced sensitivity to social cues as an adaptive response to social exclusion. In K. D. Williams, J. P. Forgas, & W. von Hippel (Eds.), *The social outcast: Ostracism, social exclusion, rejection, and bullying* (pp. 213–226). New York, NY: Psychology Press.

Pronin, E., Wegner, D. M., McCarthy, K., & Rodriguez, S. (2006). Everyday magical powers: The role of apparent mental causation in the overestimation of personal influence. *Journal of Personality & Social Psychology, 91*(2), 218–231.

Pryor, J. B., Reeder, G. D., & Monroe, A. E. (2012). The infection of bad company: Stigma by association. *Journal of Personality & Social Psychology, 102*(2), 224–241.

Pryor, J. B., Reeder, G. D., Yeadon, C., & Hesson-McInnis, M. (2004). A dual-process model of reactions to perceived stigma. *Journal of Personality & Social Psychology, 87*(4), 436–452.

Randolph-Seng, B., & Nielsen, M. E. (2007). Honesty: One effect of primed religious representations. *International Journal for the Psychology of Religion, 17*(4), 303–315.

Reed, D. (2011). *Supernatural: Bobby Singer's guide to hunting.* New York, NY: HarperCollins.

Rothbaum, F., Weisz, J. R., & Snyder, S. S. (1982). Changing the world and changing the self: A two-process model of perceived control. *Journal of Personality & Social Psychology, 42*(1), 5–37.

Rozin, P., Markwith, M., & McCauley, C. (1994). Sensitivity to indirect contacts with other persons: AIDS aversion as a composite of aversion to strangers, infection, moral taint, and misfortune. *Journal of Abnormal Psychology, 103*(3), 495–504.

Rozin, P., Millman, L., & Nemeroff, C. (1986). Operation of the laws of sympathetic magic in disgust and other domains. *Journal of Personality & Social Psychology, 50*(4), 703–712.

Saxe, R., Tzelnic, T., & Carey, S. (2007). Knowing who dunnit: Infants identify the causal agent in an unseen causal interaction. *Developmental Psychology, 43*(1), 149–158.

Schaller, M., & Park, J. H. (2011). The behavioral immune system (and why it matters). *Current Directions in Psychological Science, 20*(2), 99–103.

Shariff, A. F., & Aknin, L. B. (2014). The emotional toll of hell: Cross-national and experimental evidence for the negative well-being effects of hell beliefs. *PlosOne, 9*(1), e85251.

Shariff, A. F., Cohen, A. B., & Norenzayan, A. (2008). The devil's advocate: Secular arguments diminish both implicit and explicit religious belief. *Journal of Cognition & Culture, 8*(3), 417–423.

Shariff, A. F., Cohen, A. B., & Norenzayan, A. (2007). God is watching you: Priming God concepts increases prosocial behavior in an anonymous economic game. *Psychological Science, 18*(9), 803–809.

Shenhav, A., Rand, D. G., & Greene, J. D. (2012). Divine intuition: Cognitive style influences belief in God. *Journal of Experimental Psychology: General, 141*(3), 423–428.

Shilling, A. A., & Brown, C. M. (2016). Goal-driven resource redistribution: An adaptive response to social exclusion. *Evolutionary Behavioral Sciences, 10*(3), 149–167.

Shtulman, A. (2013). Epistemic similarities between students' scientific and supernatural beliefs. *Journal of Educational Psychology, 105*(1), 199–212.

Solomon, S., Greenberg, J., & Pyszczynski, T. (1991). A terror management theory of social behavior: The psychological function of self-esteem and cultural worldviews. In M. Zanna (Ed.), *Advances in experimental social psychology* (Vol. 24, pp. 91–159). San Diego, CA: Academic Press.

Stanford, M. S. (2007). Demon or disorder: A survey of attitudes toward mental illness in the Christian church. *Mental Health, Religion & Culture, 10*(5), 445–449.

Subbotsky, E. (2011). The ghost in the machine: Why and how the belief in magic survives in the rational mind. *Human Development, 54*(3), 126–143.

Subbotsky, E. (2014). The belief in magic in the age of science. *SAGE Open, 4*(1), 2158244014521433.

Todd, M., & Brown, C. (2003). Characteristics associated with superstitious behavior in track and field athletes: Are there NCAA divisional level differences? *Journal of Sport Behavior, 26*(2), 168–187.

Van Raalte, J. L., Brewer, B. W., Nemeroff, C. J., & Linder, D. E. (1991). Chance orientation and superstitious behavior on the putting green. *Journal of Sport Behavior, 14*(1), 41–50.

Waytz, A., Epley, N., & Cacioppo, J. T. (2010a). Social cognition unbound: Insights into anthropomorphism and dehumanization. *Current Directions in Psychological Science, 19*(1), 58–62.

Waytz, A., Morewedge, C. K., Epley, N., Monteleone, G., Gao, J. H., & Cacioppo, J. T. (2010b). Making sense by making sentient: Effectance motivation increases anthropomorphism. *Journal of Personality & Social Psychology, 99*(3), 410–435.

Wesselmann, E. D., & Graziano, W. G. (2010). Sinful and/or possessed? Religious beliefs and mental illness stigma. *Journal of Social & Clinical Psychology, 29*(4), 402–437.

Whitson, J. A., & Galinsky, A. D. (2008). Lacking control increases illusory pattern perception. *Science, 322*(5898), 115–117.

Windholz, G., & Diamant, L. (1974). Some personality traits of believers in extraordinary phenomena. *Bulletin of the Psychonomic Society, 3*(2), 125–126.

Wiseman, R. (2010). *Paranormality: Why we see what isn't there.* Lexington, KY: Spin Solutions.

Wiseman, R., & Watt, C. (2004). Measuring superstitious belief: Why lucky charms matter. *Personality & Individual Differences, 37*(8), 1533–1541.

Woolley, J. D. (1997). Thinking about fantasy: Are children fundamentally different thinkers and believers from adults? *Child Development, 68*(6), 991–1011.

Xygalatas, D. (2013). Effects of religious setting on cooperative behavior: A case study from Mauritius. *Religion, Brain & Behavior, 3*(2), 91–102.

## Notes

1. Episode 1–17, "Hell House" (March 30, 2006).
2. Hood (2009), p. xvii.
3. Hood (2009); Lindeman & Aarnio (2007); Subbotsky (2014).
4. e.g., episodes 9–20, "Bloodlines" (April 29, 2014); 12–11, "Regarding Dean" (February 9, 2017).
5. Episode 1–12, "Faith" (January 17, 2006).
6. Florian & Mikulincer (1998); Greenberg et al. (1986); Solomon et al. (1991).
7. Episodes 1–1, "Pilot" (September 13, 2005); 1–9, "Home" (November 15, 2005); 1–10, "Asylum" (November 22, 2005); 1–22, "Devil's Trap" (May 4, 2006); 2–1, "In My Time of Dying" (September 28, 2006); 3–2, "The Kids Are Alright" (October 11, 2007); 4–1, "Lazarus Rising" (September 18, 2008); 4–7, "It's the Great Pumpkin, Sam Winchester" (October 30, 2008); 5–10, "Abandon All Hope . . ." (November 19, 2009).
8. Cohen et al. (2005); Dechesne et al. (2003); Jonas & Fischer (2006); Lifshin et al. (2016); Lundh & Radon (1998); Osarchuk & Tatz, (1973).
9. Episodes 3–16, "No Rest for the Wicked" (May 15, 2008); 5–16, "Dark Side of the Moon" (April 1, 2010); 5–22, "Swan Song" (May 13, 2010); 7–23, "Survival of the Fittest" (May 18, 2012); 8–19, "Taxi Driver" (April 3, 2013).
10. Episodes 2–18, "Hollywood Babylon" (April 19, 2007); 3–7, "Fresh Blood" (November 15, 2007); 4–18, "The Monster at the End of This Book" (April 2, 2009); 6–11, "Appointment in Samarra" (December 10, 2010).
11. Piaget (1928); Woolley (1997).
12. Keinan (2002); Lobato et al. (2014); Pronin et al. (2006); Rozin et al. (1986); Shtulman (2013); Subbotsky (2011; 2014); Woolley (1997).
13. Kerr & Levine (2008); Lieberman (2013); Pickett & Gardner (2005); Shilling & Brown (2016).
14. Boyer (2001); Epley et al. (2007); Waytz et al. (2010a; 2010b).
15. Episode 3–13, "Ghostfacers" (April 24, 2008).
16. Abell et al, 2000; Heider & Simmel (1944); Markson & Spelke (2006); Over & Carpenter (2009).
17. Atran & Norenzayan (2004).
18. Episode 1–17, "Hell House" (March 30, 2006).
19. Cosmides & Tooby (1992).
20. Episodes 1–2, "Wendigo" (September 20, 2005); 1–3, "Dead In The Water" (September 27, 2005); 1–8, "Bugs" (November 8, 2005); 1–11, "Scarecrow" (January 10, 2006); 2–6, "No Exit" (November 2, 2006); 2–15, "Tall Tales" (February 15, 2007); 3–6, "Red Sky at Morning" (November 8, 2007); Irvine (2011); Reed (2011).
21. Episode 1–16, "Shadow" (February 28, 2006).
22. Bering (2006); Hood (2009); Pepitone & Saffiotti (1997); Wiseman (2010).
23. Episodes 1–9, "Home" (November 15, 2005); 1–14, "Nightmare" (February 7, 2006); 1–16, "Shadow" (February 28, 2006).
24. Episode 2–13, "Houses of the Holy" (February 1, 2007).
25. Episodes 1–1, "Pilot" (September 13, 2005); 3–13, "Ghostfacers" (April 24, 2008); 4–6, "Yellow Fever" (October 23, 2008); 4–17, "It's a Terrible Life" (March 26, 2009).
26. Episodes 1–4, "Phantom Traveler" (October 4, 2005); 1–16, "Shadow" (February 28, 2006); 1–22, "Devil's Trap" (May 4, 2006); 4–18, "The Monster at the End of This Book" (April 2, 2009).
27. Episodes 1–20, "Dead Man's Blood" (April 20, 2006); 2–3, "Bloodlust" (October

12, 2006); 3–7, "Fresh Blood" (November 15, 2007); 6–5, "Live Free or Twihard" (October 22, 2010).

28. Irvine (2011); Episodes 1–1, "Pilot" (September 13, 2005); 1–2, "Wendigo" (September 20, 2005); 1–8, "Bugs" (November 8, 2005); 1–16, "Route 666" (January 31, 2006); 2–4, "Children Shouldn't Play with Dead Things" (October 19, 2006); 3–2, "The Kids Are Alright" (October 11, 2007).

29. Barrett & Nyhof (2001); Boyer & Ramble (2001); Norenzayan et al. (2006).

30. Guiley (2005); Melton (1994).

31. Irvine (2007); Knight (2014); episodes 1–20, "Dead Man's Blood" (April 20, 2006); 2–3, "Bloodlust" (October 12, 2006); 3–7, "Fresh Blood" (November 15, 2007); 6–5, "Live Free or Twihard" (October 22, 2010).

32. Irvine (2007; 2011); Knight (2014); Reed (2011).

33. Episodes 1–7, "Hook Man" (October 25, 2005); 1–11, "Scarecrow" (January 10, 2006); 1–12, "Faith" (January 17, 2006); 2–4, "Children Shouldn't Play with Dead Things" (October 19, 2006); 2–8, "Crossroad Blues" (November 16, 2006); 2–11, "Playthings" (January 18, 2007); 3–9, "Malleus Maleficarum" (January 31, 2008).

34. Burger (1992); Peterson & Seligman (1984).

35. Rothbaum et al. (1982); Whitson & Galinsky (2008).

36. Ciborowski (1997); Dag (1999); Davies & Kirkby (1985); Foster et al. (2006); Todd & Brown (2003); Van Raalte et al. (1991).

37. Episode 3–3, "Bad Day at Black Rock" (October 18, 2007).

38. Damisch et al. (2010); Keinan (1994; 2002); Padgett & Jorgenson (1982); Whitson & Galinsky (2008); Wiseman & Watt (2004).

39. Episodes 1–22, "Devil's Trap" (May 4, 2006); 2–8, "Crossroad Blues" (November 16, 2006); 3–4, "Sin City" (October 25, 2007); 4–18, "The Monster at the End of This Book" (April 2, 2009); Reed (2011).

40. Episodes 1–4, "Phantom Traveler" (October 4, 2005); 1–16, "Shadow" (February 28, 2006); 2–11, "Playthings" (January 18, 2007).

41. Boyer (2001); Frazer (1890/1959).

42. Hood (2009).

43. Frazer (1890/1959); Mauss (1902/1972).

44. Episode 2–11, "Playthings" (January 18, 2007).

45. Irvine (2007).

46. Rozin et al. (1986).

47. Episode 1–21, "Salvation" (April 27, 2006).

48. Brown (2011); Chevalier & Gheerbrant (1996).

49. Episodes 1–7, "Hook Man" (October 25, 2005); 1–10, "Asylum" (November 22, 2005); 1–22, "Devil's Trap" (May 4, 2006); 2–16, "Road Kill" (November 2, 2006); 3–13, "Ghostfacers" (April 24, 2008); 4–17, "It's a Terrible Life" (March 26, 2009); Irvine (2007; 2011); Knight (2014); Reed (2011).

50. Episodes 1–5, "Bloody Mary" (October 11, 2005); 1–9, "Home" (November 15, 2005); 1–16, "Route 666" (January 31, 2006); 1–19, "Provenance" (April 13, 2006).

51. Schaller & Park (2011).

52. Rozin et al. (1986); Rozin et al. (1994).

53. Episodes 1–1, "Pilot" (September 13, 2005); 1–21, "Salvation" (April 27, 2006); 2–2, "Everybody Loves a Clown" (October 5, 2006).

54. Hood (2009); Piaget (1928).

55. Bretherton et al. (1981); Saxe et al. (2007).

56. Bos et al. (2013).

57. Frable (1993).
58. Corrigan (2004); Lundberg et al. (2007).
59. Kurzban & Leary (2001).
60. Episode 2–3, "Bloodlust" (October 12, 2006).
61. Bastian & Haslam (2006); Gelman (2004).
62. Pryor et al. (2012); Rozin et al. (1994).
63. Episodes 2–1, "In My Time of Dying" (September 28, 2006); 2–21, "All Hell Breaks Loose (Part 1)" (May 10, 2007); 4–4, "Metamorphosis" (October 9, 2008); Irvine (2011).
64. Episode 4–18, "The Monster at the End of This Book" (April 2, 2009).
65. Episodes 1–1, "Pilot" (September 13, 2005); 2–3, "Bloodlust" (October 12, 2006); 2–16, "Road Kill" (November 2, 2006).
66. Irvine (2007; 2011); episodes 2–3, "Bloodlust" (October 12, 2006); 4–17, "It's a Terrible Life" (March 26, 2009).
67. Bouvet & Bonnefon (2015); Gervais & Norenzayan (2012a); Pennycook et al. (2012); Shariff et al. (2008); Shenhav et al. (2012);
68. Pryor et al. (2004)
69. Irvine (2011); Reed (2011); episodes 1–2, "Wendigo" (September 20, 2005); 1–17, "Hell House" (March 30, 2006); 2–16, "Road Kill" (November 2, 2006).
70. Episode 2–3, "Bloodlust" (October 12, 2006).
71. Boyer (2001); Hood (2009).
72. Episode 2–2, "Everybody Loves a Clown" (October 5, 2006).
73. Episodes 4–6, "Yellow Fever" (October 23, 2008); 4–17, "It's a Terrible Life" (March 26, 2009); 4–18, "The Monster at the End of This Book" (April 2, 2009).
74. Boyer (2001); Johnson & Bering (2006).
75. Bering & Johnson (2005); Bering et al. (2005); Gervais & Norenzayan (2012b); Piazza et al. (2011); Randolph-Seng & Nielsen (2007); Shariff & Norenzayan (2007); Xygalatas (2013).
76. Episode 1–12, "Faith" (January 17, 2006).
77. Episodes 1–17, "Hell House" (March 30, 2006); 3–13, "Ghostfacers" (April 24, 2008).
78. Pryor et al. (2004).
79. Episodes 1–2, "Wendigo" (September 20, 2005); 1–9, "Home" (November 15, 2005); 1–12, "Faith" (January 17, 2006); 2–13, "Houses of the Holy" (February 1, 2007); 2–14, "Born under a Bad Sign" (February 8, 2007); 4–17, "It's a Terrible Life" (March 26, 2009).
80. Bering (2006).
81. Pargament et al. (2005); Subbotsky (2014).
82. Asser & Swan (1998); Stanford (2007).
83. Gray & Wegner (2010); Pargament & Hahn (1986); Wesselmann & Graziano (2010).
84. Episode 1–12, "Faith" (January 17, 2006).
85. Knight (2014), p. 39.

## CHAPTER TWENTY-ONE

# The Message is in the Music:
# The Psychological Impact of
# Music in *Supernatural*

SUSAN NYLANDER, AMANDA
TAYLOR, AND LYNN S. ZUBERNIS

*"Driver picks the music; shotgun shuts his cakehole."*
—Dean Winchester[1]

*"You may know that what you hear is 'just music,' but
the mechanisms that evoke your emotions do not."*
—music psychologist Patrick Juslin[2]

Music has been associated with better physical and mental health and higher levels of psychological and emotional well-being for people of all ages. One of the benefits of music appears to be that listening to it helps us regulate our emotions.[3] That is, we dampen, maintain, or intensify our emotional experience and learn strategies to cope with overwhelming emotion. Emotional regulation is considered essential for healthy psychological adjustment. Music can be an effective means of regulating emotion both by creating positive emotional reactions and by helping us cope with negative ones through engagement instead of emotional suppression. Music also can help us understand our emotions, thus increasing our self-awareness.[4]

In media, music is used in a similar way to enrich the atmosphere of a scene unfolding on the screen. *Supernatural* uses both original music composed for the show and classic rock songs to enhance, highlight, and clarify viewers' emotional experience of the characters and story. Many television shows use music, often passively, to add to the intensity of a scene, cue the audience to impending doom, or create pathos, but the music in *Supernatural* creates more than ambience; it creates relationships between the characters, relationships with the viewers, and relationships to the show itself.[5] Creator Eric Kripke was so adamant that the music on the show reflect his own taste in music, he wrote it into the pilot so that it would be established from the beginning.[6]

## The Music So Far

Music affects people emotionally, cognitively, and physiologically. Whether intuitively or strategically, music composers and performers create music that influences people at every level. Through means that include *sensory interaction* (in which one physical sense alters the way we perceive stimuli detected by a different sense) and *sensory-cognitive interaction* (in which perceptions influence mental processes and vice versa[7]), music can create expectations, influence evaluation, heighten suspense, lighten the moment, and guide those who hear it as they process characters, stories, and stimuli of many kinds.[8]

## The Emotional Impact of Familiarity

Certain features and content of music, as well as our familiarity with a piece of music, affect how we can use the music for emotional regulation; more familiar music can feel like an "old friend."[9] *Supernatural* has two musical directors who share the composing duties: Christopher Lennertz and Jay Gruska. Not only do Lennertz and Gruska set the mood of the series, their original compositions have become signature tunes in their own right, in particular Gruska's "Americana,"[10] pieces of which play in familial scenes and act as emotional touchstones for the viewer. "Americana" and the classic rock songs played on the show evoke positive autobiographical memories because of their familiarity.

"The Road So Far" recaps that begin each episode utilize famous rock songs not only to review the previous episodes but to set the tone of the story arc as it has progressed to that point. The first such recap used featured "Carry on, Wayward Son" by Kansas.[11] This song has become the show's unofficial theme song,[12] used in every finale episode from season 2 onward. (Triumph's "Fight the Good Fight"[13] is used in the finale of season 1, a rallying cry both for what's come before and for what the boys and their father, finally reunited, must face when they try to confront the yellow-eyed demon.)

The use of familiar popular music in the recaps increases the emotional impact and also adds to the narrative, telling more of the story.[14] Ted Nugent's "Stranglehold"[15] demonstrates the dire straits the Winchesters find themselves in as the second season begins, and when the recap gives way to the episode showing the boys and their father severely injured in the wrecked Impala, Creedence Clearwater Revival's "Bad Moon Rising"[16] takes over to further the sense that this is only the beginning of their troubles. Using popular music to open the first three episodes of season 2 establishes this as part of the show's motif and creates a tradition for years to come.

## The Emotional Impact of Instrumentation

Adding to the poignancy of the family theme is the instrumentation used when that theme plays, which has varied from episode to episode. Psychologist Teun Lucassen looked at the connection between instrumentation and emotions.[17] His experiment explored the impact of different musical instruments on the emotions perceived by a listener. To do this, he wrote an original composition that contains descending notes (mostly rated sad) and ascending notes (mostly rated happy) as well as minor and major chords. According to Lucassen, the composition is emotionally neutral as written, and so it is the instrumentation that affects the emotional value. He played the composition with each instrument—cello, marimba, piano, and alto sax—and measured the emotional response of each participant.

The study found that the piano (often used in renditions of "Americana") was the most difficult to assign a specific emotion to. This may be the case because it is the performer who adds the emotion to a piano composition; some researchers note that "expert musicians rarely play a score as written; instead, they introduce intentional variations in timing, amplitude, and timbre." The musician's "expressivity in musical performance can serve the function of . . . signaling the presence of a particular emotion such as happiness, sadness, or fearfulness."[18] The other instruments were assigned an emotion more easily. The marimba was rated the highest in joy, potentially as a result of its generally higher pitch and staccato feel. Unsurprisingly, Lucassen found that the cello and sax were rated highest in sadness, anger, and fear;[19] even non-musically trained viewers are attuned to the use of stringed instruments to evoke deep emotion. Heartbreaking scenes in any drama are often underscored by strings. When someone complains about all the things going wrong in his or her life, someone else may mimic playing the violin while affecting a sad expression; we are familiar with the power of instrumentation even if we do not know all of the theory behind it.

This innate reaction to instrumentation is utilized in the varied renditions of the "family theme" in "Americana." Although the piano version of the theme is presented most often in the show, it also has been played by French horn and cello, which evoke sadness and melancholy. However, with the cello rendition that plays when Sam tries to cure Dean after he has become a demon,[20] we also sense nostalgia, longing, and regret as well as a strengthening of Sam's resolve to continue the attempted cure. The use of the cello's rich, deep tones—lower than a violin but not as low as a bass—instead of the piano's lighter touch reflects both Sam's strong brotherly love and his anguish about what Dean has become and is going through.

Music evokes these emotional reactions through several different cognitive mechanisms. Certain aspects of music (abrupt changes in rhythm or volume or an accelerating pace, for example) are interpreted by the brain as signaling something that needs attention. Other aspects, such as rhythm, influence listeners because they increase arousal or because listeners adjust their heart rate and breathing accordingly. These reflexive decisions take place in a very old part of the brain, and so the reactions are automatic. Manipulating these musical aspects produces varying emotional responses in listeners.[21] Other reactions involve learning: We all perceive a particular piece of music differently, depending on which aspects of the music are perceptually salient and what our own individual associations with the music are. When fans are all immersed in the same episode of *Supernatural*, however, those aspects will be more similar than different. When a piece of music is paired repeatedly with a type of event (as with "Americana" and family relationships), through conditioning the music itself eventually comes to evoke the emotional response.[22] That explains why just the first few notes of the piano portion of "Americana" can make fans tear up.

## Cognitive Absorption and Engagement

Although many *Supernatural* fans would probably say they are highly engaged when watching their favorite show, the frequent use of music on the program can intensify that experience. Listening to music can result in engagement, an intense focus on something that changes the way a person thinks and feels. The idea of engagement or *flow* is the loss of self-consciousness during an activity that captures our intrinsic attention so thoroughly that we feel a sense of immersion. Engagement and flow states are associated with psychological well-being.[23] This idea of absorption has been connected to listening to music and also to being a fan, and so when viewers watch their favorite television show and it is accompanied by familiar music, the tendency to lose oneself and become absorbed in a healthy way may be magnified. When people are absorbed in the experience, music very simply can make them happy. Listening to music perceived as pleasurable produces changes in the frontal cortex of the brain that eventually reach the brain's reward centers, releasing the neurotransmitter dopamine.[24] This is especially true when the music is personally meaningful to the listener, as with some of the classic rock songs commonly used on *Supernatural* or an original piece such as "Americana."

Arguably, the best-known portion of "Americana" is referred to as "Dean's family dedication theme" or the "family theme."[25] This segment marks familial moments within the series, most often with one or more Winchesters present, and serves to strengthen the emotional bonds viewers may have with the characters.[26] At times, the use of the theme reminds viewers of the family bond in connection with loss, as when John sits silently at a dying Dean's bedside[27] or when Sam has taken a knife to his back and is dying in Dean's arms.[28] At other times, hearing the theme brings great joy, such as when "Americana" plays while Dean tells a newly resurrected Mary that he is her son.[29] Both fans' familiarity with the song and the emotionality of the piece contribute to fans' engagement in the scene as it plays.

### Physiological and Psychological Responses

Music can have a significant impact on emotion and mood,[30] partly because it is recognized by the brain as meaningful. For early humans, survival depended on the ability to detect patterns in sounds and create meaning from those sounds, which allowed them to fight or flee or relax.[31] We evolved to experience sound and music as being invested with meaning. Music is a means of social and emotional communication between people, and so being able to communicate subtle shades of emotional meaning by using melody and sound conferred an evolutionary advantage.[32] In other words, we may be perfectly aware that what we're hearing is "just music," but the mechanisms in the brain that produce emotions are not.[33]

At the level of brain functioning, our perception of melodies and rhythm creates a simulation of an emotional state when we listen to music. We hear the music as an emotional expression and unconsciously construct a representation of that emotion, and this in turn produces physiological and emotional responses.[34] Thus, when a rock song or an instrumental score is played on *Supernatural*, certain emotions are automatically aroused in the viewer. Several cognitive mechanisms influence reactions to music such as this. Sometimes music-induced emotions are caused by aspects of the music that have been paired with positive or negative experiences in the past or aspects of the music bring to mind a personal memory; alternatively, emotions can be induced by music when the person listening perceives the emotional content in the music itself and then mimics that emotion internally, a process known as emotional contagion.[35] All three mechanisms may be at work when fans watch a scene with its musical sound track.

As the music people are hearing changes, their emotional state changes with it; in other words, the music regulates our emotions.[36] Neuroimaging studies have shown that the limbic system, which evolved to help us survive by modulating our basic emotions, is involved in our emotional responses to music.[37] For example, the experience of a piece of music "giving you chills" is associated with activity in the limbic system.[38] The combination of music and images, such as on a television show, produces even stronger activation. When music plays simultaneously with a film clip of an emotionally neutral situation, for example, the film elicits stronger reactions.[39] It is no wonder, then, that the music of *Supernatural* resonates so much with viewers, as it adds significantly to the story.

In fact, changing the music can change the characterization as well as the overall feel and emotional impact of a scene in the show.[40] This is most apparent in season 1, for which the Netflix version of the season does not have the same songs as the original broadcast version. The episode "Skin" is one of the clearest examples of this musical mismatch.[41] The post-recap opening scenes of "Skin" take place at night in a darkly lit room and offer us images of threatened torture and clear fear on the victim's face.[42] The opening alternates between these and the approaching police officers who then search the house to find the victim, ending with the police officers confronting a knife-wielding Dean Winchester. Viewers have had different emotional experiences with the episode in these first two minutes because they use different music; certain attributes of the music result in different emotional reactions.[43] The Netflix version opens with "Good Deal" by Mommy and Daddy.[44] It is a high-energy, guitar-driven, percussion-filled indie rock song with a tempo of 160 beats per minute. The singer's voice is in a tenor range, and it is sung relatively cleanly, which gives the song a more upbeat feel even though the lyrics tell a serious story.

In contrast, the original broadcast version of "Skin"[45] uses a very different piece of music, Iron Butterfly's "In-A-Gadda-Da-Vida."[46] The Iron Butterfly song has a slower tempo (119 beats per minute) and is guitar-driven with steady percussion. It is also in a minor key and is sung in a medium baritone range. The singer's voice is gritty and raw, matching the drive of the guitar and adding to the dark edge and timbre of the episode. The slower tempo contrasts with the quick action in the episode and offers a much darker ambience, changing the impact of the music.[47]

## Supernatural's Effective Use of Music

Music itself increases engagement and absorption,[48] and so Supernatural's frequent use of music encourages fans' passion for the show. Since music that is familiar has the greatest emotional impact,[49] Supernatural utilizes several different types of music that are familiar to its viewers: classic rock songs that fans already know and love and original compositions that have become familiar to fans through their repeated use in certain

# INTERVIEW: *SUPERNATURAL* MUSIC COMPOSER JAY GRUSKA

### Lynn Zubernis

**Zubernis:** How do you see music impacting humans both psychologically and emotionally?

**Gruska:** At its base, it's wordless communication amongst humans. If you're privileged enough to have hearing, it can be something that transcends written language and becomes a conduit to human emotion and experience.

**Zubernis:** When you compose for *Supernatural*, are you creating something with the explicit intention of evoking certain emotional reactions?

**Gruska:** When scoring for television, the tone and the emotional nature of the music completely has to do with what that moment in the film is asking for. Let's take an example of the family theme. People have called it *Americana*, the brothers theme, the family theme. In that instance, my thought was "Let me see if this can also from now on start to express whenever you have that family thing going on," whether it's the brothers to each other or with their parents, or in some cases with the brothers and another character if there was a family pull. And maybe then there would be a variation in the harmonic approach or a little shift in the melody or something like that. That's one of the few times I went, "Oh, let me write for this scene because it's got a deep inherent emotionalism to it," kind of a lump in your throat kind of feeling. And I thought, "We'll be able to go here again because so much of the subtext of the show is about loss and how to cope with it and how to fight the good fight through your pain."

**Zubernis:** When scoring for a scene, are you portraying the emotion the character is feeling or the emotion you want the viewer to feel?

**Gruska:** Often one wants to be careful of gilding the lily of the character's emotion. We have good actors on this show, and if they're sitting there really in a moment, I don't want to hit people with the music over the head too hard. Maybe there's a context where you do want to play the emotion that you want the audience to get even though the actor might not be portraying it, but more often than not, it's to go hand in hand. If the performance is making a statement enough, then maybe that implies that the music can be that much more subtle. Other times, if the music is subtle enough, it can bring out the subtlety of the text or even the subtlety of a look on an actor's face.

types of (usually emotionally intense) scenes. The show's composers also employ variations in instrumentation, tempo, and rhythm that evoke various emotional responses.[50] Through the intentional use of music, viewers become more absorbed in the show, feel a closer connection to the characters, and experience both the characters' emotions and their own more intensely.

Even the goddess Calliope, when describing what makes *Supernatural* so special, recognizes the importance of music to the show: "Why *Supernatural*? *Supernatural* has everything. Life. Death. Resurrection. Redemption. But, above all, family. All set to music you can really tap your toe to. It isn't some piece of meandering genre dreck. It's epic!"[51]

## References

Baumgartner, T., Esslen, M., & Jäncke, L. (2006). From emotion perception to emotion experience: Emotions evoked by pictures and classical music. *International Journal of Psychophysiology, 60*(1), 34–43.

Bhatara, A., Tirovolas, A. K., Duan, L. M., Levy, B., & Levi, D. (2011). Perception of emotional expression in musical performance. *Journal of Experimental Psychology: Human Perception & Performance, 37*(3), 921–934.

Boltz, M. G. (2001). Musical soundtracks as a schematic influence on the cognitive processing of filmed events. *Music Perception, 18*(4), 427–454.

Chin, T., & Rickard, N. S. (2013). Emotion regulation strategy mediates both positive and negative relationships between music uses and well-being. *Psychology of Music, 42*(5), 692–713.

Costable, K. A., & Terman, A. W. (2013). Effects of film music on psychological transportation and narrative persuasion. *Basic & Applied Social Psychology, 35*(3), 316–324.

Croom, A. M. (2015). Music practice and participation for psychological well-being: A review of how music influences positive emotion, engagement, relationships, meaning, and accomplishment. *Musicae Scientiae, 19*(1), 44–64.

DeCaro, R., Peelle, J. E., Grossman, M., & Wingfield, A. (2016). The two sides of sensory-cognitive interactions: Effects of age, hearing acuity, and working memory span on sentence comprehension. *Frontiers in Psychology, 7*, Article D, 236.

DeNardo, A. (2013, October 7). *"Supernatural" premieres new season.* The DA: http://www.thedaonline.com/arts_and_entertainment/music/article_2139a8d6-2fc6-11e3-becd-001a4bcf6878.html.

Eldar, E., Ganor, O., Admon, R., Bleich, A., & Hendler, T. (2007). Feeling the real world: Limbic response to music depends on related content. *Cerebral Cortex, 17*(12), 2828–2840.

Hoeckner, B., Wyatt, E. W., Decety, J., & Nusbaum, H. (2011). Film music influences how viewers relate to movie characters. *Psychology of Aesthetics, Creativity, & the Arts, 5*(2), 146–153.

Juslin, P. N. (2013). From everyday emotions to aesthetic emotions: Towards a unified theory of musical emotions. *Physics of Life Reviews, 10*(3), 235–266.

Juslin, P. N., & Vastfjall, D. (2008). Emotional responses to music: The need to consider underlying mechanisms. *Behavioral & Brain Sciences, 31*(5), 559–621.

Koelsch, S. (2010). Towards a neural basis of music-evoked emotions. *Trends in Cognitive Sciences, 14*(3), 131–137.

Krueger, J. (2014). Affordances and the musically extended mind. *Frontiers in Psychology, 4*, Article 1003, 1–13.

Lucassen, T. (2006). Emotions of musical instruments. *4th Twente Student Conference on IT.*

Morinville, A., Miranda, D., & Gaudreau, P. (2013). Music listening motivation is associated with happiness in Canadian late adolescents. *Psychology of Aesthetics, Creativity, & the Arts, 7*(4), 384–390.

Nakamura, J., & Csikszentmihalyi, M. (2009). Flow theory and research. In S. J. Lopez and C. R. Snyder (Eds.), *Oxford Handbook of Positive Psychology* (2nd ed.) (pp 195–206). New York, NJ: Oxford University Press.

Overy, K., & Molnar-Szakacs, I. (2009). Being together in time: Musical experience and the mirror neuron system. *Music Perception, 26*(5), 489–504.

Paley Center (2009, June 29). *Supernatural—Kripke on classic rock.* Paley Center for Media: https://youtu.be/d8SfyBccpCs.

Ratcliffe, A. (2014, July 9). *We are possessed by the music of Supernatural.* Nerdist: http://nerdist.com/we-are-possessed-by-the-music-of-supernatural/.

Reybrouck, M. (2012). Musical sense-making and the concept of affordance: An ecosemiotic and experiential approach. *Biosemiotics* 5(3), 391–409.

Schafer, T., Sedlmeier, P., Stadtler, C., & Huron, D. (2013). The psychological functions of music listening. *Frontiers in Psychology, 4*, Article 611, 1–33.

Shannon, A Girl Called (2009, September 9). *SPN score: Gruska motifs—"Dean's Family Dedication Theme."* Zimshan: http://zimshan.livejournal.com/177317.html.

Van Goethem, A., & Sloboda, J. (2011). The functions of music for affect regulation. *Musicae Scientiae, 15*(2), 208–228.

Vastfjall, D. (2002). Emotion induction through music: A review of the musical mood induction procedure. *Musicae Scientiae, 6*(3), 173-211.

## Notes

1. Episode 3–1, "No Rest for the Wicked" (May 15, 2008).
2. Juslin (2013), p. 238.
3. Morinville et al. (2013).
4. Chin & Rickard (2013).
5. Boltz (2001); Hoeckner et al. (2011).
6. Paley Center (2009).
7. DeCaro et al. (2016).
8. Costable & Terman (2013).
9. Van Goethem & Sloboda (2011).
10. Written by J. Gruska (2005).
11. Written by K. Livgren (1975); first played in episode 1–21, "Salvation" (April 27, 2006); every season finale from 2–22, "All Hell Breaks Loose," part 2 (May 17, 2007); and at the end of every episode of *Supernatural: The Animation* (2011)..
12. DeNardo (2013); Ratcliffe (2014).

13. Written by R. Emmett, G. Moore, & M. Levine (1981); played in episode 1–22, "Devil's Trap" (May 4, 2006).
14. Van Goethem & Sloboda (2011).
15. Written by T. Nugent & R. Grange (1975); played in episode 2–1, "In My Time of Dying" (September 28, 2006).
16. Written by J. Fogerty (1969); played in episode 2–1, "In My Time of Dying" (September 28, 2006).
17. Lucassen (2006).
18. Bhatara et al. (2011), p. 921.
19. Lucassen (2006).
20. Episode 10–3, "Soul Survivor" (October 21, 2014).
21. Vastfjall (2002).
22. Juslin (2013).
23. Nakamura & Csikszentmihalyi (2009).
24. Schafer et al. (2013).
25. Shannon (2009).
26. J. Gruska, personal interview (March 20, 2016).
27. Episode 1–22, "Devil's Trap" (May 4, 2006).
28. Episode 2–21, "All Hell Breaks Loose (Part 1)" (May 10, 2007).
29. Episode 12–1, "Keep Calm and Carry On" (October 13, 2016).
30. Koelsch (2010).
31. Reybrouck (2012).
32. Schafer et al. (2013).
33. Juslin & Vastfjall (2008).
34. Overy & Molnar-Szakacs (2009).
35. Croom (2015).
36. Krueger (2014).
37. Koelsch (2010).
38. Eldar et al. (2007).
39. Baumgartner et al. (2006).
40. Croom (2015).
41. Episode 1–6, "Skin" (October 18, 2005).
42. Episode 1–6, "Skin" (October 18, 2005).
43. Vastfjall (2002).
44. Written by V. Sarratt & E. Hallas (2005); played in episode 1–6, "Skin" (October 18, 2005), Netflix version.
45. Episode 1–6, "Skin" (October 18, 2005).
46. Written by D. Ingle (1968); played in episode 1–6, "Skin" (October 18, 2005).
47. Vastjfal (2002).
48. Schafer et al. (2013).
49. Van Goethem & Sloboda (2011).
50. Lucassen (2006).
51. Episode 10–5, "Fan Fiction" (November 11, 2014).

# Acceptance

*"Life's short. And ours are shorter than most."*
—Dean Winchester[1]

*"No one wants to die. Even people who want to go to
heaven don't want to die to get there. And yet death is
the destination we all share. No one has ever escaped it."*
—entrepreneur Steve Jobs[2]

Life ends. Whatever comes next remains the great mystery even to those with faith in an afterlife. Though we know about death throughout our lives, objective knowledge is not synonymous with subjective acceptance, cognitively or emotionally. *Mortality salience*, when the fact of our own mortality becomes prominent in our thoughts and feelings, can cause us to pause, alter our views, change our actions, and treat others differently, if only in those moments.[3] While people can dwell on death without imminent threat, mortality tends to grow more salient in dangerous situations, during old age, and when diagnosed with terminal illness.[4] Like soldiers, first responders, and others in high-risk professions,[5] *Supernatural*'s monster hunters face death repeatedly in the course of their lives and therefore seem to accept it to some degree, but true acceptance does not require extensive avoidance, sublimation, thought suppression, and alcohol abuse. When Dean makes a deal with a demon in order to bring his brother back to life, he says that he accepts the fact of his own impending doom, that "it's like there's a light at the end of the tunnel,"[6] but he's in denial again. Avoidance of the issue is not acceptance, and in time Dean admits as much: "I'm scared, Sam. I'm really scared."[7]

What, then, is acceptance of death? For all its shortcomings, psychiatrist Elisabeth Kübler-Ross's model of the five stages of grief remains popular because each stage makes intuitive sense.[8] Based on her experiences treating and studying terminally ill individuals, she came to see acceptance of their fate as the peaceful, possibly even hopeful, outcome for those who navigated the path through denial, anger, bargaining, and depression.[9] As this book's previous Morgue Files illustrate, the characters in *Supernatural* demonstrate them all from denial through depression.

When a legal secretary asks Sam to kill her so that she won't turn into a werewolf again[10] or when Tessa the Reaper kills herself with Dean's blade because she can no longer bear to hear the cries of earthbound spirits locked out of Heaven,[11] that is not acceptance of death. That is active pursuit of death specifically to escape from something in life. Seeking death through suicidal or risky behavior is more about testing reality or escaping from life situations than it is about accepting death. Many suicidal individuals are ambivalent about dying, not typically wishing to be dead but very much wanting to get out of unpleasantness in their lives.[12]

The characters in *Supernatural* tend not to accept their own deaths because they live in a world where bargaining and fighting to the bitter end can pay off and gain an individual continued life. In real life, refusal to accept death is sometimes rewarded when the individual gets a second diagnosis, successfully undergoes experimental treatment, or keeps surviving out of sheer will to live.[13] Living characters are less likely to show acceptance than are some ghosts, such as Bobby, who resisted death and lingered until the time came to accept his fate and move on.[14] Perhaps the example that best fits Kübler-Ross's acceptance stage is Layla, who comes to terms with the fact that a brain tumor will kill her within six months but finds peace through her religious faith even though no miracle has saved her.[15]

When one is looking at how first responders, soldiers, and others whose lives make mortality salient without any terminal illness involved, Kübler-Ross's model may be less useful than other perspectives. *Existential psychology* looks at the way we face our questions about our own existence, and *existential therapy* seeks to help people overcome the fear of death by finding meaning in life.[16] Even though many (though not all) existential psychologists feel that there ultimately is no meaning to it all, they see value in *making meaning* (finding purpose and making sense out of life[17]) and believing that the individual has purpose in life. Some people find meaning while living in the moment, such as when Dean says, "My peace is helping people, working cases." People who focus on the present experience less depression than do those who ruminate over the past and less anxiety than do those who fret over the future,[18] which is where death eventually awaits, but others find ways to experience peace or hope instead of despair while looking ahead. Acceptance of one's own mortality can be part of an individual's life view without requiring the stages of grief.

> *"Guys like us, we're not exactly the type of people they write about in history books, but the people we saved, they're our legacy and they'll remember us. Then I guess they'll eventually fade away, too. That's fine, because we left the world better than we found it. You know?"*
> —Sam Winchester[19]

> *"As a well-spent day brings happy sleep, so life well used brings happy death."*
> —artist Leonardo da Vinci[20]

## References

Belmi, P., & Pfeffer, J. (2016). Power and death: Mortality salience increases power seeking while feeling powerful reduces death anxiety. *Journal of Applied Psychology, 101*(5), 702–720.

Caplan, R. D., Tripathi, R. C., & Naidu, R. K. (1985). Subjective past, present, and future fit: Effects on anxiety, depression, and other indicators of well-being. *Journal of Personality & Social Psychology, 48*(1), 180–197.

Carmel, S., Baron-Epel, O., & Shemy, S. (2007). The will-to-live and survival at old age: Gender differences. *Social Science & Medicine, 65*(3), 518–523.

Chapman, A. L., & Dixon-Gordon, K. L. (2007). Emotional antecedents and consequences of deliberate self-harm and suicide attempts. *Suicide and Life-Threatening Behavior, 37*(5), 543–552.

Chappell, N. L. (1975). Awareness of death in the disengagement theory: A conceptualization and an empirical investigation. *Omega: Journal of Death & Dying, 6*(4), 325–343.

Chochinov, H. M., Tataryn, D., Clinch, J. J., & Dudgeon, D. (1999). Will to live in the terminally ill. *The Lancet, 354*, 816–819.

Corr, C. A. (1993). Coping with dying: Lessons that we should and should not learn from the work of Elisabeth Kübler-Ross. *Death Studies, 17*(1), 69–83.

Davidson, R. J., Kabat-Zinn, J., Schumacher, J., Rosenkranz, M., Muller, D., Santorelli, S. F., Urbanoswki, F., Harrington, A., Bonus, K., & Sheridan, J. F. (2003). Alterations in brain and immune function produced by mindfulness meditation. *Psychosomatic Medicine, 54*(4), 564–570.

Eysenck, M. W., Payne S., & Santos, R. (2006). Anxiety and depression: Past, present, and future events. *Cognition & Emotion, 20*(2), 274–294.

Fortunato, V. J., & Furey, J. T. (2011). The theory of mindtime: The relationships between future, past, and present thinking and psychological well-being and distress. *Personality & Individual Differences, 50*(1), 20–24.

Frankl, V. (1963). *Man's search for meaning.* Boston, MA: Beacon.

Hayslip, B., Jr., Schuler, E. R., Page, K. S., & Carver, K. S. (2014). Probabilistic thinking and death anxiety: A terror management based study. *Omega: Journal of Death & Dying, 69*(3), 248–270.

Ignelzi, M. (2000). Meaning-making in the learning and teaching process. *New Directions for Teaching & Learning, 82*(1), 5–14.

Jobs, S. (2012, June 12). Commencement address. Stanford University, Stanford, CA. Transcript: http://news.stanford.edu/2005/06/14/jobs-061505/.

Karppinen, H., Laakkonen, M. L., Strandberg, T. E., Tilvis, R. S., & Pitkälä, K. H. (2012). Will-to-live and survival in a 10-year follow-up among older people. *Age & Ageing, 41*(6), 789–794.

Kelley, N. J., & Schmeichel, B. J. (2015). Mortality salience increases personal optimism among individuals higher in trait self-control. *Motivation & Emotion, 39*(6), 926–931.

Kübler-Ross, E. (1969). *On death and dying.* London, UK: Routledge.

Kübler-Ross, E. (2005). *On grief and grieving: Finding the meaning of grief through the five stages of loss.* New York, NY: Simon & Schuster.

Li, X., Liu, Y., Luo, S., Wu, B., Wu, X., & Han, S. (2015). Mortality salience enhances racial in-group bias in empathic neural responses to others' suffering. *NeuroImage, 118*, 376–385.

Little, M. (2004). The skull beneath the skin: Cancer survival and awareness of death. *Ethics & the Law in Medicine, 13*(3), 190–198.

Mahoney, M. B., Saunders, B. A., & Cain, N. M. (2014). Priming mortality salience: Supraliminal, subliminal, and "double-death" priming techniques. *Death Studies, 38*(10), 678–681.

May, R. (1983). *The discovery of being: Writings in existential psychology.* New York, NY: Norton.

McCurdy, E. (1908). *Leonardo da Vinci's note-books.* London, UK: Duckworth.

O'Connor, S. S., Jobes, D. A., Yeargin, M. K., Fitzgerald, M. E., Rodriguez, V. M., Conrad, A. K., & Lineberry, T. W. (2012). A cross-sectional investigation of the suicide spectrum: Typologies of suicidality based on ambivalence about living and dying. *Comprehensive Psychiatry, 53*(5), 461–467.

Roos, S. (2013). The Kübler-Ross model: An esteemed relic. *Gestalt Review, 17*(3), 312–315.

Yalom, I. (2008). *From staring at the sun: Overcoming the terror of death.* San Francisco, CA: Jossey-Bass.

Zaleskiewicz, T., Gasiorowska, A., & Kesebir, P. (2015). The Scrooge effect revisited: Mortality salience increases the satisfaction derived from prosocial behavior. *Journal of Experimental Social Psychology, 59*, 67–76.

## Notes

1. Episode 6–16, "And Then There Were None" (March 4, 2011).
2. Jobs (2012).
3. Belmi & Pfeffer (2016); Kelley & Schmeichel (2015); Li et al. (2015); Zaleskiewicz et al. (2015).
4. Chappell (1975); Little (2004); Mahoney et al. (2014).
5. Hayslip et al. (2014).
6. Episode 3–1, "The Magnificent Seven" (October 4, 2007).
7. Episode 3–14, "Long Distance Call" (May 1, 2008).
8. Corr (1993); Roos (2013).
9. Kübler-Ross (1969; 2005).
10. Episode 2–17, "Heart" (March 22, 2007).
11. Episode 9–22, "Stairway to Heaven" (May 13, 2014).
12. Chapman & Dixon-Gordon (2007); O'Connor et al. (2012).
13. Carmel et al. (2007); Chochinov et al. (1999); Davidson et al. (2003); Karppinen et al. (2012).
14. Episode 7–23, "Survival of the Fittest" (May 18, 2012).
15. Episode 1–12, "Faith" (January 17, 2006).
16. Frankl (1963); May (1983); Yalom (2008).
17. Ignelzi (2000).
18. Caplan et al. (1985); Eysenck et al. (2006); Fortunato & Furey (2011).
19. Episode 12–18, "The Memory Remains" (April 13, 2017).
20. McCurdy (1908), pp. 18, 51.

# FINAL WORD

# Peace

## TRAVIS LANGLEY

*"My peace is helping people, working cases.
That's all I want to do."*
—Dean Winchester[1]

*"There is no need to go to India or anywhere else to find
peace. You will find that deep place of silence right in
your room, your garden, or even your bathtub."*
—psychiatrist Elisabeth Kübler-Ross[2]

Inner peace can be elusive. When found, it may be brief. Moments of mental and spiritual calm and strength in the face of stress or discord might occur only sporadically with spells of turmoil in between, but that's not all bad. *Intermittent reinforcement* (reward received only sometimes) can exert powerful influence over us and lead to more enduring patterns of behavior than can *continuous reinforcement* (getting rewarded for our actions every time we do them).[3] Helpful behavior is considered to be more genuinely altruistic when it is done without expectation of reward.[4] Even though hunting monsters is frequently a thankless task and the world keeps spinning full of people unaware they've been saved from something monstrous or even apocalyptic, Sam and Dean Winchester keep hunting long after they avenge their parents' deaths. As Dean puts it, "What I do, I do because it's the right thing to do."[5] Doing what's right can be its own purpose and its own reward,[6]

# ROAD MUSIC

### "Carry On, (My) Wayward Son" by Kansas"[7]

We don't exactly know where *resilience*, the common capacity to adapt to adversity and keep going with competent functioning, comes from.[8] Research has identified some *correlates*, factors that vary with how resilient a person is (such as having social support or focusing one's efforts on specific tasks[9]), but correlation is not causation. *Supernatural*'s unofficial anthem[10] suggests that the person who will persist despite grief, pain, and tears (despite, not without) can eventually achieve fulfillment in life with a promise of serenity at the end. Resilient individuals employ a variety of coping behaviors in order to face crisis and deal with difficulties, often through sheer *grit* (perseverance and passion for goals).[11]

thereby providing a measure of inner peace deep in the eye of an emotional storm.

Many people we consider to be heroes insist that they are not,[12] but they don't make that determination. Heroism "is a social attribution, never a personal one"[13]—meaning that other people decide who the world's heroes are, and a hero to one generation or population might be seen as a villain by another. When the Winchester brothers wind up in Heaven after yet another of their many deaths, they're astonished to find themselves there because neither considers himself worthy. In fact, each sees the other as the better person, more deserving of heavenly reward. "Last I checked," Sam says, "it wasn't the road to Heaven that was paved with good intentions."[14] Yet we do judge actions by the intentions behind them.[15] Risking personal loss or even expecting to suffer or die as a result of doing what's right is considered more heroic.[16] Who's more saintly and truly deserving of eternal peace, the pious believer who helps others out of an expectation that every person aided adds another jewel to the believer's heavenly crown or the ruffian who helps others while expecting no reward even in the long run?

We need some heroes as *role models*, examples to inspire hope that others will do the right thing and belief that we might do it, too.[17] Within their fictional world, most people know nothing about Sam and Dean. In our world, these are famous characters on a popular TV show but also something more: They are inspirational and aspirational, as are their wayward sisters and many other characters throughout their stories.[18] Their heroics give hope to other characters and lead some to emulate them, following heroic paths of their own even though, as Charlie Bradbury says, the lifestyle "mostly ends in Sophie's choices, death, or tears—usually all of the above, huh?"[19] Greater than the role models' power within the fiction, though, may be their power in our world, where the actors and crew and fans unite and encourage one another to "always keep fighting."

Regarding how the series should one day end, actor Jensen Ackles expressed this wish: "They go out in a blaze of glory! I want the heartbreaker ending. The great thing about these characters is they'll fight to the end."[20] Heroes keep going. Persistence may be the great lesson of most heroic tales, even more so than courage, in both fiction and fact. The hero goes above and beyond the call of duty.[21] "The only way I'd be happy for the show to end is *Butch Cassidy and the Sundance Kid*-style," actor Jared Padalecki said,[22] which Jensen's character Dean later echoes to Sam on the show: "I always thought we'd go out Butch and Sundance style."[23] For some, inner peace is not about expecting a calm and externally peaceful fate but instead about accepting that an end will come while fighting until that end to make it and the life that led up to it count. No matter how that goes for Sam and Dean, though, we know they'll just be on their way to the next adventure, and maybe we will, too.[24]

Always keep fighting.

*"Did you know people tell stories about us?"*
—Sam Winchester[25]

*"Death is not the end. Death can never be the end. Death is the road. Life is the traveler."*
—spiritual leader Sri Chinmoy[26]

## References

Allison, S. T., & Goethals, G. R. (2011). *Heroes: What they do & why we need them.* New York, NY: Oxford University Press.

Barasch, A., Levine, E. E., Berman, J. Z., & Small, D. A. (2014). Selfish or selfless? On the signal value of emotion in altruistic behavior. *Journal of Personality & Social Psychology, 107*(3), 393–413.

Batchelor, K. (2015, October 4). *Top 11 musical moments in "Supernatural."* Michigan Daily: https://www.michigandaily.com/section/arts/top-11-musical-moments-supernatural.

Baumann, D. J., Cialdini, R. B., & Kendrick, D. T. (1981). Altruism as hedonism: Helping and self-gratification as equivalent responses. *Journal of Personality & Social Psychology, 40*(6), 1039–1046.

Chinmoy, S. (2000/2004). *The wisdom of Sri Chinmoy.* Delhi, India: Motilal Banarsi-dass.

Duckworth, A. L., Peterson, C., Matthews, M. D., & Kelly, D. R. (2007). Grit: Perseverance and passion for long-term goals. *Journal of Personality & Social Psychology, 92*(6), 11087–11101.

Ferster, C. B., & Skinner, B. F. (1957). *Schedules of reinforcement.* New York, NY: Appleton-Century-Crofts.

Franco, Z. E., Blau, K., & Zimbardo, P. G. (2011). Heroism: A conceptual analysis and differentiation between heroic action and altruism. *Review of General Psychology, 15*(2), 99–113.

Friedman, H. (1999) *I'm no hero: Journeys of a Holocaust survivor.* Seattle, WA: University of Washington Press.

Hanks, R. A., Rapport, L. J., Waldron-Perrin, B., & Mills, S. R. (2016). Correlates of resilience in the first 5 years after traumatic brain injury. *Rehabilitation Psychology, 61*(3), 269–276.

Hiatt, B. (2003). *Jessica Lynch: I'm no hero.* Entertainment Weekly: http://ew.com/article/2003/11/07/jessica-lynch-im-no-hero/.

Hilliard, M. E., McQuaid, E. L., Nabors, L., & Hood, K. K. (2015). Resilience in youth and families living with pediatric health and developmental conditions:

Introduction to the special issue on resilience. *Journal of Pediatric Psychology, 40*(5), 835–839.

Javors, I. R. (2008). Redefining heroes. *Annals of the American Psychotherapy Association, 11*(1), 35.

Knight, N. (2014). *The essential Supernatural: On the road with Sam and Dean Winchester.* San Rafael, CA: Insight Editions.

Kronisch, L. (1976, November–December). Elisabeth Kübler-Ross: Messenger of love. *Yoga Journal, 1*(11), 18–20.

MacDonald, J. M., Ahearn, W. H., Parry-Cruwys, D., Bandcroft, S., & Dube, W. V. (2013). Persistence during extinction: Examining the effects of continuous and intermittent reinforcement on problem behavior. *Journal of Applied Behavior Analysis, 46*(1), 333–338.

Morgan, D. L. (2010). Schedules of reinforcement at 50: A retrospective appreciation. *Psychological Record, 60*, (1), 151–158.

Papadopoulos, C., & Hayes, B. K. (2017). What matters when juding intentionality-moral conent or normative status? Testing the rational scientist model of the side-effect. *Psychnomic Bulletin & Review.* https://link.springer.com/article/10.3758%2Fs13423-017-1312-x [epub ahead of print.]

Prudom, L. (2015, February 17). *Kansas discuss the song that changed their lives in new documentary.* Variety: http://variety.com/2015/music/news/kansas-carry-on-wayward-son-miracles-out-of-nowhere-documentary-video-1201435065/.

Rosenberg, A. R., & Yi-Frazier, J. P. (2015). Commentary: Resilience defined: An alternative perspective. *Journal of Pediatric Psychology, 41*(5), 506–509.

Weiss, R. F., Boyer, J. L., Lombardo, J. P., & Stich, M. H. (1973). Altruistic drive and altruistic reinforcement. *Journal of Personality & Social Psychology, 25*(3), 390–400.

Weiss, R. F., Buchanan, W., Alstatt, L., & Lombardo, J. P. (1971). Altruism is rewarding. *Science, 171*(3977), 1262–1263.

Windle, M. (1999). Critical conceptual and measurement issues in the study of resilience. In M. D. E. J. Glantz & L. Jeanette (Eds.), *Resilience and development, positive life adaptations* (pp. 161–176). New York, NY: Springer.

Yazici, S., & Aslan, M. (2011). Using heroes as role models in value education: A comparison between social studies textbooks and prospective teachers' choice of hero or heroines. *Kuram vs Uygulamada Egitim Bilimleri [Educational Sciences: Theory & Practice], 11*(4), 2184–2188.

Zubernis, L. S. (2017). *Family don't end with blood: Cast and fans on how Supernatural has changed lives.* Dallas, TX: BenBella.

## Notes

1. Episode 10–13, "Halt and Catch Fire" (February 10, 2015).
2. Quoted by Kronisch (1976).
3. Ferster & Skinner (1957); MacDonald et al. (2013); Morgan (2010).
4. Barasch et al. (2014); Weiss et al. (1971; 1973).
5. Episode 9–13, "The Purge" (February 4, 2014).
6. Baumann et al. (1981); Weiss et al. (1971).
7. Written by K. Livgren (1975); played in episode 1–21, "Salvation" (April 27, 2006); every season finale from 2–22, "All Hell Breaks Loose," part 2 (May 17, 2007); and at the end of every episode of *Supernatural: The Animation* (2011).
8. Hilliard et al. (2015); Rosenberg & Yi-Frazier (2015); Windle (1999).
9. Hanks et al. (2016).

10. Batchelor (2015); Prudom (2015).
11. Duckworth et al. (2007).
12. e.g., Friedman (1999); Hiatt (2003).
13. Franco et al. (2011), p. 99.
14. Episode 5–16, "Dark Side of the Moon" (April 1, 2010). Sam's reply to Dean after this exchange. Sam: "You, I get, sure. But me? Maybe you haven't noticed, but I've done a few things." Dean: "You thought you were doing the right thing."
15. Papadopoulous & Hayes (2017).
16. Allison & Goethals (2011); Franco et al. (2011).
17. Allison & Goethals (2011); Javors (2008); Yazici & Aslan (2011).
18. Zubernis (2017).
19. Episode 10–18, "Book of the Damned" (April 15, 2015).
20. Knight (2014), p. 217.
21. Franco et al. (2011).
22. Knight (2014), p. 217.
23. Episode 12–22, "Who We Are" (May 18, 2017).
24. John 16:33.
25. Episode 12–6, "Celebrating the Life of Asa Fox" (November 17, 2016).
26. Chinmoy (2000/2004), p. 37.

# ABOUT THE EDITOR

**Travis Langley, PhD**, is a psychology professor who teaches courses on crime, media, and mental illness at Henderson State University. He received his bachelor's from Hendrix College and his graduate degrees from Tulane University in New Orleans. Dr. Langley is the series editor and lead writer for the Popular Culture Psychology books *The Walking Dead*, *Game of Thrones*, *Doctor Who*, *Star Wars*, *Star Trek*, *Captain America*, *Iron Man*, *Wonder Woman*, *Daredevil*, and more. He regularly speaks on media and heroism at universities, conferences, and conventions throughout the world. *Necessary Evil: Super-Villains of DC Comics* and other films have featured him as an expert interviewee, and the documentary *Legends of the Knight* spotlighted how he uses fiction to teach real psychology. He authored the acclaimed book *Batman and Psychology: A Dark and Stormy Knight*. *Psychology Today* carried his blog, "Beyond Heroes and Villains."

Follow him as **@Superherologist** on Twitter, where he ranks among the ten most popular psychologists. You can also keep up with him and this book series through **Facebook.com/ThePsychGeeks.**

Travis remains confident that Charlie Bradbury's hacker predecessor Frank Devereaux faked his death and, true to character, simply went deeper off the grid. He decided to be fine.

# ABOUT THE CO-EDITOR

**Lynn S. Zubernis, PhD**, is a clinical psychologist and professor at West Chester University. She earned her bachelor's degree from Rosemont College and her graduate degrees from Bryn Mawr College in Pennsylvania. In addition to publishing a psychology textbook and a variety of articles on psychological topics, Dr. Zubernis has published five books that celebrate being a fan—*Family Don't End With Blood: Cast and Fans on How Supernatural Has Changed Lives, Fangasm Supernatural Fangirls, Fan Phenomena Supernatural, Fandom At The Crossroads*, and *Fan Culture: Theory/Practice*. She has written for *Slate, The Conversation*, and *Supernatural Magazine*, is a regular contributor to articles, podcasts and documentaries on fandom, and has appeared on NPR. Dr. Zubernis was also co-writer and associate producer for the documentary *Squee: The Fangirl Project*. She chairs the Stardom and Fandom area of the Southwest Popular Culture Association and blogs at fangasmthebook on Wordpress. That's her academic half; the fangirl half writes fanfiction whenever she can, collects *Supernatural* gifs on Tumblr (yes, we have a gif for everything), and has purchased way too many photo-ops at *Supernatural* conventions. Follow her as **@FangasmSPN** on Twitter, Tumblr and Facebook!

# ABOUT THE CONTRIBUTORS

 **Travis Adams,** MSW, received his degree from the University of Southern California. He is a Marine Corps veteran and peer support specialist working with U.S. military veterans diagnosed with PTSD and other conditions. He utilizes various types of therapy to aid veterans in their recovery and has incorporated the use of popular culture in conjunction with standardized treatment models. You can find Travis on Twitter @themarine_peer.

 **Jennifer Bonds-Raacke**, PhD, is the Dean of the Graduate School and Office of Scholarship and Sponsored Projects at Fort Hays State University (FHSU). She holds the rank of tenured professor in the Department of Psychology. Her primary research interests are the psychology of mass communication, decision-making, and the psychology of teaching. Dr. Bonds-Raacke obtained her BA from Christian Brothers University and her PhD and MS from Kansas State University in experimental psychology.

 **Colt J. Blunt,** PsyD, LP, has worked as a forensic examiner throughout his career and serves as a guest lecturer and trainer for a number of organizations and educational institutions. His academic interests include the intersection of psychology and law, including the study of criminal behavior. He previously contributed to most books in this series.

**Melanie Boysen** was completing her master's degree in clinical psychology at the University of Northern Iowa at the time this chapter was written. She earned a bachelor's degree in psychology at Buena Vista University. She is a youth counselor at the Human Services Center in Yankton, South Dakota.

**Jenna Busch** is a writer, host, and founder of Legion of Leia, a website that promotes and supports women in fandom. She co-hosted *Cocktails with Stan* with Spider-Man creator and comic legend Stan Lee. Busch has appeared in the film *She Makes Comics* and as a guest on *Attack of the Show*, NPR, Al Jazeera America, and multiple episodes of *Tabletop* with Wil Wheaton. She is a comic book author and associated editor at ComingSoon.net. Busch has co-authored chapters in most books in the Popular Culture Psychology series and in one way or another has helped with them all. Her work has appeared all over the web. She can be reached on Twitter @JennaBusch.

**Erin Currie,** PhD, LP, is an instructor, therapist, and consultant by day. Driven to use her psychology superpowers for good, she founded the consulting practice MyPsychgeek, LLC, to help individuals and small businesses find their own superpowers through professional and team development. She also wrote for *Game of Thrones Psychology, Doctor Who Psychology,* and *Wonder Woman Psychology.*

**Christine M. Dickson**, MS, LAC, works with her husband, who is a pilot, rescuing and rehabilitating dogs and converting them for various forms of service. She lives a life full of diverse passions, interests, and hobbies. She uses her love of comics and anime therapeutically.

**William Blake Erickson,** PhD, is a researcher and lecturer at the University of Arkansas. His research interests include eyewitness memory and face recognition. He has published in journals such as *Applied Cognitive Psychology, Psychonomic Bulletin and Review, Psychology, Psychiatry and Law,* and *Journal of Police and Criminal Psychology.*

**Larisa A. Garski**, MA, LMFT, is a licensed marriage and family therapist. She works with geeks, superheroes, and their families at Empowered Therapy in Chicago. Larisa blogs on geek wellness and related topics for Blue Box Counseling. She and Justine Mastin are developing a book on geek-focused narrative therapy. Larisa can be reached at empoweredtherapy.org.

**Wind Goodfriend,** PhD, is a professor of psychology and assistant dean of graduate studies at Buena Vista University. She earned a bachelor's degree at Buena Vista University and a master's and PhD in social psychology from Purdue University. Dr. Goodfriend has won BVU's "Faculty of the Year" award several times and won the Wythe Award for Excellence in Teaching, and she is the principle investigator at the Institute for the Prevention of Relationship Violence.

**Lara Taylor Kester,** MA, holds a degree in counseling psychology as well as a certificate in traumatology and treatment from Holy Names University. A registered marriage and family therapy intern who works with at-risk and foster youth in the San Francisco Bay Area, she is the co-host of the Geek Therapy podcast and serves as a contributing editor at GeekTherapy.com. She has authored chapters in most books in the Popular Culture Psychology series. Find her on Twitter @geektherapist.

**Elizabeth Kus,** PsyD, is a psychologist in the prison system, specializing in working with sex offenders. She uses her love of nerdy topics to help connect with clients and help them connect with their own issues. For her self-care she runs NerdLush.com and loves running around conventions. She can be found on Twitter @NerdLushDiva.

**Scott Jordan**, PhD, is a cognitive psychologist who conducts research on the roots of cooperative behavior. He often uses popular culture in in his classes in order to illustrate the relevance of social-cognitive psychology to daily life. He has contributed chapters to *Captain America vs. Iron Man: Freedom, Security, Psychology*; *Wonder Woman Psychology: Lassoing the Truth*, *Star Trek Psychology: The Mental Frontier*, and the forthcoming *Daredevil Psychology: The Devil You Know*. He is very proud of his international comic book collection.

**Jonathan Maberry** is a *New York Times* bestselling author, 5-time Bram Stoker Award-winner, and comic book writer. He writes in multiple genres including suspense, thriller, horror, science fiction, fantasy, and action, for adults, teens, and middle grade. His works include the *Joe Ledger* thrillers, *Glimpse*, the *Rot & Ruin* series, the *Dead of Night* series, *The Wolfman*, *X-Files Origins: Devil's Advocate*, *Mars One*, and many others. Several of his works are in development for film and TV. He is the editor of high-profile anthologies including *The X-Files*, *V-Wars*, *Scary Out There*, *Out of Tune*, *Kingdoms Fall*, *Baker Street Irregulars*, *Nights of the Living Dead*, and others. He lives in Del Mar, California. Find him online at jonathanmaberry.com.

**Justine Mastin,** MA, LMFT, is the owner of Blue Box Counseling in Minneapolis. She specializes in working with clients who self-identify as being outside the mainstream, such as those in the geek, secular, and LGBTQ communities. Justine is the fearless leader of YogaQuest, a business that blends geek narratives with yoga. She appears at pop culture conventions, teaching yoga and speaking on geek wellness topics. Justine takes a holistic approach to healing: mind, body, and fandom. Follow her on Twitter @mindbodyfandom.

**Denisse Morales,** PsyD, is a licensed clinical psychologist in southern California. She works with children, adolescents, and adults with depression, anxiety, trauma, and developmental disorders. She conducts psychological evaluations of children with special needs and adults with traumatic brain injury. Her special interests include helping girls get through issues of low self-esteem and self-harm behaviors. Find her blog at www.psycholo-geek.com and find her on Twitter @Super-SaiyanDrM.

 **James S. Nairne**, PhD, is the Reece McGee Distinguished Professor at Purdue University. Specializing in the cognitive science of human memory, he is keenly interested in the role that evolution and natural selection have played in the development of cognition. He teaches a course on Dracula and the psychology of the supernatural and has led three study abroad trips to Transylvania to trace the roots of the vampire legend.

 **Susan Nylander** (as her pseudonym Susan Landers) worked in broadcast radio as air talent and music director. Now a full-time professor of English composition and literature at Barstow College, a passionate *Supernatural* fan and scholar, Susan is working with Mandy Taylor on an edited collection of essays about Death in Supernatural.

 **John B. Pryor**, PhD, is an Emeritus Distinguished Professor at Illinois State University. His research interests include social stigma and sexual harassment. He is a past-president of the Midwestern Psychological Association and a fellow of the American Psychological Association and the Association for Psychological Science.

 **John Raacke**, PhD, is chair and associate professor in the Department of Criminal Justice at Fort Hays State University. His primary research interests are juror/jury decision-making, team decision-making, and the impact of social networking sites. Prior to joining the faculty at FHSU, Raacke served as an associate dean at the University of North Carolina at Pembroke. Raacke earned his BA from Christian Brothers University and his PhD and MS from Kansas State University in experimental psychology and his.

 **Billy San Juan**, PsyD, works as a psychosocial rehabilitation specialist in San Diego, CA. In his spare time, he is a proud member of the Psych Geeks, Horror Writers Association, and *Magic: The Gathering* judge community. He also has spoken on panels at San Diego Comic-Con, LA Comic Con, WonderCon, and other conventions. Follow him on Twitter @Billi_sense or read his thoughts about life's dichotomies on trilobits.net.

 **Janina Scarlet**, PhD, is a licensed clinical psychologist, a scientist, and a full-time geek. She uses superhero therapy to help patients with anxiety, depression, chronic pain, and PTSD at the Center for Stress and Anxiety Management. Dr. Scarlet is the author of *Superhero Therapy* with Little Brown Book Group and has authored chapters in every book in the Popular Culture Psychology series. She can be reached via her website at superhero-therapy.com or on Twitter @shadowquill.

 **Stephan Schaffrath**, PhD, has worked for various universities as an instructor in writing, literature, German, academic skills, and career exploration courses. His critical academic work focuses on comparative literature, particularly in regard to chaotics (i.e., chaos theory), Mikael Bakhtin, vampirism, Templar-themed literature, war, and violence. He dabbles in independent publication of his children's books and historical fiction.

 **Amanda Taylor**, MA, is a lecturer at CSU San Bernardino where she teaches writing for the English and Natural Science departments. She has presented several papers on the series and is co-editing a collection of essays on death in Supernatural with Susan Nylander. She has a background in both vocal and piano performance and is a fan of almost all types of music.

 **Paul VanPortfliet**, PsyD, is a registered psychologist and certified core adjunct faculty at National University in San Diego, California. He received the Mental Health Services Act Fellowship, has published in the *Journal of Research in Innovative Teaching,* and has presented at the Society for Personality Assessment Annual Conference. He received a BA from Ferris State University and his MA and PsyD from Alliant International University, San Diego.

 **Eric D. Wesselmann** is an associate professor of psychology at Illinois State University. He publishes research on various topics, such as social exclusion, stigma, and religion/spirituality. He has been a horror enthusiast as far back as he can remember; he fondly recalls staying up late to watch *Chiller Theater*–style B movies on TV during grade school, and made his first horror movie in the fourth grade (he played a vampire). Eric continues to feed his fandom by spending way too much money at horror conventions.

# INDEX